USING BAR CODE

WHY IT'S TAKING OVER

Second Edition

David Jarrett Collins

Nancy Nasuti Whipple

DATA CAPTURE INSTITUTE

Duxbury, Massachusetts

CREDITS

Cover   Hannus Design Associates
Production Coordinator   Sandra Rigney
Illustrations   Peter Collins
Tables/Charts   Data Design

REGISTERED TRADEMARKS

AIM is a registered trademark of the Automatic Identification Manufacturers.

Datacode is a registered trademark of International Data Matrix, Inc.

dBase IV, Paradox are registered trademarks of Borland International, Inc.

IBM, IBM PC, AT, XT, OS/2, SQL, SNA/SDLC are registered trademarks of International Business Machines Corporation.

ID Expo is a trademark of Advanstar Expositions.

KERMIT is a trademark of Henson Associates.

Mac-Barcode® is a registered trademark licensed to Data Capture Institute, Inc.

Macintosh is a registered trademark of Apple Computer Company.

Microsoft, MS, MS-DOS, Works, Word, Windows are registered trademarks of Microsoft Corporation.

Oracle is a registered trademark of Oracle Corporation.

Partnership for Integration and Autofact are registered trademarks of the Society of Manufacturing Engineers.

Scantech is a trademark of Reed Exhibitions.

Symphony is a registered trademark of Lotus Corporation.

UCC is a trademark of the Uniform Code Council.

UNIX is a registered trademark of American Telephone and Telegraph Bell.

U.P.C. is a trademark of the Uniform Code Council. In this book U.P.C. will be referred to as UPC.

WordPerfect is a registered trademark of WordPerfect Corp.

Library of Congress Catalog Card Number: 90-083564
ISBN: 0-9627406-1-6

Printed in the United States of America   1 2 3 4 5   98 97 96 95 94

Contents

ABOUT THE AUTHORS

DAVID JARRETT COLLINS is widely recognized as the founder of the bar code industry. As a pioneer in the development of sophisticated control systems, he holds patents on several of the industry's earliest inventions. He is a graduate engineer from Villanova University and received a master's degree in Industrial Management from the Sloan School of MIT. In 1968, he founded Computer Identics Corporation (listed on NASDAQ), the first company to develop and market bar code products and systems. As CEO for 18 years, he directed solutions to over 1000 industrial data collection problems. He was also a co-founder of the Automatic Identification Manufacturers (AIM) trade association. In 1987, he established Data Capture Institute, a company specializing in research and education in automatic identification technology. He is a frequent lecturer, author of numerous articles, and a highly regarded consultant to major corporations, automatic identification manufacturers, and financial investors in the industry. He was the 1992 recipient of the Dilling Award, AIM's highest honor, for his bar code pioneering. In 1993 he received the prestigious Stanley J. Morehouse Award, Villanova University's highest honor to an engineering alumnus.

NANCY NASUTI WHIPPLE holds a master's degree in Computer Science from Boston University and has held senior professional positions in programming and analysis with several automatic identification and data collection companies, including Motorola/Codex Corporation and Computer Identics Corporation. She is currently Program Manager with Data Capture Institute, responsible for overseeing the successful installation of automatic data collection systems for major corporations. She also lectures at Data Capture Institute's seminars.

ACKNOWLEDGMENTS

We wish to thank Sandra Rigney for coordinating and supervising the production of this second edition and Margaret Kearney for her editorial support.

Thanks also go to Joan Hacker, our publisher, for her professional guidance and personal encouragement.

Peter Collins contributed by taking our arcane concepts and system examples and converting them into crisp illustrations.

Finally, the men and women who adopted pioneering bar code applications when this technology was young deserve our thanks, as well. Bar code development owes much to them.

Introduction

Bar codes — or those little black and white lines that most people first saw on grocery packaging — seem to be on everything today. As you will learn in Chapter 1, there are great benefits to be gained from applying bar code sensibly to many day-to-day procedures. You've probably begun to wonder whether your organization is missing out without bar code, and how you can learn more about it, painlessly, if possible. This book has been written to serve that need.

The structure of *Using Bar Code — Why It's Taking Over* has evolved from the many seminars the authors have given and the questions that attendees most wanted to have answered. Every industry and service group has been represented in the seminar audience, with individuals ranging from nontechnical owners and presidents to experienced bar code users preparing for their second or third bar code application. At one level, bar code is a simple way to write and read messages that computers find easy to understand. At another level, for someone planning a companywide conversion to bar code driven data collection, there are many intricate system design and integration steps that have to be provided if the bar code investment is to achieve its full potential.

Let's briefly review the way *Using Bar Code — Why It's Taking Over* is organized to see how it deals with these differing levels of interest. The book is divided into four parts, with Part One devoted to the technology of bar code. Chapter 1 presents history and background, a few interesting examples that are representative of broader applications, and a look into the future uses of bar code. Chapter 2 covers the bar code symbologies you are likely to choose from (there are several), and steers you toward the most sensible choice for your application. Scanners and printing devices are covered in Chapters 3 and 4. Since the marketplace offers many different types and suppliers, these chapters give instruction in the operating principles of each scanner and printing method and explain their relative strengths and weaknesses.

Part Two covers components of a bar code system — the pieces needed to make an application of bar code friendly and successful. Software is the focus of Chapter 5, since bar code data collection usually drives new or existing computer programs. Chapter 6 covers bar code communication components, both local and extended. Taken together, these two chapters give the perspective necessary to design a very elaborate bar code system. Selecting scanning terminals is complicated by the numerous choices of features and options that are available, and Chapter 7 treats this subject matter in depth, with advice based on the experience of other users. Chapter 8 deals exclusively with bar code labels and explains why label design is the most important step in the development of a bar code project.

The most commonly adopted bar code applications are presented in Part Three. Chapter 9 focuses on inventory control, Chapter 10 covers all phases of retail operations using bar code, and Chapter 11 presents the range of bar code tracking applications. These chapters also include the key choices to be made in hardware, software, and label design, along with the advice and experience of other users.

Whether you go forward with a simple bar code application or take the first step along a multiyear path of interrelated bar code uses, you will find the information in Part Four most helpful. Chapter 12 presents the five necessary steps to assure a successful bar code project. Chapter 13 covers the vendor sources or combinations for components and services and then lists and describes the institutions that promote or support bar code users. Chapter 14 goes beyond the simple data collection use of bar code and shows how bar code integration into electronic data interchange can multiply the benefits of both technologies. It also covers the emerging use and future potential of Application

Identifiers which assist in distinguishing and formatting complex bar code messages. Finally, this chapter discusses an alternative technology to bar code scanning, Radio Frequency Identification and its appropriate applications. A useful list of acronyms and a glossary appear at the back of the book.

While *Using Bar Code — Why It's Taking Over* evolved from our seminar series, it goes much further in scope and detail than is possible in a two-day classroom situation. On the one hand, this book may be read quickly as a bar code overview and reference by managers who merely wish to understand bar code and its interrelationship with data systems and operations. On the other hand, for those with the responsibility of designing and implementing a bar code system, the wealth of technical detail will be a resource to study, as well as a reference to turn to again and again during and after the installation of each bar code application.

Part One

TECHNOLOGY

Part One presents a comprehensive explanation of bar code technology. Chapter 1 contains a brief history of how bar code originated, where it is going, and why so many organizations have chosen bar code to control and refine their data collection requirements. A presentation of the most popular bar code symbologies in use today, as well as several which have recently been introduced, follows in Chapter 2.

The remainder of Part One explains bar code scanning technology (Chapter 3) and printing technology (Chapter 4), taking the reader through theory and current practice. The emphasis in these chapters is to advise and clarify so that bar code tools can be quickly and effectively applied to solve real problems.

Chapter 1

Why Bar Code Is Taking Over

What if bar code had never been invented? How would our world be different today? Without grocery scanning, check-out lines would certainly be longer and food prices higher. Fewer product choices would be on the shelves, since store inventory could not be taken every day. Restocking from the distribution center to the local store would take an extra day or more without bar code carton labels and automatic laser scanning. Cars would cost more, too. Today's new Ford or Chevy has over twenty bar code labels on component parts, which are read by dozens of laser scanners from the time an engine block starts down the assembly line until your custom-made new Blazer is delivered to the dealer down the street.

Bar code has also begun to infiltrate our personal lives. For example, the New York City Marathon has over 25,000 runners competing on a Sunday each November. Every runner wants his or her exact finish time listed in the paper the following morning. Using bar code, each competitor's time in hours, minutes, and seconds, in exact finish order, reaches the New York newspapers by 7:00 P.M. that evening, minutes after the last runner crosses the finish line. In another example, nine years before AIDS was identified as the scourge of our time, some farsighted administrators in health care began a worldwide program to bar code whole blood donations and strictly control their testing, processing, and distribution. Without bar code control the AIDS epidemic would have brought far more grief and devastation to society than it has.

Chapter 1 begins by placing the reader in the historical context of bar code as a useful control technology. Then the chapter highlights the benefits bar code brings to applications like those mentioned above. Finally, the chapter takes a look ahead several years to see where bar code will play a further role in refining our organizational processes.

■ HISTORY AND DEVELOPMENT OF BAR CODE

Starting in the mid-1950s, the development and ever-expanding use of the digital computer has been generating a requirement for faster and more accurate methods to input data for analysis and orderly event reporting. A great deal of research and development work has been devoted to a search for the perfect industrial data collection technology. Back in 1959 a group of railroad R&D managers organized a meeting in Boston to bring together technology specialists from the defense supply community to listen to descriptions of unsolved rail industry problems. Chief among these problems was the need to read rail car owner and serial number information from moving trains to enable accurate car tracing and to provide accounting reports for interrailroad freight car rental.

Among the audience were members of the Sylvania/GTE Applied Research Lab, which had a number of pattern recognition projects under way for military and commercial customers. By 1962 Sylvania had designed a system that the rail industry could adopt to solve its freight car control problem. This was an optical scanning system using white light to illuminate a label with horizontal bars of reflective red, white and blue on a nonreflecting black background. The color bars and black background were coded to represent each car's owner and serial number. The Sylvania scanning design included the innovation of broadcasting the scan beam at right angles to the traveling freight train, allowing label reading at any speed or even when the train had stopped in front of a scanner. Exhibit 1.1 illustrates this system.

Over twenty alternative proposals for freight car identification techniques were submitted to the railroad industry by capable high-tech suppliers like GE and RCA. These proposals covered the entire range of energy-sensing technology from optical through ultrasonic, including radio frequency (RF) transmission and microwave reflection. The four most promising systems were field tested for a year on trains in Pennsylvania. Then, in 1967, Sylvania's color bar code technology

Exhibit 1.1
Automatic Freight Car Identification

(Courtesy of Data Capture Library)

was selected as the freight car control system for use throughout North America. None of the other competing systems was selected for commercial use.

In 1968, Computer Identics Corporation was formed as a spin-off of Sylvania, with the intention to advance this bar code technology with two important improvements. First, in order to simplify the label, the requirement for color coding (red and blue) was eliminated. Then the size of the label was reduced by 99 percent using ordinary paper or other conventional label media. Computer Identics used the emerging, but still exotic, helium-neon (HeNe) laser as the scanning source in place of the white light used with the earlier railroad system. It was this change that made the breakthroughs possible. Modern bar code, as we know it now, developed from that point forward.

Commercial use of bar code first began with grocery carton scanning for conveyorized order picking at a distribution center in early 1970. This application was followed within several months by the first of many automotive component tracking applications. Throughout this book there are references to many other companies that contributed to this technology over subsequent years. Today, the bar code industry has grown to be a $5 billion international market for scanning and printing devices, label media, specialized software, and packaged application solutions. The bar code market is expanding at the rate of 25 percent per year, and while there is a place for non-bar code data collection technology in retail and factory applications, over 90 percent of automatic data collection is accomplished by bar code systems today. Let's look at some of the reasons why bar code has left competing technology far behind.

With any new technology, the lower the application cost to develop a benefit, the easier the project justification will be. When competing technologies emerge in parallel as they did in the 1960s and 1970s within automatic identification, the system with the least expensive label will gain more customers. Bar code with paper labels had a strong advantage over any nonoptical tag-based system, since the cost of a paper label is low to negligible. Optical character recognition (OCR) also uses paper labels, but bar code is much more prevalent than OCR for data collection. Why? The answer lies in the simplicity of bar code scanning compared with scanning and interpreting human readable fonts through OCR. Exhibit 1.2 illustrates a human readable character and a bar code.

Exhibit 1.2

Character vs. Bar Code

As will be explained in detail in Chapters 2 and 3, a single pass of an 0.008-inch scan spot almost anywhere across a bar code is sufficient to read 20 or more characters of data. More important, a bar code can even be read at a distance of a foot or more from the scanner. By contrast, to interpret each human readable character with an acceptable degree of certainty involves generating 20 to 40 individual scan lines across that character, or performing an equivalent amount of electro-optic imaging. This is costly and imprecise compared to bar code label scanning, which is hundreds of times simpler than OCR scanning. As a further disadvantage, OCR is based on contact scanning, with no practical ability to read labels at a distance. However, bar code was at a disadvantage for several years, after its invention, compared to OCR, due to the limited availability of label printers. Chapters 4 and 8 explain how this situation has changed in favor of bar code.

Pioneering companies that first used bar code had to invest far more for scanning and decoding devices than the market charges for more sophisticated products today. In addition, the cost of integrating bar code scanners into early computer networks and application programs in order to get a new application on-line, was magnified by the requirement to write custom software in assembly language for minicomputers or 8-bit microprocessors. By contrast, today, many bar code applications are running under menu-driven, user-configurable, prewritten software with "popular" databases embedded for easy activity reporting. Chapters 5 and 6 cover this subject matter in detail.

An acceleration in the spread of technology is sometimes provided unintentionally by government law or policy. This happened in the case of bar code. When the Environmental Protection Agency (EPA) began testing and certifying automobile engines to conform to the Clean Air Act, it was mandated under the act to impose a fine of $10,000 each time a car engine's serial number and component configuration were not recorded and made available for federal inspection. Not long after this bill was passed, an auto company was fined $90 million for failure to record 9000 engine builds. This task is an easy one for bar code laser scanning, and it's called component tracking, so all automotive manufacturers quickly installed bar code systems. In the dozen years since this incident, auto makers have installed hundreds of additional component tracking systems, strictly for internal benefits.

The next few pages contain examples of other benefits of bar code and why "doing business as usual" without bar code can put an organization at a serious disadvantage.

■ BENEFITS OF BAR CODE

Tens of thousands of organizations here and around the world have turned to bar code over the twenty years of its existence as a data collection technology. Chapter 1 has already referred to four early applications of bar code that are commonplace today.

- Supermarket check-out — a retail point-of-sale application
- Automotive assembly control — a production control application
- Marathon race management — a personnel time and attendance application
- Health care — a specimen tracking application

In Part Three of this book, Solutions, the reader is presented with a design path to follow in adopting the four applications listed above, as well as a design path to follow for a number of additional mainstream bar code applications. Calculating benefits from the use of bar code can be an exercise each user approaches individually, but all benefits rely on two well-known attributes of bar code: speed and accuracy. All bar code applications benefit from at least one of these attributes, and most users of bar code rely on both speed and accuracy to improve their operations.

Supermarket Check-out Application

In the supermarket check-out application, the benefits of using bar code accrue to both the merchant and the customer. Every grocery store puts a high value on its product stocking and display space and on serving as many customers as possible. By innovative advertising and merchandising, a store can continually increase its customer traffic, but eventually will reach a time when more check-out lanes need to be added to handle the additional customers. Adding check-out lanes, though, removes some valuable product and display space. By installing bar code scanning to existing lanes, the grocery check-out process is speeded up and product stocking and display space is not reduced. As a customer benefit to using bar code, check-out receipts are very detailed, which permits item-by-item verification by the shopper. As a benefit, the shopper saves check-out time, especially when coupon redemption is incorporated into the bar code application.

The grocery merchant's other major benefit of using bar code is in avoiding stockouts, or the situation of customers finding an empty shelf where their favorite product should be. The computer supporting the check-out scanner is connected to the supermarket's headquarters computer. Every night the exact number of grocery items sold that day is replaced by the distribution center, and the store's shelves can be replenished the next morning. This process is so exact that lower stock levels can be established for each store, bringing higher profits to the grocery chain due to lower inventory costs. This book describes a number of related retail store bar code applications that enhance point-of-sale scanning. Each application dovetails with other applications, providing a systematic way to further increase bar code derived benefits.

Automotive Application

Taking a simple view of the benefits of an automotive engine component tracking system, balance the cost of 50 or 100 bar code scanning stations with avoiding a $90 million EPA fine, and even the most hard-bitten financial controller would rush to sign an approval for that investment. Looking at customer benefits, a customer for a new car would like to be sure that the specified six-cylinder engine had the matching air conditioner attached to it, not the air conditioner for the four-cylinder engine. Bar code systems make sure all the right parts go on the car that was ordered.

Automotive assembly control, or any production control bar code system, has benefits that go far beyond detailed build recording or higher customer satisfaction. Today, bar code use begins when the auto manufacturer sends a purchase order to a supplier for components. The components are individually bar coded, and the shipment container is bar coded as well. These labeling procedures trigger the movement of the components from the manufacturer's receiving dock directly to the assembly line without intermediate parts storage. The reduction in inventory and its related carrying cost can generate savings of 10 percent or more of the manufacturing cost of complex products. Bar code driven material receiving and bar code driven shop floor management produce accurate data in a format that integrates with existing production planning programs.

After automobiles are built, the need for detailed control procedures increases. Next, bar code assures the matching of each auto with the proper transport carrier, and, if shipment damage occurs, bar code scanners record this information during delivery inspection. If product warranty claims are made, or if a product recall is initiated, bar code is the tool that assembles all the claim records. Every new car built after 1990 has a bar code vehicle identification number (VIN) which can be scanned from outside the car with a hand-held laser gun. This benefit permits law enforcement officials to establish a quick and error-proof record of the 21 alphanumeric characters that define a car, down to the serial number, country, assembly plant, and day that car was built. Many benefits throughout the product life cycle are possible through the use of a well-designed bar code data collection system.

Time and Attendance Application

The New York City Marathon is now a part of our sports culture, but in 1977 there was a serious limitation to its ability to grow and satisfy the desire of tens of thousands of runners from around the world who applied to race. At that time only 5000 runners, a quarter of those applying to race, could be registered and scored by the manual methods used by race organizers. That's when Fred Lebow, President of the New York Road Runners Club (NYRRC), the sponsors of this classic race, turned to bar code for assistance.

Since the adoption of bar code control, five times as many runners are now racing in this major marathon, all confident that their finish time and position will be accurately recorded and formatted for publication in the next morning's newspaper. The first user benefit is in providing better service to the running public which applies each year in greater numbers to be accepted in this most prestigious race. Benefits extend far beyond the accurate scoring of the runners, though. Bar code accelerates runner registration because each runner's acceptance document contains vital bar code messages which are scanned during runner check-in and trigger the creation of the bar-coded runner's bib. Beyond this, bar code determines who rides the bus to the starting line, who gets admitted to the pasta party before the race and the disco party after the race, and who can claim an athletic equipment bag.

Using bar code to control a road race represents a personnel time and attendance application, and any organization can profit from similar system design and bar code control principles. Once employees have been assigned a bar code identification badge and a network of scanning stations has been set up, the potential for constructive monitoring of employee activity yields great return. The collection of more accurate cost accounting detail for refined client billing in professional offices is one benefit. More accurate cost information for bidding on future contracts is another. Employee facility use can be improved by better scheduling of access to shared resources such as cafeterias or parking garages. Chapter 11 of this book discusses personnel time and attendance system design in some detail and proposes system short-cuts that can benefit many organizations that adopt bar code to improve their personnel management.

Health Care Application

Unfortunately, bar code can't cure AIDS, but its early role in health care has helped control the spread of AIDS. Whole blood collection and tracking by bar code dates back almost fifteen years, here and overseas. A blood transfusion can be a lifesaving procedure if a donor is properly matched to the patient. Eliminating all systematic error is vital in performing transfusions. Since manual recording of repetitive information is thousands of times more error prone than using bar code for the same task, whole blood and other specimen tracking applications in health care have been popular for many years.

Putting a value on avoiding a fatal mistake in health care delivery is easy because life is priceless. Many health care applications of bar code have been adopted where benefits aren't as dramatic, however. Throughout health care, from clinic admission and insurance recording to x-ray tracking and pharmacy replenishment, hundreds of applications of bar code are in place today. Health care expense consumes more than 15 percent of the gross national product of our country today. It is important in our society to streamline health care delivery. While countless lives have been spared to date by the use of bar code to control blood supplies and eliminate mistakes in medicine production, applications such as the more precise scheduling of nurses and other scarce health care workers are important, too. Improving accuracy in patient billing by using bar code scanners on every hospital floor to record patient procedures and medicine dispensing is increasing hospital revenue and reducing accounting expenses. Exhibit 1.3 shows a nurse scanning a patient's bar-coded identification band. Medical economists look to bar code as a prime tool for future cost and error avoidance, which each of us can benefit from.

Exhibit 1.3

Bar Code Scanning in the Hospital

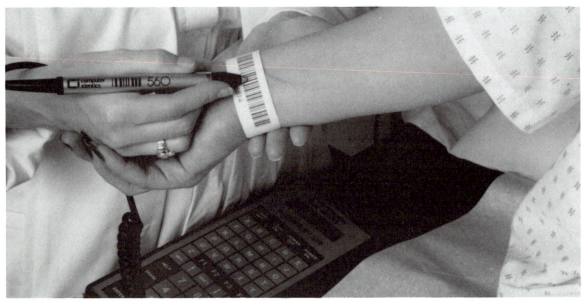

(Courtesy of Computer Identics)

■ LOOKING AHEAD

The first use of modern bar code by a group of companies, including suppliers and customers, was for point-of-sale recording within the grocery industry. Here, a small symbol carries information from the producer of a product to the cash register where a scanner uses it to determine price and set a number of related activities in motion. Although this system was created in 1973 and has enjoyed widespread use since then, many linking pieces that could harmonize commercial processes even further still need to be adopted. Exhibit 1.4 illustrates a flow of activity which has retail point-of-sale (POS) in the middle. The use of bar code before and after the product sale will increase dramatically over the next five years to permit radical changes in the industrial production cycle.

Bar code is now used extensively in the stages prior to retail within individual companies and organizations. Through interindustry activities, as described in Chapters 13 and 14, bar code label standards are emerging to coordinate material and data transactions among a broad

Exhibit 1.4

Future Bar Code Information Cycle

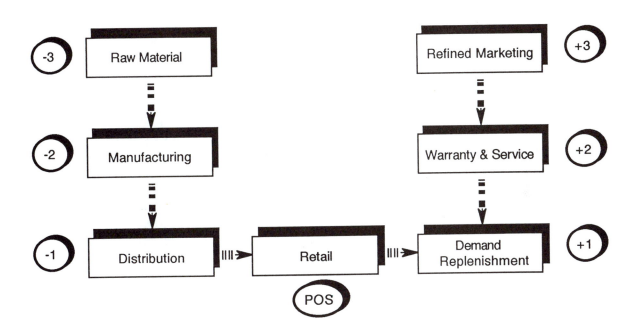

group of primary and secondary suppliers to the food and general merchandise retail industries. Within a few years, suppliers who choose not to cooperate with bar code labeling will be locked out of many markets.

Another trend that will grow rapidly is the use of bar code after the retail POS as is illustrated in Exhibit 1.4. Manufacturers are beginning to receive daily product sales reports from selected retail locations, which lets them measure their products' demand very precisely, and then tune the product distribution channel to eliminate excess or misallocated inventory. The implications of this trend within the U.S. economy are healthy and efficient. Fifteen percent or more of producers' inventory can be reduced as this trend grows, lowering business investment and increasing profits.

Farsighted companies are now beginning to use bar code to link themselves more closely to their customer group, by population segment or directly to individual customers in many instances. Bar-coded warranty return cards and bar code support to product service are

becoming common practices. Today, a field engineer servicing appliances for several manufacturers can scan a bar code on an appliance,
send this message immediately to a remote computer by phone, and
receive back detailed service history and repair instructions for the
exact model under repair.

Although the cost of mailing has risen rapidly in recent years, many
consumers now receive bulky catalogues containing a broad selection
of clothing, appliances, and hobby equipment. Only 1 to 5 percent of
catalogues sent will produce an order, however, so the bulk of the
merchandising effort is wasted. In the future, target mail marketing
based on a consumer's history of previous bar-coded purchases will be
accumulated in a database, and individualized mail campaigns will
direct information only of interest to each consumer, eliminating a
great deal of waste.

The following thirteen chapters of this book will expand on every
important aspect of bar code technology. It is indeed taking over many
important jobs in our society. When used intelligently, bar code can
eliminate boring and error-prone activities and instead build a constructive bridge to efficient management.

Chapter 2

Popular Symbologies

A symbology is a language in bar code technology. In certain countries people speak, write, and read the French language in order to communicate. In other countries the language of choice and custom might be English, German, or Chinese. In the bar code field, a symbology is a language that we use to print and read messages. When a symbology is used to print a message, we call that message a bar code label. Information in a bar code label is read through the eyes of a scanner, but the scanner and the label have to communicate through the same symbology rules or the message will not be understood. There are a number of bar code symbologies, some primitive and some quite sophisticated. Chapter 2 describes five symbologies in some detail and explains why you might decide to use a certain symbology to control one portion of your business and a different symbology to control another portion.

GENERAL SYMBOLOGY CHARACTERISTICS ■

Over forty bar code symbologies have been developed during the history of bar code technology. We will examine only a few in this book. These several symbologies give sufficient flexibility in providing efficient control for 99 percent of the automatic data collection applications adaptable to bar code use. Before presenting the interesting differences between these bar code symbologies, it is appropriate to present the similarities each shares.

19

"X" Dimension

The smallest element of interest in a bar code is called the "X" dimension. This is the narrowest bar or space in the "picket-fence-like" array which carries your message. In designing your bar code driven data collection system, you must first decide what this dimension should be. In the range of practical applications of bar code in use today, you may choose from an "X" of 5 mils to an "X" of 50 mils. A mil is one-thousandth of an inch. Each symbology you choose for your bar code language will have a number of its own rules for the representation of each character in your message. A character is made up of bars and spaces, some of which will be a single "X" in width, and others, two, three, or four "Xs" wide. Exhibit 2.1 illustrates a character in Code (or symbology) 128.

Generally speaking, the larger the "X" dimension, the more forgiving the bar code is when read by a scanner. On the other hand, a larger "X" dimension requires a larger label area. Most applications use "X" dimensions in the range of 10 mils to 20 mils, representing a trade-off among a number of considerations in bar code technology, including printer resolution.

Exhibit 2.1

Character "A" in Code 128

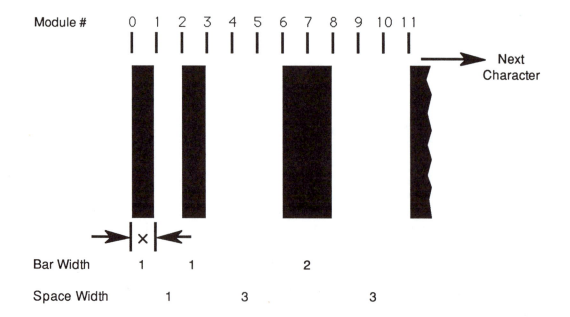

Quiet Zone and Contrast

In order to read a bar code label dependably, a scanner must make a series of sensitive measurements of the contrast between a black (or dark) bar and the white (or light) background space between each bar. To complicate this problem, the scanning instrument projects a spot of energy that can be moving very fast, challenging the capabilities of today's most responsive electronic circuits. Symbology designers have, therefore, specified a zone just to the left and right of the bar code that shall be free of all printing. This "quiet zone" gives the scanning device time to adjust its opto-electronic measurement circuits in order to properly determine the critical width of each bar in the message.

Bar code is most frequently expressed as black bars on white paper. This combination gives the greatest contrast and the most reliably scanned message. However, bar code continues to work effectively when certain other combinations of color and background are used. You see this in supermarket packaging. What is important is the contrast between bars and spaces as viewed by the scanner. Bar code technology is designed to function best with a red light as the scanning spot. The first red-light scanner was a helium-neon laser with a beam projection of 633 nanometers in the light spectrum. Bar code standards have grown up with laser energy as the contrast point of reference. As a result, you must avoid using paper or background label stock that contains any significant blue component which reduces contrast with the bars. Black on white labels are best.

Start, Stop, and Parity Characters

From the earliest applications of bar code, system designers have insisted that bar code symbologies be bi-directional. This means that the bar code message can be read from left to right, or right to left, with no difference in performance. Actually, many bar codes have bars arranged vertically from top to bottom, or vice versa, when applied to cartons or conveyorized objects. The principle remains the same: these bar codes should be as easily read from top to bottom as from bottom to top.

To accomplish this bi-directionality, every symbology provides a separate start and stop character, in addition to the message characters. By convention, we refer to the start character as the unique character to the left of the bar code and the stop character as the unique character to the right of the bar code. In a vertical label, the start would be the top character and the stop would be the bottom character. In some symbologies, the start character may convey some additional information, as you will see later in this chapter.

The symbology designer may also specify a mandatory or optional parity, or check, character in the bar code message. This parity character is included in the bar code to minimize the risk of misreading the message. It does not add any information to the message itself. Usually this parity character is stripped by the decoding portion of the scanner and not passed along to the information network supporting the application. The start, stop, and parity characters (if present) are collectively referred to as bar code message overhead. The quiet zone should be thought of as overhead also and provided for in your label space, even though no transaction information is carried there.

Bar Code Message Composition

Now that we've covered the prerequisites for a bar code message, let's look at how a bar code would typically appear. Exhibit 2.2 represents a horizontal, or picket fence, bar code message. Exhibit 2.3 represents a vertical, or ladder, bar code. As these two exhibits illustrate, the zones to the left and right (or top and bottom) of the symbology are free from all printing so that the scanner can have time to calibrate. The distance set aside for this quiet zone is somewhat variable. Most symbologies require that the quiet zone be ten times the "X" dimension of the symbol, or one-quarter of an inch, whichever is greater. Since most industrial bar codes are printed with an "X" dimension of 20 mils or less, the requirement for one-quarter of an inch of quiet zone on each side is the most common rule. Of course, for large "X" dimensions of 40 or 50 mils, such as warehouse bin labels or

Exhibit 2.2

Horizontal Bar Code, Code 39

Quiet Zone · Start · AB123 Data · Stop · Quiet Zone

shipping container labels, the quiet zone will grow proportionately. While the quiet zone is literally needed on only one side of the bar code, the side from which a scan is initiated, the specification requires a quiet zone on both sides since the scan can begin from either side.

> **NOTE:**
>
> In the authors' experience, a principal cause of poor performance in bar code systems is the failure of many bar code labels to allow for a sufficient quiet zone. Either the data content grew after the application was first initiated without an allowance for additional labeling space, or the label material shifted in the printer, and the subsequent bar codes had their quiet zone clipped from one side.

Exhibit 2.3
Vertical Bar Code, Code 39

After the quiet zone, the start character will appear. Following the start character, the message characters are represented with the most significant characters to the left (or top, in a vertical bar code). This means that the characters are arranged in a horizontal bar code message the same way they are presented in the Roman alphabet. The bar code represented in Exhibit 2.2 is the message AB123. Finally, a stop character is placed at the end of the message, which means to the right side of the horizontal bar code (or at the bottom of the vertical bar code).

In some symbologies, the space between the characters can vary slightly from the normally tight print tolerances of the bars that form a character. Other symbologies demand precise bar-to-bar tolerance throughout the label. Where the space between characters is allowed to vary somewhat, the symbology is referred to as a "discrete" symbology, and the intercharacter variance is called an "intercharacter gap." When the space between characters is held to tight character tolerances, the symbology is said to be "continuous." As a bar code user, you needn't worry about such details. When certain symbologies were developed, the selection of bar code printers may have dictated the need for a variable intercharacter gap. Today, for most print technologies that need has disappeared, but the symbology feature remains.

■ MODERN SYMBOLOGIES

This book has been written to guide the reader in understanding the productive role that bar code plays in data collection dependent applications for organizations processing many items or documents. While many useful symbologies have been introduced since 1970 when industrial bar code first appeared, most users of bar code need only to consider five bar codes for their ongoing applications. Without intending to diminish the role of pioneering symbologies or the companies which introduced them, we have simplified this chapter to focus on mainstream facts and advice, while stripping unnecessary detail from the presentation of currently useful symbologies.

Symbology Standards

Anyone can invent a bar code. All that is necessary is to state how many "X" widths you intend to use to represent each character, and how to arrange those widths between the choices of black and white. Assuming you have not duplicated a character and have allowed for a separate start and stop grouping, you have created a symbology. Unless some scanner manufacturer decides to support your symbology and produce a scanner and decoder to read and process this new code, your symbology will never go into actual use. Every year several new symbologies are created.

From the dozens of symbologies introduced in the bar code field to date, only a handful have achieved broad support. Even those that have achieved this support have typically waited from four to seven years before that support reached an acknowledgment of permanent standards recognition. To gain support for a new bar code today, the symbology creator has to offer the marketplace some dramatic new feature not available in earlier symbologies. As time passes, meeting this criterion becomes more difficult.

In the United States, the process of choosing surviving bar code symbologies is accomplished in the marketplace. A large number of printer and scanner suppliers must be willing to support a symbology before it will gain standards committee approval. The suppliers' usual motivation for investing in the modification of their equipment to print or scan a new symbology is to sell their equipment for projects that only this new symbology can unlock. There is a circular logic in this thinking, and the process of building symbology support takes time.

The need for a standards authority first arose in 1972 when the supermarket industry decided to mark each of the grocery point-of-sale packages with a unique identifier to speed check-out transactions. The grocery industry created an organization that today is called the Uniform Code Council (UCC). The UCC are the keepers and publishers of the UPC symbology, the bar code on the grocery package. Now, any company processing food or manufacturing nonfood items for retail sale in the grocery industry can label its product with a bar code that can be read at the check-out stand.

Unlike the grocery marketplace, industrial codes do not have a single application to serve, so providing the valuable standards keeping and publishing of symbology information fell to a group called AIM (Automatic Identification Manufacturers), which has stepped in to fill that role for nongrocery symbologies. The AIM symbology committee, elected from a field of industry experts annually by the 150 member companies of AIM, meets and reviews symbology submissions. If a symbology proves to have a valuable uniqueness and is supported by a majority of the AIM member companies, a new symbology standards document, called a Uniform Symbology Standard, or

USS, is published. Any printer manufacturer, scanner supplier, or end user of bar code systems can obtain this specification document and produce devices, or a system, confident in the knowledge that it will interface successfully with any other user of the same symbology.

Eventually, the most popular symbologies are given ANSI (American National Standards Institute) standards consideration and approval. After that, international standards approval by the International Standards Organization (ISO) usually follows. Bar code has been an American development from its inception. Over the last seven years, AIM, the bar code equipment manufacturers association, has diligently set up affiliated AIM organizations in Europe, the Pacific Rim, and throughout the industrial world. The result has been a proliferation of true international symbology standards. For example, if you have a product manufactured in Central Europe for retail sale through K-Mart, you can specify the symbology you require on each item and the message content. A Polish or Hungarian producer can turn to its local AIM standards association for that symbology description and comply with your bar code label requirements in every detail.

Universal Product Code/ European Article Numbering Code

The Universal Product Code (UPC) is the symbology used throughout the American grocery industry. Related to this symbology is the European Article Numbering Code (EAN). While the EAN message is not directly translatable by most domestic point-of-sale scanners, this shortcoming will eventually be corrected. In time, these two similar symbologies will essentially merge to be interchangeable within American and European marketplaces. Meanwhile, think of EAN as UPC, with two extra characters in the message it carries.

In 1972, the supermarket industry set out to adopt a symbology that would speed and simplify check-out at the point-of-sale counter. The symbology chosen closely resembled an IBM code of that time called Delta Distance. The industry associations that pioneered in bar code for consumer price look-up established the rules for this symbology and created a numbering system that would permit individual grocery producer identification and individual product identification within the message. A field of five digits was set on the left half of the bar code for producer identification, and a field of five digits was set on the right half of the bar code for product identification. Exhibit 2.4 illustrates a UPC bar code on a popular grocery item.

Exhibit 2.4
UPC Symbology

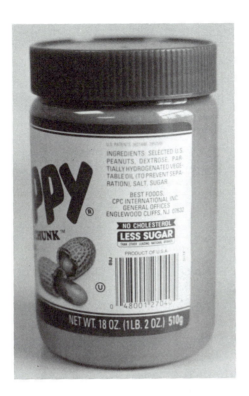

INGREDIENTS: SELECTED U.S.
PEANUTS, DEXTROSE, PAR-
TIALLY HYDROGENATED VEGE-
TABLE OIL (TO PREVENT SEPA-
RATION), SALT, SUGAR.

BEST FOODS,
CPC INTERNATIONAL INC.
GENERAL OFFICES
ENGLEWOOD CLIFFS, NJ 07632

▶ NO CHOLESTEROL ◀
LESS SUGAR
THAN OTHER LEADING NATIONAL BRANDS

PRODUCT OF U.S.A.

0 48001 27040

NET WT. 18 OZ. (1 LB. 2 OZ.) 510g

(Skippy is a registered trademark
of CPC International Inc.)

The UPC symbology is intended for use only in the structured
environment of retail point of sale. Originally planned for groceries,
UPC is now used extensively in convenience and specialty stores, and
in general merchandise retailing. In addition to the ten digits in the bar
code message assigned to the producer identification and the product
identification, the UPC symbology has a left-most character for a
classification number. This number is used for special categories such
as identifying cents-off coupons or meat and produce. The UPC
message contains a right-most check character as well. In any event,
this symbology is used as a fixed-length message system with 11
characters for unique identification and an embedded check digit as a
nonprinting 12th character.

Since some retail items are very small and bar code label area is
difficult to reserve, a short version of the UPC symbology is permitted,
with only six characters of numeric information in its message. The
producer and product information is still available, but zeros within the
producer and product numbering sequence have been squeezed out of
the bar code. The missing zeros are reconstructed again after scanning
within the decoding device at the cash register, for price look-up. This
shortened UPC symbol is called UPC-E.

To summarize UPC, it is an all-numeric, fixed-length (11-character), highly structured symbology, developed for point-of-sale price look-up. You should not consider using this symbology as the bar code element of a data collection application other than retail price look-up. A number of special characteristics of this symbology have been designed in, or enhanced, for maximum effectiveness in retail scanning applications. The UPC symbology anticipated precise print reproduction, and it is difficult to print accurately on certain surfaces such as corrugated container stock, where other symbologies are much more adaptable.

Codabar

Codabar is the earliest symbology still in widespread use today, dating back to 1972. Developed by Pitney Bowes Corporation, it differs from UPC in two important characteristics. While UPC is a fixed-length, all-numeric bar code containing 11 numeric characters in the standard message, Codabar is a variable-length symbology capable of encoding 16 different characters within any length message. Codabar can represent the digits 0 through 9, as well as six special nonalpha characters. There are also four start/stop code choices with Codabar, giving this symbology additional coding ability. With Codabar, in addition to permitting messages to be of variable length, the message can be divided into two bar codes, which are concatenated into a single message after scanning.

Codabar is not considered to be a sophisticated symbology by today's standards, but it has served several user groups well for over a decade. Many library circulation systems are built around Codabar labels. More important, whole blood collection, processing, and distribution is monitored through Codabar symbology in a program initiated during the middle 1970s. And many years ago Federal Express overnight package delivery service adopted Codabar for shipment tracing. Users of bar code who apply data collection to order fulfillment systems should have a scanner programmed to read this code if they intend to append a Federal Express package trace number to their shipment record. Exhibit 2.5 shows a package waybill with a Codabar label in the upper-right-hand area.

System designers should not use Codabar symbology for new applications today, except under unusual circumstances. When Federal Express was choosing a symbology, Codabar had the advantage of allowing serial numbers to be printed by an indexing impact print

Exhibit 2.5

Waybill with Codabar Symbology

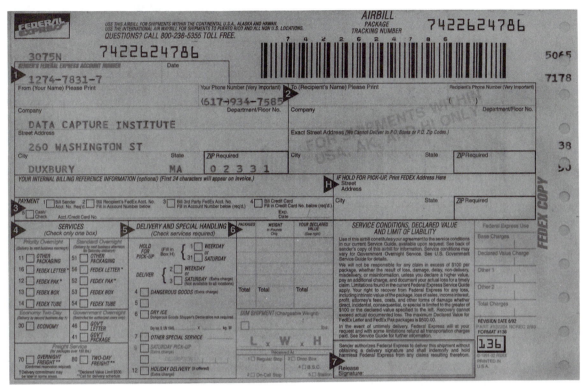

(Courtesy of Federal Express Corporation)

wheel system since it is not held to tight tolerance between characters. With a print wheel numbering system printing millions of documents per year, normal bushing wear between numbering wheels spinning to create each bar code would have prohibited the use of a symbology with more demanding tolerances.

As shown in Exhibit 2.9 on page 37, Codabar messages take more space than Code 128 to express the same information, and space for bar code is limited in most applications. Many bar code applications today would suffer from the limited character set offered with this symbology. For these reasons new bar code applications using Codabar are rare.

Interleaved 2of5 Code

Interleaved 2of5 Code is another symbology developed early in the history of commercial bar code use. It dates back to 1972 and was developed by Computer Identics. An earlier symbology called Straight 2of5 Code expressed numeric information by using two wide black bars out of a cluster of five total black bars per character. The white separator bars in this symbology were all narrow. Interleaved 2of5 used the same coding scheme but permitted the white separator bars to vary in width as well. Two wide spaces out of five total spaces encode a second character, interleaved within the character coded in black. I 2of5 is an all-numeric symbology, and messages encoded with this code have to use an even number of characters since two numeric characters are interleaved together.

Interleaved 2of5 permits users to express a numeric bar code message in a small label, as shown in Exhibit 2.9 on page 37. However, this symbology has a coding weakness in that it is prone to create short reads of long messages when the scan beam crosses the bar code at an angle, running off the bars before the entire message is scanned. For this reason, it should only be used as a fixed-length symbology within any application. Short-length I 2of5 messages should not be intermixed with longer-length I 2of5 messages, since message editing by checking the label length for each scan is recommended for safe practice. It is also wise to include a check digit in your I 2of5 message for additional security. The check digit would appear at the right of the message, just before the stop character.

Exhibit 2.6 shows a carton with a 14-numeric character label using I 2of5 symbology. This photograph illustrates several interesting points. Notice the black border surrounding the bar code. The horizontal black line at the top of the bar code must touch all the bars, and in this way serves the purpose of interrupting a partial or diagonal scan of the symbol, preventing a short message scan. The message format illustrated for this carton label is called the UPC Shipping Container Code and is one option specified by the Uniform Code Council for shipping container marking. Although the I 2of5 was chosen by the UCC for marking corrugated shipping cases, only a few companies adopted this practice and still fewer companies scanned the bar codes. The development of the UCC/EAN-128 symbology, which can incorporate a UPC shipping container code, will eventually eliminate the use of the I 2of5 case code.

Setting aside its ability to express numeric data within a short label, there are several reasons to be cautious when using I 2of5. As an early

Exhibit 2.6
Interleaved 2of5 Shipping Container Code

(Skippy is a registered trademark of CPC International Inc.)

symbology, I 2of5 lacks the sophistication of newer symbologies, limiting the user to all-numeric character representation. Since bar code systems tend to grow over time and encompass new data collection responsibilities not anticipated at a project's initiation, this limitation can become serious. Also, in addition to the tendency of I 2of5 to create false short messages within long messages, I 2of5 can trigger a misread situation when used interchangeably with Code 39, which is currently the most widely used symbology in industrial/commercial bar code applications.

Code 39

The most frequently used symbology in industrial bar code systems today is Code 39. Developed by Intermec Corporation in 1975, this symbology has as its principal feature the ability to encode messages using the full alphanumeric character set. In fact, Code 39 can

also express seven more special characters and, under certain circumstances, ASCII characters as well.   The ASCII feature, however, is
cumbersome and rarely employed.

The widespread popularity of Code 39 began with its selection by
the Department of Defense (DOD) as the bar code label designating the
contents of every package in every shipment delivered to all U.S.
military agencies by suppliers. This DOD directive, which was made
in 1981, called for 40,000 vendors to use Code 39 bar code labels to fulfill
their contract shipping requirements. Exhibit 2.7 illustrates the label,
referred to by the military as the LOGMARS label.

Exhibit 2.7

Code 39 LOGMARS Label

5360022546548

5360-02-254-6548

FSCM 86403 MFR P/N 3492666

SPRINGS RESISTORS

1000 EACH

DLA500 86 P 9191

(Courtesy of Monarch Marking Systems)

During the 1980s, when bar code technology was spreading rapidly, Code 39 was most frequently selected for use by leading companies and industry trade associations, where applications required
alphanumeric message content. The automotive industry chose Code
39 symbology when it designed a standard vendor label for parts
shipment. This had the effect of further spreading the use of Code 39
by 20,000 companies that are suppliers of components to auto manufacturers.   Over all, Code 39 has been the workhorse of the bar code
marketplace for ten years. This symbology can be used in any message
length and has a satisfactory level of data security, with the exception
of the situation referred to earlier in this chapter regarding Code 39 and
Code I 2of5 at the same scan station. To further enhance the security of
Code 39, some users add a message check character just before the stop
character.

The worst that can be said about Code 39 is that it uses a lot of label space — more than any other popular symbology. Over the history of bar code applications, there has been continuous growth in data within a bar code message, which is creating a label space problem for many users of this symbology. Ten years ago a 6-character bar code message was the norm. Today, 20-character messages are typical, and 30 or more character bar code labels are not uncommon. The emergence of data identifiers preceding many bar codes messages exaggerates the label size problem with Code 39 as this development moves forward. Refer to Chapter 14 for more information on the role of data identifiers.

NOTE:

By analogy, when the PC first appeared, the 360-kilobyte, 5-1/4-inch floppy disk seemed to have ample capacity for loading simple programs to a PC, or for data storage. Today, 3-1/2-inch floppy disks containing 1.4 megabytes of data are required by PCs for current program capacity and data storage. CD-ROM disks can hold 600 megabytes of information on a compact 4.72 inch platter. Bar code labels have grown, too, and their symbologies must adapt to new capacity requirements.

Code 128

Code 128 was introduced in 1981 by Computer Identics Corporation. This symbology has a number of features that set it apart from the older symbologies, making Code 128 the preferred code for most new bar code applications. These special features include the following:

- Encodes all 128 ASCII characters without cumbersome procedures.
- Uses the least amount of label space for messages of six or more characters.
- Tested to be the most easily read code with the highest message integrity, due to several separate message check routines.
- Contains function codes that can increase the power of complex data collection processes.

Code 128 fits the general bar code structure illustrated in Exhibit 2.3, including a mandatory check character. However, instead of having a single start character, Code 128 gives users the choice of the following three start characters:

- *Start Code A*. Encodes all following characters into upper-case alphanumeric and ASCII control characters.
- *Start Code B*. Encodes all following characters into upper- and lowercase alphanumeric characters.
- *Start Code C*. Encodes all following characters into pairs of numbers, 00 to 99, producing a "double-density" expression of numeric information within the symbology.

Each separate start character puts the following portion of the message in a different character set. Also, the three start characters act as character set shift codes when used within the message.

With properly designed Code 128 printing software, alphanumeric messages will be expressed in each label by the shortest possible bar code expression. The choice of start codes (or shift codes) will be made by the print software and inserted in the symbology automatically, minimizing label length. Anyone designing a bar code data collection application today should consider Code 128 first. After selecting Code 128, if one of your objectives is to produce a very short bar code label, an all-numeric message format should be the choice. Where this option is not practical, consider using the alpha characters at one end of your message or the other, so only one shift character will have to be inserted between the alpha portion of the message and the numeric (double-density) field. Remember, too, using the double-density field gives two numeric values in a single character, so an even number of numeric digits is required.

> **NOTE:**
> The authors have discovered a number of print software packages on the market that do not optimize Code 128 for the shortest message length. You should avoid using such products since the suppliers lack insight into modern bar code symbology and have omitted an important coding feature from the program.

Exhibit 2.8

UCC/EAN-128 Serial
Shipping Container Code

(00)0001234566666666667

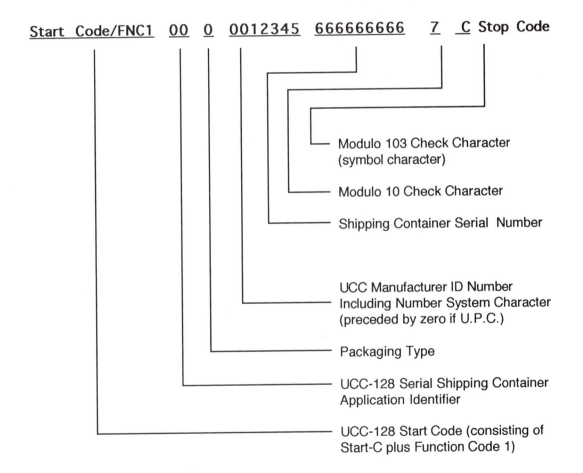

Start Code/FNC1   00   0   0012345   666666666   7   C Stop Code

Modulo 103 Check Character
(symbol character)

Modulo 10 Check Character

Shipping Container Serial Number

UCC Manufacturer ID Number
Including Number System Character
(preceded by zero if U.P.C.)

Packaging Type

UCC-128 Serial Shipping Container
Application Identifier

UCC-128 Start Code (consisting of
Start-C plus Function Code 1)

Exhibit 2.8 illustrates an example of Code 128 that rapidly increased
its use. This symbology has been chosen by several standards authori-
ties for the representation of container information through the UCC-
128 Serial Shipping Container Code. This voluntary use of a bar code

label was developed by buyers and sellers within the retail industry but also has broad industrial application, both here and throughout the world. Code 128 has earned widespread acceptance, making it the symbology of choice for the next decade. Conversion to this symbology has been simplified because scanner and decoding devices with built-in "autodiscrimination" capability permit gradual symbol migration, through the intermixing of old and new symbologies.

UCC/EAN-128

UCC/EAN-128 is the name given to a specially defined subset of Code 128 which is used for application assignments by the UCC and EAN. UCC/EAN-128 inserts a unique, reserved start code, Function Code 1 (FNC1), which ensures that software processing the data treats the initial digits as Application Identifiers (AIs). FNC1 also supplies security to the codes in mixed symbology environments. Code 128 is a symbology standard, whereas UCC/EAN-128 with AIs is a symbology standard plus a labeling standard. As these are relatively new standards, there may be some initial confusion. The important point to remember is that although UCC/EAN-128 is a symbology, it is only used with AIs as a labeling standard. It is important to look for printers, hardware, and software which support UCC/EAN-128 when purchasing new equipment. Older scanners may be able to decode Code 128 but may not recognize the FNC1 code.

UCC/EAN-128 with AIs has been adopted as a labeling standard by a wide variety of industries. Following Function Code 1 and preceding each subsequent data field, the AI distinguishes the content and form of each field. Refer to Chapter 14 for more information on Application Identifiers. Exhibit 2.8 illustrates an example of UCC/EAN-128.

Code Densities

Label space available for the presentation of a bar code is always scarce. While this statement may seem too general, the exceptions are few. Within a typical organization, many departments vie for label space to express instructional or legally mandated information. Beyond this, there are often aesthetic or cosmetic considerations that influence where a bar code may appear on an item or document. Exhibit 2.9 shows the five symbologies covered in this chapter; each expresses

UPC-A

0 12345 67890 5

12 digit Codabar

012345678901

12 digit Code I 2of5

012345678901

12 digit Code39

012345678901

12 digit Code 128

012345678901

12 digit alphanumeric Code 128

0123456789ab

an equivalent numeric message with a similar "X" dimension. Note the
dramatic difference in the label length of each symbology for the same
message. Since Code 128 takes a different amount of label space for an
all-numeric message and an alphanumeric message of the same character length, we have included one of each.

The message density of each symbology is different, and other symbology characteristics vary as well. Choose a symbology for bar code application carefully, and then select print software from a dependable source. These steps will let you create easily scanned bar codes and provide a successful data collection application.

Before leaving the symbologies subject, it would be helpful to look at some special codes that are gaining attention for applications where message content is extremely high.

Stacked and Matrix Bar Codes

The appetite for including more and more detail in bar code messages seems to have no limit. In general, the space available on an item label or form for bar code expression is limited, and because of this, the system designer is forced to compromise an application from time to time. With the growing pressure for more information in limited label space, stacked and checkerboard bar codes have been developed as illustrated in Exhibit 2.10. These codes are sometimes referred to as two-dimensional or matrix codes.

Exhibit 2.10

Stacked and Matrix Bar Codes

Code 1

Code 49

Code 16K

PDF-417

(Code 49, Code 16K and PDF-417 courtesy of PowerLabel ® software by StrandWare, Inc.)

A symbology called Code 49, the first stacked bar code to receive widespread interest, was introduced by Intermec Corporation in 1987. The following year, Laserlight Systems, Inc. introduced Code 16K as an entry in this symbology category. Since then, several additional stacked symbologies have been introduced, including PDF 417 and Code 1. In addition, several proprietary matrix symbologies such as Softstrip and Vericode have been developed. The encoding and decoding of the symbols is proprietary so that the symbol should not be used without obtaining the author's permission.

Checkerboard or matrix symbologies can encode as many as several thousand characters in a small amount of space. Small, stacked symbols such as Code 16K and Code 49 can be read with a laser scanner. However, area scanners are preferred when larger, stacked symbols are used, such as Code 1, Datacode, and MaxiCode.

Area scanners use raster-scanned laser or area CCD camera technology. The cost of these scanners is now competitive with laser scanners. Code 1 was the first checkerboard symbology to be placed in the public domain; therefore, we will discuss its features. Each Code 1 symbol has bars running through the center which are used to identify the symbol and measure the size and rotation. Data is encoded in rectangular tiles comprised of eight squares in a four-wide by two-high array to encode an 8-bit byte. These bytes can represent ASCII data, error correction data, function characters, or binary encoded data. Binary encoded data can represent three alphanumeric characters for two bytes, three digits in ten bits, or user-defined 8-bit bytes. The user-defined byte mode can be used to encrypt data for secrecy.

Code 1 has eight different sizes. The smallest, Code 1A, can encode up to 13 alphanumeric characters or 22 digits. The largest, Code 1H, can encode up to 2,218 alphanumeric characters or 3,550 digits.

Stacked and matrix bar code applications are not yet in the mainstream of bar code technology. They do represent the direction toward which the technology is headed in some industries. They have been widely discussed in health care, for instance, where each unit dose of medicine requires lengthy documentation but where very little label area is available for a bar code. Matrix codes have also been used on patient identification bracelets. Another use is in electronics manufacturing where there is a need to track product, lot number, or serial numbers on small products such as integrated circuits and circuit boards. Stacked codes are also used in distribution centers with a shipping computer system and an omni-directional camera to route each box to the correct loading dock automatically, and to generate an accurate manifest and customer invoice. Finally, the recycling industry has used two-dimensional (2-D) symbologies in high-speed sortation systems that separate bottles by unique plastic composition.

> **NOTE:**
> Until the development of stacked codes, all symbologies were referred to simply as "bar codes." Now you sometimes hear the distinction between "stacked," "linear," and "matrix" bar codes, with "linear" referring to the symbologies where the complete message is expressed in a single line of bars.

■ CHOOSING A SYMBOLOGY

Although Chapter 2 presents a number of symbologies and references the fact that over forty have been developed over the course of bar code history, your choice of a symbology need not be too difficult. The first consideration in approaching symbology choice is to strive for ease and accuracy of scanning. To achieve this goal, the bar code presentation must sometimes trade among the following desirable virtues that are sometimes in conflict:

- Keep the bar code short — label space is always scarce.
- Make the bar code as square as possible — this makes it easier to scan, whether using a wand or moving beam laser device.
- Use the largest "X" dimension that will fit in the label area (after allowing for quiet zones) — this increases scanning depth of field.

Exhibit 2.11 illustrates a successful bar code from the point of view of compromising these qualities. Here we see a 10-character label in Code 128, with an all-numeric message structure. The bar code is 2.5 inches long and 1.25 inches high, giving a 2:1 aspect ratio, which is a reasonable goal to shoot for with hand-scanned item, tag, or document bar codes. This label's "X" dimension is 24 mils, which should provide

Exhibit 2.11

Well-Proportioned
Code 128 Bar Code

0123456789

good depth of field using hand-held laser scanners. The greater the depth of field, the more quickly data collection can take place, even when scanning a bar code through several layers of clear stretch wrap with the label set back from the wrapping surface by several inches. Labels with aspect ratios beyond 6:1 (the length is six times the bar code height) require more operator care in scanning, since the scan wand or laser beam will frequently fall off the bar code before all bars have been crossed. This problem lowers the "first-read rate," slowing data collection, and can become an operator morale factor in extreme cases. There seems to be a "squeeze-the-bar-code-in" mentality in many bar code applications, which produces a long narrow bar code, often with the code placed in a label area difficult to position for easy scanning.

The most efficient symbology in practical use today is Code 128, and it should be the first symbology choice to consider, unless an application requires a different symbology to comply with an industry standard such as LOGMARS. Within Code 128, the use of all-numeric information gives the shortest bar code. Otherwise, clustering any necessary alpha characters to the right or left of the message would be desirable in order to minimize bar code length. Occasionally, you may be required to bar code a numeric message with a special character in the middle, such as a dash or comma. Rather than use three character spaces in Code 128, consider inserting this special character through a formatting procedure when the bar code message reaches the host, or even at the decoding terminal. This technique may save a great deal of label space overall.

If there is a requirement to print a message of 50 characters or more, or if label space forces the message into a stack with no quiet zone available, the 2-D symbologies should be considered. Otherwise, the authors advise using the simpler linear bar codes.

■ SUMMARY

The first bar code symbologies began with simple binary representations of data using wide and narrow black bars separated by white spaces of constant dimension. Today, modern symbologies use sophisticated representations of ASCII characters through as many as eight bar and space values, with check characters embedded in each message, and function codes available to link bar code messages or trigger special processing routines. Users of bar code technology today inherit twenty years of evolutionary development in the field of symbology.

The power of the microprocessor is key to the accurate printing and decoding of modern symbologies, as many measurements and calculations must be performed to create or decode a single character. Beyond this, the bar code user has the ability to mix symbologies and read each reliably with state-of-the-art scanning devices through a technique called autodiscrimination. This permits orderly transition from one symbology to another within an application, and should put an emphasis on message collection and application performance using bar code, instead of a preoccupation by designers with symbology choice.

Chapter 3

Scanners

A bar code is a data message expressed through a special language called a symbology. The bar code message is carried, via a label, to many data collection locations where it will be "read." This message, together with time, place, and additional information recorded at the reading point, will combine to become a record in a database. The collective information in the database will enable an organization to operate a department or function more efficiently through timely and accurate detailed reports of activities.

The purpose of Chapter 3 is to explain how bar code scanners "read" the data messages on labels and what characteristics scanners should have to perform bar code reading effectively. There are a variety of scanning devices to choose from in the marketplace today, with promising developments reported for more choices to come. This chapter will highlight the scanning technology rather than present technical details. Guidelines, where applicable, will be offered to assist in matching scanner technology with different bar code applications.

GENERAL PRINCIPLES OF SCANNING ■

Bar code presents data messages through arrangements of varying width black bars and white spaces. Modern symbologies express bar code information by clustering bars and spaces as characters comprising the data message, and by requiring certain overhead (nonmessage) characters called start codes and stop codes and sometimes a check digit to assure reliable reading. As we learned in Chapter 2, there also has to be a quiet zone on either side of the bar code. Contrast between the black bars and the white spaces between the bars must conform to a minimum standard.

Spot Size

A bar code scanner is a device that projects a tiny spot of light crossing the bars and spaces of a label and then precisely measures the reflectance back from that spot. Scanners create an electrical signal (voltage) that is proportionate to the strength of the reflected light and amplify and shape this signal for reliable transmission to a data entry terminal. Data entry terminals are described in greater detail in Chapter 7.

Chapter 2 explained that a bar code is controlled by its "X" dimension, which is the narrowest bar in the array of bars that carries each message. To achieve the most dependable results from bar code data collection you must match the "X" dimension of the symbol with a scan spot of proportionate diameter. In other words, your scanner can project a spot that is too large, too small, or ideally matched for your bar code. To help understand this concept, look at Exhibit 3.1. The scan spot indicated to the left of the bar code is surrounded by a circle that represents an optical sensor positioned to collect the reflected energy from each bar and space in the code. As the scan spot moves across the bar code, reflections from each white space and light absorption from each black bar, in combination, produce a voltage variation through the scanner's electronic sensor. This voltage variation is illustrated underneath the bar code in Exhibit 3.1.

The ideal relationship between the scanning spot and the "X" dimension of the bar code would have the spot at 80 percent (in diameter) of the "X" value. In other words, if you have chosen your symbology, and decided to print bar codes with a 10-mil "X" dimension, then your scan spot should be 8 mils. Scanning problems can arise if the spot size is too large or too small, relative to the "X" dimension. Since bar code does not normally misread, this spot size mismatch will result in a poor "first-read rate." This type of problem is more noticeable with a wand scanner than a laser scanner, which scans tens or hundreds of times per second, and often finds a good read path relatively quickly. A gross mismatch between the bar code "X" dimension and the scan spot will produce a "no read" at that scan station.

Exhibit 3.1

Scanning a Bar Code

SCAN

SPOT OF LIGHT

RECEIVER'S VIEW

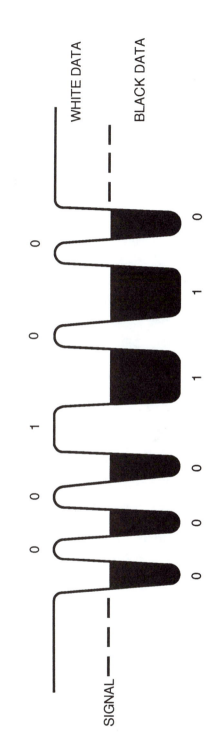

WHITE DATA

BLACK DATA

SIGNAL ---

Scan Rate

As we will see later in this chapter, a wide choice of scanning instruments is available in today's marketplace. Different scanners have been developed to respond to the variety of bar code applications which have emerged over twenty years of practice. Many devices are tailored to the practices of specific user groups. One way in which scanners differ is in scan rate, which may be as low as 1 scan per second using a wand scanner, or as high as 1000 scans per second with a fixed-mounted laser scanner. Also, to decode a bar code message properly the speed of the scan spot over the bars and spaces of a symbol must be relatively constant across the entire symbol. A speed variation by the scan spot of more than two to one will challenge the best decoding logic, since the shape of the signal produced by the spot reflection will be distorted.

Light Source

The earliest bar code scanners were developed around the helium-neon (HeNe) laser tube as the energy source. These lasers emit red light at 633 nanometers (nm) wavelength, which has influenced the choice of bar colors and space (background) colors ever since. Most industrial and nonfood applications of bar code revolve around black bars on white label stock. Prepackaged grocery products may incorporate colored bars and contrasting color background into their symbol presentation. The Uniform Code Council has published strict, clear guidelines to limit the choice of colors to conform with the signal contrast generated by the HeNe scanners. Where appropriate in the description of some scanners, we will comment on limitations of certain devices if the scanner light source varies from HeNe and creates a reading compromise.

Depth of Field

Bar code technology "won" the competition for industrial data collection technology twenty years ago, in large part due to the distance bar code could be read from a fixed-mounted scanning station adjacent to an automatic conveyor. Later, when many bar code labels were in circulation, contact scanning was developed with significant additional benefits. As you will see, different scanning devices operate at different distances from the bar code. The variation in distance that a bar code can be read from a scanner is called "depth of field." The scanner marketplace offers scanners with "zero" depth of field, called contact scanners, as well as remote scanners with depths of field of several feet.

SCANNER TYPES ■

In designing your bar code driven data collection system, it is important to anticipate your organization's future bar code uses over the broadest range of applications. In this way the symbology decision, as well as your choice of "X" dimension and communications network architecture, will give your system its longest productive life. Later, when you choose scanning devices for a specific application, you will find available an agreeable variety that can be tailored to your needs. Presented next are the general categories of scanners on the market now. Most have changed little in the last several years, although price tends to come down about 10 percent per year, as with other electronic devices. Many scanning devices purchased five, or even ten, years ago still serve well, so you should expect many satisfactory years of use from scanners purchased today.

Wand Scanners

In the opinion of the authors, the most cost-effective method of manual bar code scanning is the wand scanner, or light pen, as it is sometimes called. This method of scanning was developed for bar code use by Identicon Corporation in 1972 and quickly became the most popular scanning instrument due to its low cost and ruggedness. Exhibit 3.2 illustrates a modern wand scanner. The most significant change in wand scanners over the last few years is the integration of the bar code decoder into the wand itself, eliminating the need for a special decoder box or decoder software residing on the host computer. Wand scanners with built-in keyboard wedges which permit direct data input from the scanner to a computer screen are also available. These features raise the cost of the scanner, but this can be offset by easier hardware integration.

Using a wand scanner requires attention to certain details for greatest effectiveness. As in all applications, there should be great

Exhibit 3.2

Wand Scanner

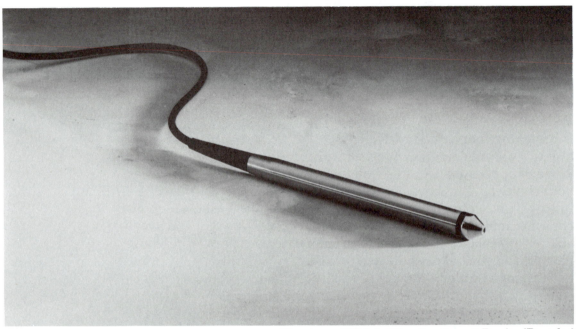

(Courtesy of Welch Allyn-Scanteam® Reader/Decoder)

emphasis on the printing excellence of the bar code message presentation. First of all, the bar code should be printed to the tolerances for the symbology chosen, and the wand user must be trained to scan a label properly. Proper scanning technique involves starting with the pen tip lightly touching the label, well to one side of the symbol, and moving across all the bars to a position well to the other side of the bar code in one continuous motion. The wand angle is important, too, as the wand should be held at an angle of about 60 degrees above the label surface. This is about the angle one would use to write with a pen, so it does not typically present a training problem. Since the wand tends to flood the bar code with light and collect the image with a lens to create the spot effect, too horizontal an angle will let light scatter into space, and too vertical an angle will bounce more light back to the wand's detector than it is calibrated to handle. As in any other manual procedure, training is important, although studies indicate that ten minutes of training is the normal period required for proficiency.

While the emphasis on excellence of bar code label presentation is a general precondition for any successful bar code system, any weakness in label printing will show up quickly with a wand scanner. The scan rate for wand scanning is dependent on the operator, but would normally be about one to two scans per second. If the label is printed poorly or has deteriorated in a rugged application or through abuse, it could take many scan attempts to find the path across the bars where a clear presentation of each bar and space is available. Operators tend to get frustrated and mistrust equipment when more than three scans are required to read a label while using a wand scanner. In addition to making sure that the bar code has been printed to exact tolerance, there should be a good match between the wand spot resolution and the "X" dimension of the symbology. Wand scanners can be purchased with a choice of spot resolutions of about 4 mils, 6 mils, and 13 mils. Often users are unaware of the wand resolution at a scan station, and the spot may not match the bar dimensions or printer type properly.

NOTE:

The majority of wands illuminate the bar code by a light-emitting diode (LED) using the bright red color region, at 660 nm wavelength, which is very close to the HeNe laser. There is a choice of infrared illumination at 940 nm, however, which may be required for reading employee badges covered with a red security filter, used to prevent copying in time and attendance systems. When using infrared wands, be sure that the bar code ink has a high carbon content. Infrared wands have difficulty reading many thermal printed labels.

Variations of the wand packaging include the slot reader shown in Exhibit 3.3 and a pistol grip scanner (not pictured). Both of these devices work on the same principles as the wand scanner and may even contain the same active components. While the power consumption of the wand scanner is very low, designers sometimes pulse the scan beam to limit power even further. This is helpful in preserving battery life when wands are used with portable data entry terminals. The pistol

Exhibit 3.3

Slot Reader
Variations

(Courtesy of LINX Data Terminals, Inc.)

grip scanners often include a press-to-scan trigger, so that power to the pen LED is only required during the scanning process. There is virtually no depth of field to a wand scanner, except enough to penetrate clear plastic label laminates which give abrasion or moisture resistance to the label. However, many users prefer the touch-and-scan feel you get with wand scanning, and operators are far less likely to collect the wrong bar code message from a menu crowded with bar codes than when using a hand-held laser gun for this same task.

The wand scanner works as well as any other type of scanner with the exception of scan rate, and it may cost as little as one-tenth the price of other manual scanning devices. If the bar code system is well designed and maintained in all respects, wand scanning is hard to improve upon for overall cost effectiveness. In approaching bar code system design, begin with the assumption that you will use one or more wand scan stations, and be careful to ensure that the labels in your system are of acceptable quality to make this type of device productive.

Hand-Held Laser Guns

When contact with the bar code label is awkward or if the nature of the application makes contact impossible, the hand-held laser gun is an alternative scanning device to consider. The general design of a laser gun incorporates a HeNe laser tube or a solid state laser diode, creating a scan line by projecting a beam of energy off a rotating prism or oscillating mirror. The scan beam then exits through a scanner window to trace across the bar code symbol, as illustrated in Exhibit 3.4. While a device of this sophistication is about six times more costly than a wand scanner, it is useful and worth the premium under certain circumstances. Scanning a bar code on a curved or irregular surface or through

Exhibit 3.4
Hand-Laser Scanning Principle

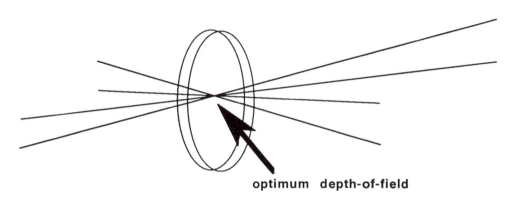

optimum depth-of-field

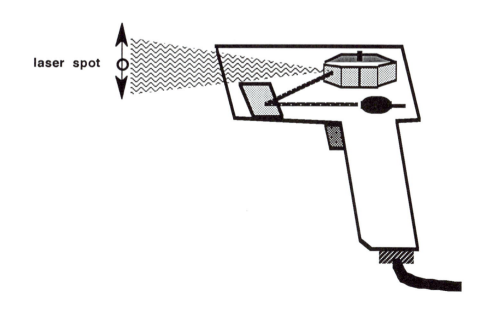

laser spot

multiple layers of stretch wrapping requires a noncontact device such as the laser gun.

Devices using an infrared laser diode (ILD) project a scan beam whose light is beyond the spectrum the eye can see. These guns require a separate beam marker light to permit the user to aim them. The visible laser diode (VLD) gun and the HeNe laser gun project visible scan beams, permitting the user to see the scan line while it covers the bar code. Of course, the scan line is actually the laser spot moving very rapidly, usually about 40 scans per second, and the spot appears as a line. When the scanner is presented with a good quality bar code label printed to approved tolerances, a single scan will suffice to read the message and the data collection will be immediate. However, if the label is damaged or poorly printed, the multiple scans generated by a laser gun will more rapidly seek and find an acceptable read path through the bar code than will a wand scanner, reducing employee frustration and accelerating data capture.

The energy radiated by laser guns is typically less than 1 milliwatt of power, but this light is focused in a concentrated spot and not scattered in all directions like the illumination from a light bulb. Even though this spot is constantly moving, protective government regulations apply to the industrial use of lasers regarding safety and warning labels. If a manufacturer wants to sell a laser gun as a Class I instrument and avoid placing a warning label on the scanner, the scan beam must be self-extinguishing after a period of about 5 seconds of use, and then remain off for several more seconds. In general practice, the scanner operator may need several seconds to bring the bar code label and the scan beam together, and if the label is damaged or out of spec, the time it takes to find a good scan path may exceed the scanning interval of the gun. Then, another scan attempt would be required by the operator after an annoying pause. By choosing a Class II laser instrument, you can have the laser beam remain on until the bar code is read, eliminating some employee frustration, especially in situations where label quality is poor. Your scan instrument, however, would have to display a warning label.

During the discussion of the "X" dimension in Chapter 2, we advised choosing a large bar width whenever label space permitted. With laser scanners, whether hand-held or fixed-mounted, the larger the "X" dimension the greater the distance the label can be read from the scanner. This is because the laser beam must be focused to a fine scan spot and will only hold that exact dimension for a short distance on either side of the scanner's focal point. With a bar code using a large "X" dimension, the scan spot will still be matched to the bar code for a greater distance on both sides of the focal point. This produces a more forgiving label. To illustrate what this improvement represents, a 7.5-mil "X" dimension will produce a 4- or 5-inch scanning range, but a label with a 40-mil bar dimension will give you a depth of field of almost 4 feet. The newest laser scanners, classified as Class IIIA, have working ranges of up to 20 feet with 70-mil bar codes. For scan operators who are performing a physical inventory using a fork-lift truck or picking orders from extended warehouse bins, this depth-of-field improvement can be the key to high system productivity.

> **NOTE:**
> It is frequently assumed that operators would always prefer a laser gun to a wand scanner, due to the scanning aggressiveness of the gun. This is not so. Since the wand has no depth of field, many employees prefer the "touch and scan" characteristics of the wand because no decision about distance from the label to the gun must be factored into the task.

The popularity of laser guns makes it clear that many users find their convenience will offset their added cost in some applications. For example, they can often be used "hands free" as shown in Exhibit 3.5. Here we see a hand laser scanner, which is periodically mounted on a stand, automatically scanning labels passed beneath the beam. This approach to scanning is popular among a number of retail point-of-sale (POS) users, and in certain operations such as tool tracking. The majority of item labels can be scanned by passing them beneath the scanner while it is mounted on the stand. However, heavy or oversized items can be scanned by removing the laser gun and reaching over to the distant label.

CCD Scanners

When bar code labels can be brought in contact with the scanning device, the user has one more choice to consider: the charge coupled device (CCD) scanning method. CCD technology has been used commercially for about ten years and is a technique whereby the bar code is entirely flooded with light (typically by a cluster of LEDs), and the image of the bar code is transferred to an array of very small photo detectors. Here, scanning differs somewhat from the method shown in

Exhibit 3.5

Stand-Mounted
Laser Gun

(Courtesy of Spectra-Physics Scanning Systems, Inc.)

Exhibit 3.1. Instead, the characteristics of the bar code are determined by electronically sampling each individual photodetector, which interprets each bar and space measurement by the number of adjacent detectors sensing black, in comparison to white. Exhibit 3.6 illustrates such a device.

The cost of a CCD scanner is about halfway between the wand scanner and the hand-held laser gun. CCD scanners are more rugged than the laser gun because they are lighter and have no moving parts. Although most CCD scanners require near contact with bar codes (an inch or less), newer CCD scanners have a depth of field of up to 3 inches. They would not be suitable for an application where labels are set back several inches behind stretch wrap, as is common in many warehouse operations. A bigger drawback to their use stems from the

Exhibit 3.6
CCD Scanner

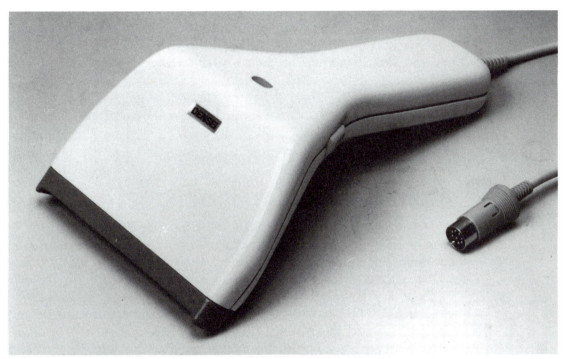

(Courtesy of Densei)

need to read a wide variety of label lengths and formats, where at least one bar code message is long, or expressed in a large "X" dimension. Here, the length of the bar code may well exceed the width of the scan head, which would make the label unreadable. Where it is practical to use CCD scanners, you will find that their training requirement is the easiest to fulfill. The concept of "taking a picture" of the label by covering it completely with the end of the scanner and tripping a switch is easy for anyone to grasp. Refer to Exhibit 3.4 for an illustration of this concept.

CCD scanners have begun to play a more important role in certain bar code data collection systems. We mentioned in Chapter 2 that another generation of scanners is needed to unlock all the potential of the stacked bar code, with the greater information density it can deliver. The CCD technology is the most practical for applications requiring this type of symbology. Another influence which would give CCD scanners a boost would be more widespread use of standard interindustry labels, such as those discussed in Chapter 13. CCD scanners are widely used here and overseas for point-of-sale scanning of general merchandise. The small UPC-type label is the standard bar code for retail transactions, and when recording a few purchases the CCD is cost-effective in comparison with the table-top laser scanner we use in U.S. supermarkets. Mixing bar code reader styles to match detailed data collection procedures and label types is an attractive option for the modern system designer. Whether you choose wands, laser guns, or CCD scanners at any data collection location will depend on bar code application details that should emerge during your system planning and design exercise.

Fixed Laser Scanners

The most advanced application of bar code data collection is illustrated by the fixed laser scanner, first developed and marketed commercially by Computer Identics Corporation in 1970. While industrial applications for fixed laser scanners first appeared in progressive factories and distribution centers, the role of fixed laser scanners in supermarkets for grocery check-out made this application more prominent with the general public. While industrial scanners and point-of-sale scanners are similar in many respects, it's worthwhile to consider their differences first.

Table-Top Scanners

Before the grocery industry adopted bar code scanners for item check-out in supermarkets, most grocery items were taken out of the shopping cart by the shopper and placed on a conveyor belt. The check-out clerk then activated the belt to bring the packages closer, reached for each package, read the price, and entered the amount into the cash register. The introduction of bar code scanning did away with the need to place a unit price on each package and added, in bar code, the producer number and product number from which the price information could be determined through a look-up table. Early scanner suppliers to this application designed a laser instrument that would fit between the check-out clerk and the conveyor belt, permitting the clerk to pass each item above a window from which the laser beam was emitted. Exhibit 3.7 illustrates this type of scanner. It is interesting to note that usually two or more beam paths are projected through the

Exhibit 3.7

360-Degree
Supermarket
Scanner

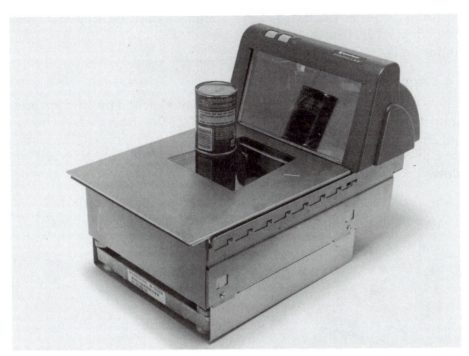

(Courtesy of Spectra-Physics Scanning Systems, Inc.)

table-top window. This use of multiple traces increases the likelihood that the bar code will intersect a laser beam. Food packagers are asked to place their bar code on the package bottom, or on a side of the package near the bottom to keep the label close to the scanner window, within the several-inch depth of field of this type of device. Since laser scanners are U.S. Bureau of Radiological Health (BRH) Class I (as are many laser guns), the scanner will remain on for only a few seconds, and then it will shut itself off. For this reason, a clerk will key enter the grocery identification if the bar code fails to read after making several passes above the scan window.

With the spread of bar code into general merchandise and convenience stores, other laser scanning packages have been developed. Hand-held laser guns, used manually or mounted in a stand as seen in Exhibit 3.5, have found a place in data collection. The footprint of the table-top scanner is considered too large for many busy check-out counters outside the supermarket, so a narrow profile side-view scanner has begun to appear in some stores. This design is somewhat similar to the table-top scanner rotated 90 degrees, so that the laser beam exits across the counter instead of up from the counter surface.

Again, several scan traces are used to minimize the time needed for the bar code label and the laser trace to intersect. Exhibit 3.12 is an example of this design.

Conveyor-Mounted Scanner

As mentioned earlier, the warehouse conveyor and production line were instrumented with laser scanning before the supermarket checkout lane. Progressive companies have continuously increased automation in material movement and found they frequently stopped or slowed conveyors to permit a clerk to key in a package destination or

Exhibit 3.8

Fixed Scan Station

(Courtesy of Computer Identics Corp.)

to record an item's product or serial number. The advent of the laser bar code scanner has eliminated the need to slow or stop automatic material-handling equipment, since bar code labels can express this information, and scanners can read each data message at a much higher speed than can an individual, and without mistakes.   Exhibit 3.8 illustrates a fixed scan station beside a conveyor.

The remainder of Chapter 3 discusses considerations that are important in the use of fixed-mounted scanners. Certain application choices and trade-offs go beyond the obvious and require more detailed systems analysis than do manual scanners. While hand-held laser guns are like fixed scanners but packaged with smaller components and a trigger for activation, the fixed conveyor scanners cost three to thirty times as much to purchase. The price difference is partly explained by the lower volume of devices sold for automated applications, and partly explained by the higher-quality laser, optics, and more rugged housing these instruments possess. Beyond that, fixed laser scanners include a number of specialized interfaces for photoelectric relay sensing and activation of conveyor controls.

> **NOTE:**
>
> In applications of fixed-mounted conveyor scanning of bar code, the success of such systems depends equally on the material-handling skills directed at the problem and data collection expertise. Make sure that a competent conveyor engineer looks at your design, especially from the vantage point of the electromechanical interfaces required and event timing.

Special Scanning Features

As we know from the discussion of hand-held laser guns, scanning energy radiates from a laser as a column of red light spreading very slowly as the laser spot moves out from the laser tube. Engineers then place focusing lenses in the beam path so that the scan spot will have its optimum size at a predictable distance from the face of the scanner, called the focal point. We also know that, depending on the "X" dimension of the bar code, a label can be read somewhat closer to and farther from the scanner than just at the focal point. In fixed-mounted conveyor scanners, this distance within which the label can be read is called the depth of field. Fixed laser scanners are engineered to deliver as much depth of field as possible. By employing a longer HeNe laser tube in a fixed-mounted scanner, the laser spot can be broadcast with less beam spread, helping to extend the depth of field. Better lenses in these instruments also contribute an improvement.

Sophisticated techniques are now being added to fixed laser scanners to provide variable scan spot focus capability. For example, distance sensors developed from self-focusing photographic cameras have been added to some scanner designs; they sense the distance to the approaching carton and adjust the spot focusing lenses as needed. Other suppliers are using holographic focusing scanners; these focus the scan spot at a number of focal distances on successive scans. In this case there is an expectation that the bar code label will be within the ideal field of view of the scanner for one of the set focal distances. When considering these scanner choices, make sure the scanner vendor explains the focusing design completely. Scanning experts prefer two or more bar code reads across the same label to compare together before accepting data from an automatic scanner. If the scan focusing technique has the effect of slowing the scan rate down, you may not achieve the goal of several identical scans at high conveyor rates.

NOTE:

By using more and more refined laser tubes and focusing optics, a bar code can be read at greater distances when combined with a larger "X" dimension. However, this process has a limit. While little laser energy will be lost on the path from the scanner to the bar code, the return reflected signal will get rapidly weaker with more distant bar codes. As a rule of thumb, to read a bar code 20 inches away with a well-designed fixed laser scanner, your bar code should have at least a 20-mil "X" dimension. Likewise, to read a bar code at 40 inches from the scanner, the bar code should have at least a 40-mil "X" dimension. This label distance is about the farthest practical distance from which you should attempt to read under sound design practices.

Another application consideration requires matching the data rate from automatic scanners with the host computer's capacity to accept information. Fixed-mounted laser scanners are often engineered into a materials management system at a time when a conveyor is first installed. Over time, additional bar code labels may be applied to scanned items — for example, adding product weight information when only product type had been previously scanned. If production volume increases in a scanning application, the conveyor line speed may be increased or item spacing may be reduced. All these actions have the effect of increasing the data rate of information flow from the scanning station to the host computer. At some point the capacity of the network will be exceeded, or the host computer cycle time will become greater than the interval between messages, and bar code information will be lost. It is not possible to describe all the symptoms of this kind of data rate conflict, due to the number of ways that data collection systems can be designed. However, fixed laser scanners are very aggressive data collection devices and can overload your upstream communications and processing components in an automated factory or warehouse.

Label Orientation

Most fixed laser scanners are single-trace devices mounted beside a conveyor positioned to read all bar code labels of interest passing by that station. Since the scan trace must cross all bars and spaces in a single pass, the labels must have the bars and spaces at right angles to the scan trace. There are two traditional ways to mount these scanners. The preferred method is to have the scanner create a vertical scan beam or "curtain" across the conveyor through which the item or container will pass. Then all vertical or "ladder" bar codes will be scanned and the bar code messages collected. Exhibit 3.9 illustrates this mounting method.

Exhibit 3.9

Ladder Bar Code and Scanner

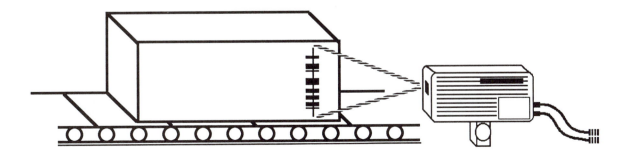

Exhibit 3.10

Picket Fence Bar Code and Scanner

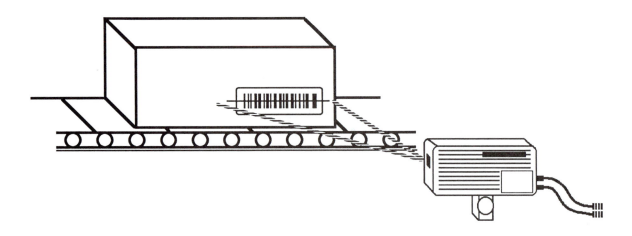

The second method of mounting fixed laser scanners is to have a horizontal or "picket fence" bar code positioned at a fixed height above the conveyor surface with the laser scanner mounted so that the beam is parallel to the conveyor and aimed at the middle of the label. This method is illustrated in Exhibit 3.10. Here, the effectiveness of the bar code scanner is reduced somewhat from the use of a ladder code shown above. Since this scanner can only look at a single height on the passing container, any misalignment of the scanner or labeling error that changes the label height will produce a "no read" and reduce the system effectiveness. As an additional weakness, a lot of good bar code information is ignored by horizontal scanning of a picket fence label. A fundamental virtue of bar code scanning comes from the data redundancy represented by the bar height, which repeats each message many times if different scan paths are taken across the label. This gives the technology forgiveness, working around common deficiencies in certain bar code print methods. Using a ladder bar code and a vertical scan trace, the same bar code may be scanned dozens of times while the label passes through the beam. This repetitive scanning is not accomplished with picket fence labels. Since some items or containers are too short to carry a vertical bar code, compromises are occasionally unavoidable.

Multiple Trace Scanners

As we saw earlier in this chapter, the commercial supermarket scanners use a single laser tube to create multiple scan traces, shortening the time required for a check-out clerk to read the bar code. Fixed laser scanners used in conveyor data collection have been designed with multiple trace capability as well. A modification of the horizontal scan beam reading a picket fence label shown in Exhibit 3.10 contains a scanning polygon with slightly angled reflecting mirrors to generate four, eight, or twelve scan lines, spaced slightly apart at the bar code target distance and providing several different scan heights at the symbol. While this feature improves the readability of poorly printed labels, or compensates for labels applied above or below the ideal height, breaking the scan line apart will slow the scan rate down considerably.

To this point we have described fixed conveyor scanning stations which have scanners mounted alongside the conveyor. Increasingly, scanners are mounted above the conveyor, aiming down at items or packages passing beneath the scan station. Large order processing systems frequently employ high-speed tray conveyors with picked items moving underneath one or more scanners at high speed. Adding to the scanning challenge is the problem that there is no fixed orientation for the bar code labels. The omnidirectional label in Exhibit 3.11 is an illustration of this design. For this type of data collection system you have several choices to consider when using bar code scanners. A single-line scanner, positioned with the scan beam across the conveyor, will be capable of scanning each item if its identifying bar code is printed twice, in two oversquare patterns, as shown in Exhibit 3.11.

ZIP DESTINATION

02332

Exhibit 3.11
Omnidirectional
Label

The omnidirectional label, however, requires a lot of label space, and choosing this approach may not be practical. As an alternative, several scanner manufacturers are offering multiple-trace scan instruments, with a single laser creating two or more lines, as with the supermarket scanner. Also available are scanners that contain several lasers which create an elaborate raster of scan lines varying by as little as 16 degrees around an axis. While this type of scanner may cost as much as ten times a normal fixed laser scanner, it permits a small bar code label to be used. In high-volume mail order houses, for instance, avoiding the cost of hundreds of thousands of square inches of label stock each day will easily recapture the price of a multiple-trace scanner. Exhibit 3.12 illustrates this technology.

Exhibit 3.12

Omnidirectional Scanner Trace

(Courtesy of Metrologic Instruments, Inc., Blackwood, NJ)

> **NOTE:**
>
> In determining how to design an overhead scan station and choosing an omnidirectional scanner or an omnidirectional label, consider a third choice: You may be able to position two or more standard fixed laser scanners above the conveyor at varying angles relative to the conveyor direction. This approach to conveyor data collection might be the least expensive to implement and the most reliable.

SUMMARY ■

Bar code scanning devices first appeared in 1970 and have steadily advanced in variety and sophistication since then. Today, designers of data collection systems have all the tools necessary to create application-specific scanning stations, choosing and intermixing devices to adapt any retail or industrial data entry location to this technology. Where bar code data can be acquired using fixed scan stations, the cost of this function will be very low when spread over the life of the scanner. If manual clerks or inspectors are required in a combined production and data collection task, contact or proximate hand scanners are quick and reliable. Decisions regarding the choice of various scanner features cannot be made without considering the composition of the bar code label. The "X" dimension of the label, the height and width of the entire bar code, and the range of scanning distances required will all combine to determine a scanner's effectiveness. Don't hesitate to involve the future operators of the scanning devices in your decision making. By borrowing demonstration products and simulating the intended scanning task, much of the mystery and confusion you may be experiencing with so many scanner choices will dissipate.

Chapter 4

Printing Bar Code

Over the last twenty years there has been a revolution in print technology. Bar code applications are very sensitive to the ability of printers to present their special messages in high contrast, well-dimensioned bars and spaces. The continued growth of new bar code applications in retail and industrial projects has benefited greatly from the steady advances in printer capability. The breadth of choice in modern printers may produce some initial confusion or even intimidate the newcomer to bar code. However, this situation should be considered an "embarrassment of riches" since there is available an ideal method for printing bar code labels, inexpensively and exactly, in support of all basic retail data collection tasks as well as the majority of industrial production and distribution control applications.

Chapter 4 is divided into three sections. The first section reviews the print technologies most appropriate for creating bar code in production facilities of off-site label suppliers. The second section highlights the most popular bar code print technologies to choose from if the decision is made to produce labels in-house, in batch or on demand. The last section of this chapter discusses other bar code print considerations — for example, bar code verification.

OFF-SITE PRINT TECHNOLOGY ■

If all the supermarket packages created since the grocery industry's adoption of bar code in 1973 were to be counted, then it could be said that more bar code is printed off site than in-house. Eliminating this

67

retail point-of-sale application, the division of label production shifts the other way, with about 40 percent of labels printed by off-site vendors and 60 percent of labels printed by the bar code user in close coordination with scanning applications.

If you have decided to purchase labels printed by a bar code label vendor, then you must prepare a specification that includes the technical details relating to the symbology chosen, bar code message length and content, and the position of the bar code on the form or label. Other elements to consider are covered in more detail in Chapter 8. At this point you may not care how the label is created, as long as the specification is met. On the other hand, choosing a supplier is easier if you have some understanding of the print methods in use today for bar code creation.

Ink-Based Printing

The oldest and most common form of printing transfers ink from a master plate, which holds a positive or negative representation of the image, to the paper or other media to be printed on. Once a master image is created, usually by photographic means, the printing of repeated copies of this image is fast and very inexpensive. Most UPC labels are created by generating a photographic image of the bar code, called a film master, usually in reverse image. Exhibit 4.1 illustrates a UPC film master. This film master is used to create an etched plate or drum, which physically transfers ink to paper or other compatible label media.

Variations of this principle have been developed since the sixteenth century when the Gutenberg Bible was printed on the first letterpress. Offset lithography, flexography, and rotogravure are variations of the same basic principle of ink transfer. These presses can run at tremendous speeds, as high as 1200 feet per minute. Since labels are typically small, they can be repeated across a press web, making the cost of identical labels or repetitive labeled packaging material very inexpensive. The smallest "X" dimension that should be considered when using ink-based printing is about 7 to 8 mils, which certainly poses no limitation on most bar code labels. Since there is ink spread when the drum or plate containing the bar code image comes in contact with the paper under pressure, the printing plate or drum image has to have been compensated for. This ink spread is predictable, and a professional print house should have no difficulty in producing bar codes to exact tolerance for you.

Exhibit 4.1
UPC Film Master

(Courtesy of Data Capture Library)

Ink-based print methods are less appealing as a bar code label printing choice if the labels require variable information. Often this variation is in sequential bar code numbering. A device called a numbering wheel can be combined with letterpress to present bar code segments in a predetermined manner as a part of the image to be transferred in a label. This requires that the symbology be discrete, and the most common choice is Codabar, an all-numeric code. The Federal Express waybill shown in Exhibit 2.5 (page 29) is printed using this technique.

An inking wheel is an interesting and inexpensive print instrument that can be used to print UPC case codes on corrugated cartons. A drum with a raised inked image of the bar code rolls against a carton carried on a conveyor belt, transferring the image in the process. This technique is suitable for in-house printing as well. Printing on corrugated material is a special challenge and one that has received much study. Wet ink printing on corrugated material can be quite successful if the plates have proper compensation. Special bearer bars are used above and below the bar code to even the print pressure, and 40 mil or larger "X" dimension bars are specified for the bar code.

Dry Printing

Newer production printing processes have come along and added flexibility to the creation of bar code labels printed off site. Probably the most precise labels produced today are created by photocomposition printing. In this process images are created by CRT electron projection onto photosensitive paper. CRT typesetters are extremely fast and capable of very high image resolution. If your application requires a small "X" dimension, you might consider this label production technique. Exhibit 8.4 (page 169) illustrates a printed circuit label produced this way. Since this process is computer controlled, there is no practical limitation to the composition of the bar code message or the choice of symbology. These labels can, of course, be laminated for durability and have adhesive backing. Library systems and circuit board manufacturers have shown a preference for this print technology. Label cost will be higher than for ink-based printing, however.

Another approach to high-volume, computer-generated bar code label printing is a process known as ion projection electrographic printing, or ion deposition. Ion deposition printing, developed jointly by Dennison Manufacturing Company and the Canadian Development Authority, has a number of attractive features. In addition to the full freedom of bar code composition that this print technology permits, it can also be integrated into a complete multicolor rotary printing press. Many overnight delivery bar code trace labels are produced this way, creating an attractive and inexpensive self-adhesive label, applied by the millions each day. The carbon toner used in ion deposition printing presents a very scannable bar code, and "X" dimensions of 6 to 7 mils can be reproduced satisfactorily. While this technology was originally used by off-site printers, Dennison and other licensed printer manufacturers are adapting this technology to in-house devices, where they can generate large quantities of demand labels inexpensively.

High-speed continuous form, or sheet-fed, laser printing is offered by a number of off-site label vendors. Since these printers are expensive, their high printing capacity and ability to produce precise images makes them suitable for label vendors that serve many customers. The carbon-based toner used and the laser's ability to hold 5- to 6-mil "X" dimensions have combined to produce quality labels with high first-scan rates. Laminating the resulting labels to prolong the scan life is a common practice. Customers using either ion deposition or high-speed laser off-site printing often deliver computer tapes or floppy disks to the supplier with the label data in an agreed-upon format. This method eliminates any manual input errors and makes the label printing accurate and virtually automatic. Other customers teleprocess their label details to the vendor on a weekly to monthly schedule. Many of the shelf labels used in a supermarket are printed by high-speed laser. A bar code identifies the grocery product at each shelf location to facilitate the daily inventory, and additional human readable information states price, quantity or size of package, and even certain nutritional data for the benefit of the shopper. These labels are usually replenished weekly, or when item prices change. Exhibit 4.2 shows a laser-printed label.

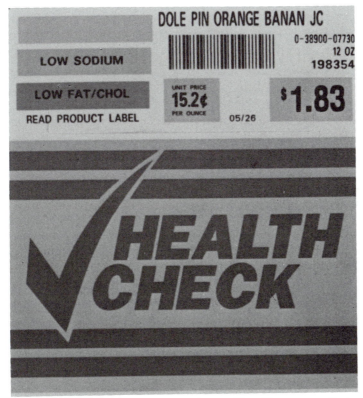

Exhibit 4.2

Laser-Printed Grocery
Shelf Label

(Courtesy of Graphic Technology, Inc. — Data Documents Systems)

There really is not a neat cut-off between bar code printing processes used exclusively by off-site vendors and printing methods used exclusively for in-house labels. As just mentioned, ion deposition is becoming available for in-house use, and the desktop laser printer makes this printing an available in-house choice as well. Some production printing houses use banks of matrix impact printers to supply bar code labels to customers; this technology will be covered in the next section of this chapter.

■ IN-HOUSE PRINT TECHNOLOGY

Bar code applications have become more integrated into the realtime processes and events of the industrial and commercial world. As a result, the need for demand-printed bar code labels to express and carry control messages has grown rapidly. Fortunately, the computerization of the office and factory has had a strong influence on the development of precise but inexpensive printers for other uses. Better and less expensive bar code label printers have appeared as a result. This section highlights the leading print technologies that one can choose from in designing a modern bar code driven data collection system. As with scanning devices, there are legitimate reasons to mix printer types in a responsive plan: some bar code applications will benefit from one print technology, and other applications or locations will benefit from another print technology. What is important to retain is constant label quality and system design integrity.

Dot Matrix Impact Printers

The first flexible printer to be adopted on a broad scale for bar code generation on demand was the dot matrix printer. Developed originally as a medium-speed (300 lines per minute), mainframe line printer, it gave a skilled programmer the ability to place a dot anywhere on a page. With the development of the graphic controller, which can be married to the printer, bar code generation and many other graphic label enhancements were easily produced by this print technology. Chapter 8 describes the role of the graphic controller more completely.

There are actually two approaches to dot matrix printer design. The faster printers employ a hammer bank that spans the width of the page to be printed. This mechanism shuttles slightly to the left and right under computer control, precisely releasing the pins that create the dots forming each element of a bar code, and the paper passes underneath. The other approach to designing a dot matrix printer employs a moving print head that rides on a track and moves back and forth across the page. The print head usually has 9 or 24 pins, which are released in clusters to form the bar code elements. A magnified example of bar code elements as created on a dot matrix printer is presented in Exhibit 4.3. As you can see, the bar code produced by this print technology has a scalloped-edge effect, and a larger "X" dimension compared with other print technologies. Depending on the printer, the minimum "X" dimension will range from 12 to 20 mils.

Several cautions are worth noting when printing bar codes with a dot matrix printer. Since these printers use multipass ribbons, it is possible to exhaust the ribbon and not deposit enough ink (carbon) to permit dependable scanning. Some printers will monitor the number of ribbon passes and display the percentage of use left. The ribbon chosen for bar code labels should be bar code or OCR grade. Also, note the voids between dots in the wide bar code. These voids can cause the scanner to "no read" when a laser gun or wand is used incorporating a high-resolution spot.

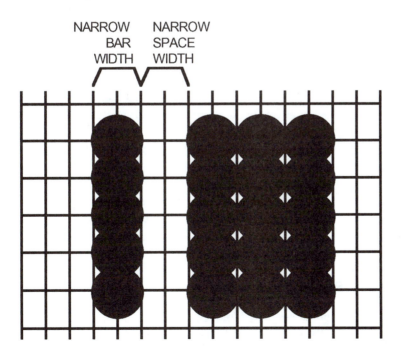

NARROW   NARROW
BAR   SPACE
WIDTH   WIDTH

Exhibit 4.3

Dot Matrix Bar Code

> **NOTE:**
>
> Dot matrix printers will usually offer two or three print speeds. The label area containing the bar code should be printed in the lowest speed, or multipass (graph) mode, to assure the greatest ink deposit in each bar and the smallest voids. You may be required to shift into and out of this graph mode each time a bar code is required.

In the design of a wide-ranging bar code system across many organizational functions, existing dot matrix printers can often be successfully converted to print new bar code messages on computer-generated forms, reducing overall cost of the bar code system considerably. Also, if bar code has to be printed on multipart forms, there are few printer choices to consider. However, be sure the bar code copy to be read is on the top page, or original print level. Some success can be had scanning the first copy level, but only if a true carbon layer is used.

Impact Drum Printers

The impact drum printer, which actually predates the dot matrix printer, was developed by Intermec Corporation about 1972. This device has each bar code element and its equivalent human readable character etched on the surface of a rotating drum. A hammer drives paper and a carbon ribbon against the drum at the moment the bar code element is in the proper print position. Repetitive hammer strikes create the elements of a bar code message. In general, a drum impact printer will only print one symbology, and in a single "X" dimension, without time-consuming modification. Another consideration is the limited number of fonts available for human readable label enhancement. However, this printer style produces precise bar code labels with dependable "X" dimensions as small as 5 mils. Drum printers are sometimes combined with label-laminating accessories to print small, precise, and durable bar codes used in rugged applications.

Engraved Band Impact Printers

As more bar code applications are integrated into mainframe-created forms and labels, traditional high-speed line printers are coming on the market with bar code capability. Exhibit 4.4 illustrates a contemporary example of this printer. An engraved band travels at high speed across the width of the paper, and hammers strike fully formed alphanumeric characters to create printed text. To print bar code, print bands are used with bar segments added, and bar segments are assembled in patterns for horizontal or vertical bar code generation. An application program from the mainframe must generate the data stream to compose the bar code as well as the human readable text. The advantages of this type of printer are speed (up to 2200 lines per minute) and the ability to handle multipart forms.

Exhibit 4.4
IBM 6262 Printer

(Courtesy of International Business Machines)

Direct Thermal Printers

Thermal printing is not a new technology, but it has been adopted as a popular method of printing bar code for 15 years. The decreasing costs of printers combined with advances in print heads and thermal papers have made this a practical technology for producing on-demand labels. The thermal printer is very simple in design, and the label paper is the only moving component in the system. It is a small device that can even be portable as shown in Exhibit 4.5. The thermal printer is also quiet — a quality especially apparent when compared with a matrix impact printer that is generating labels in a location such as an office.

To create a thermal-printed label, heat-sensitive label stock passes across the face of a print head of the same width as the paper. The print head is called a linear thermal array, and it can momentarily heat any position along its length under digital or computer control. As the

Exhibit 4.5
Hand-Held Printer

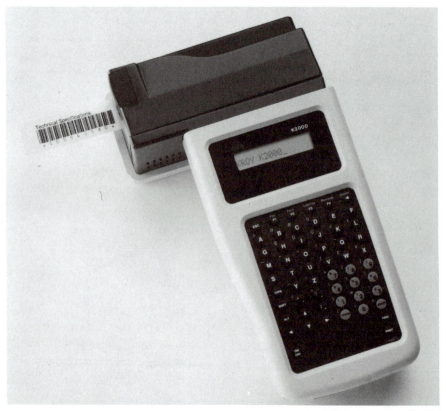

(Courtesy of KROY)

timed passage of the label progresses, tiny dark dots are created under the heated array elements, and these dots combine to produce a bar code, as well as human readable text and graphic label enhancements. The label stock has to be specially treated and matched to the print head carefully to assure the proper heat level and application time. Thermal label stock may be organic or inorganic in composition. Organic label stock has a white background and is traditional looking and attractive. However, organic label material is very difficult to scan with an infrared scanner and will not tolerate industrial chemicals. The inorganic label stock is off-white in color and therefore less attractive to some users. However, labels on this stock are more easily scanned, and the stock is much more resistant to industrial chemicals and moisture. Exhibit 4.6 shows the chemical process at work in creating a dark dot within a label.

Users who require many direct printers for labels that have a short application life find thermal print technology ideal. Thermal bar code printers are available for as little as $600 and can create "X" dimension bars as small as 5 mils. Print head width determines the label width, and print speeds are normally in the range of 2 to 5 inches per second. Some care must be taken to assure that the paper is matched to the printer characteristics. It would be appropriate to begin by purchasing the label stock directly from the printer manufacturer and varying from that only after some extended tests of an alternate source. Since the application

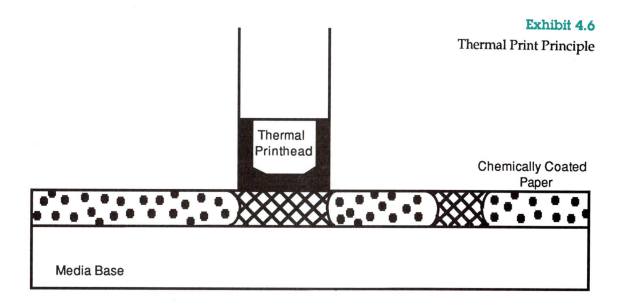

Exhibit 4.6
Thermal Print Principle

Thermal Printhead

Chemically Coated Paper

Media Base

of heat creates the bar code, thermal labels should not be exposed to heat above 140 degrees Fahrenheit or placed in direct sunlight. Contrast will be lost and the bar code may become unreadable. To further protect the thermal label, a protective overlaminate is frequently used to provide UV, chemical, and abrasion resistance.

Thermal Transfer Printers

Thermal transfer printers are closely related to direct thermal printers. They employ a thermal array print head, but instead of heating specially coated paper to change its color, thermal transfer printers melt a wax-like ink off a transfer ribbon running between the print head and the label stock to create a dot. Exhibit 4.7 illustrates this process. Some of the industrial conditions that limit the use of direct thermal-printed labels are avoided with thermal transfer technology. Direct sunlight will not shorten the life of this label, and the "X" dimension is printable to about 6 mils. On the other hand, the transfer ribbon melts the ink onto the label stock at about 150 degrees, so certain industrial heat conditions can cause a problem for thermal transfer labels. The printer is quiet and classified as medium speed. The label width is determined by the print head width and can be as wide as 10 inches. Some vendors offer machines capable of continuous label printing at rates as high as 10 inches per second.

Exhibit 4.7

Thermal Transfer Principle

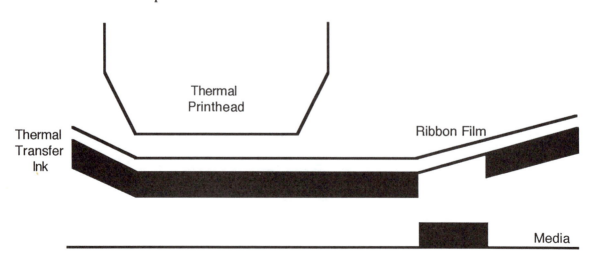

NOTE:
A great deal of chemical research is going into this technology. Modern color printers and facsimile receivers are adopting this print technology using a complex transfer ribbon that melts to create dots in cyan, magenta, and yellow colors. If used to produce a bar code label, this print technique has the ability to add graphic highlights to a label, such as color printing of human readable information. However, the black bar created by the color blend may not easily scan due to the absence of carbon.

Thermal transfer printers are very popular department-level print devices that can create on-demand labels from a local database with excellent overall scanning dependability. Since these printers do not require specially treated media, the label stock can be paper, polyester, vinyl, or other synthetic materials. Since the transfer ribbon is expensive, newer design printers are advancing this single-pass ribbon with multi-pass microprocessor control rather than advancing on a one-to-one basis with the label stock. These printers allow the user to set ribbon consumption rates. These improvements can significantly reduce the cost of labels, but with the risk of some sacrifice in print quality.

Laser Printers

Earlier in this chapter, high-speed, continuous form laser printers were presented in the context of off-site label production devices, due to their relatively high cost. The office PC and a page-based laser printer has become one of the most familiar combinations in the modern business setting. For an investment of $2000 to $4000, a PC can produce precise and appealing text, graphics, and bar coded labels running under inexpensive word processing packages. The resolution of the laser page printer permits minimum "X" dimension printing of 5 to 6 mils, and the carbon toner gives excellent contrast for reliable scanning. On the other hand, for extensive production or warehouse applications, the page format is usually less adaptable to automatic label application than a continuous spool of labels. The creation of a workstation scanning menu is a popular application for desktop laser printers. A supervisor with an inexpensive bar code software program running on a PC or Macintosh can create or modify a bar code menu in a very short period of time. To provide resistance to wand scanner abrasion, place the menu in a transparent sleeve.

NOTE:

Although it is tempting to use an office copier to reproduce laser-printed bar code menus, this process will frequently alter the bar spacing and make the bar code difficult to read. If 50 copies of a menu are needed, set your laser printer to print 50 originals.

Laser page printers are sometimes used as in-house back-up printers when off-site production is the normal label source. For example, if a local situation requires that a supermarket manager create a new shelf label to meet an immediate price change, the in-house printer can perform this task. Previously, the manager was dependent on the established weekly production and delivery schedule from the label vendor. With an in-house back-up printer, local management can remain responsive in each community.

Developments in laser printers will continue to influence the bar code label market. Continuous form laser printers are now appearing in the market below $7,000 in cost, with respectable print rates and durability. These devices will gain a larger share of the in-house label production market and shift some off-site printing back in-house. Exhibit 4.8 illustrates a moderately priced laser printer with continuous form capability. Higher-resolution laser printers at 600 dots per inch and beyond are coming into the desktop publishing market and will play some role in future bar code label printing, especially for small "X" dimension labels.

LED Array Printers

Closely related to laser printing technology is an emerging technique called LED array printing. In traditional laser printers, a digitally controlled laser beam optically "paints" a page image on a photoreceptive drum or belt which contains the image details in a positive electrical charge. Then, negatively charged toner is attracted to the charged

Exhibit 4.8
Continuous Form Laser Printer

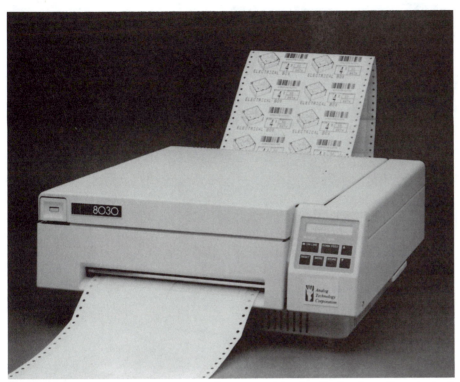

(Courtesy of Analog Technology Corporation)

portion of the drum. The toner is transferred to the label medium, where the bar code and other text and graphics are fused with heat. LED (light-emitting diode) printers use hundreds of inexpensive LEDs positioned across the width of the printer, permitting very fast and reliable electrophotographic printing as a hybrid of laser printing and matrix printing. The resolution of these printers is up to 400 dots per inch, permitting small "X" dimension labels. LED array printers are available in continuous form and page printer configurations. Exhibit 4.9 is an illustration of this type printer developed to support the Hewlett Packard minicomputer environment. LED array printers can print a narrow or full page label without affecting print speed, and LED

Exhibit 4.9
LED Array Printer

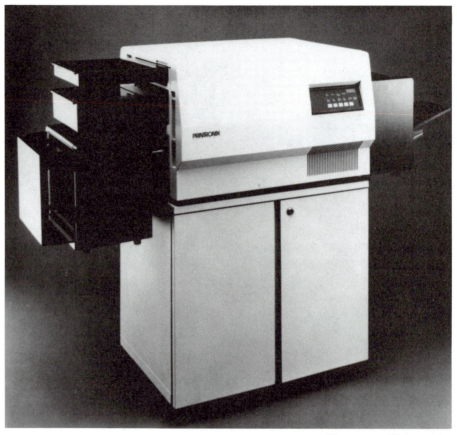

(Courtesy of Printronix)

array printers support high print rates while providing good reliability. The cost range for these devices is $7,500 to $40,000, but they do not require expensive media or supplies and can produce low-cost labels in volume.

Ink Jet Printers

Ink jet printing results from the precise projection of drops of ink a short distance to a medium surface. It is a noncontact print method based on either continuous projection of ink or controlled pulses of ink. In continuous ink jet systems, the ink is broken into tiny droplets by ultrasonic vibration. These droplets are electrostatically charged and deflected to the medium under computer control. Ink can be projected by a single nozzle or a bank of nozzles. Ink jet printers are now appearing in the desktop publishing field as a less expensive alternative to the laser printer. They can produce bar code with "X" dimensions down to 10 to 12 mils. Using multiple array print heads, ink jet printers can produce demand printout at speeds above 500 feet per minute.

In the past, demand ink jet printing was used in carton identification, both for human readable information and for bar code labeling. Exhibit 4.10 illustrates an ink jet printer used for this application. Conveyorized cartons of finished goods can have bar code printed at conveyor speeds of up to 200 feet per minute on corrugated surfaces. However, the printer resolution is very low, on the order of 10 dots per inch. This can produce a laser scannable bar code with an "X" dimension of about 50 mils. Adding variable demand information such as weight or date to a carton of produce or portioned meats is a popular application, although the use of ink jet marking is being challenged by on-demand label generation and application for cases.

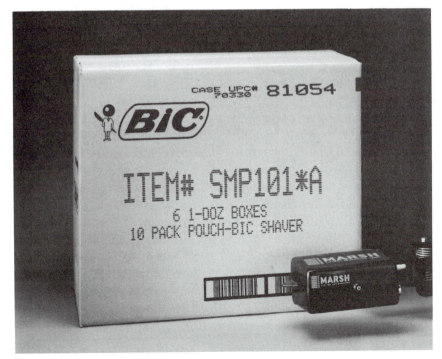

Exhibit 4.10
Ink Jet Carton Printer

(Courtesy of Marsh Company)

■ BAR CODE VERIFICATION

Bar code was developed with a great deal of message redundancy and forgiveness. A scan spot can take thousands of possible paths across the bars and spaces of the typical bar code message. A single spot passing over elements with reasonable contrast and acceptable bar tolerance is sufficient to "read" the label. The easiest first check a user can make on a bar code label is visual. An 8-power optical loupe is an excellent way to get a quick look at the details of a bar code, such as bar edge definition and black and white narrow bar comparisons. Loupes are available in photography stores or the photographic supplies section of many general merchandise chain stores. The investment for this simple magnifying inspection instrument is under $20. For about $75, a 10-power optical comparator with a reticle calibrated in 5-mil hatch marks can be purchased from a scientific supplier of optical tools such as Edmund Scientific Company of Barrington, New Jersey. This instrument permits you to make a very detailed inspection of any label, in its mechanical dimensions. Certainly, either of these optical inspection aids will give you a quick first impression of your printer's performance and possible drift from ideal adjustment.

Verifying instruments on the bar code market offer other levels of inspection, including interpreting the symbology in your bar code, presenting the message content, quantifying relative bar and space contrast, and other tests. The ANSI grade for a sample of labels may be required by some trading partners. An example of a modern verifier in-line with the printer is illustrated in Exhibit 4.11. Test data can be displayed immediately on a screen, test results can be stored, or a signal can be sent to the printer to stop operation until the cause of the failure can be determined and the problem corrected.

Bar code quality has become increasingly important. Labels applied at one location may be scanned at many other locations and by trading partners around the world. For twenty years, the determination of bar code print quality has been mostly by subjective analysis. Sometimes, symbols which met published specifications failed to scan. Others which appeared to be outside the specifications could be scanned. With publication by ANSI of the "Guideline for Bar Code Print Quality" (ANSI X3.182-1190) in 1990, print quality could be defined in precise scientific terms.

Verifier instruments designed to evaluate printed bar code in accordance with the new ANSI guidelines are available from a number of quality suppliers. These devices not only indicate whether a printed bar code passes or fails, but also gives it a score on a five-point scale. More detailed data from the verifier indicates the type and severity of printing problems so that a knowledgeable operator can take appropriate corrective action. Some verifiers can be programmed to evaluate printed symbols in accordance with one or more of the older quality standards as well.

When choosing a verifier, it is necessary to match the verifier's wavelength of light and scanning aperture size to the label(s) to be checked and to the application. Industry application standards for bar

Exhibit 4.11

In-Line Bar Code Verifier

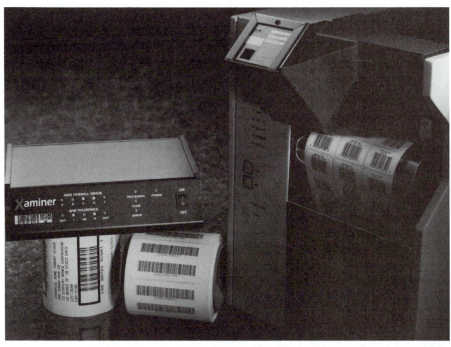

(Courtesy of Bar Code Systems, Inc. Atlanta, GA)

codes specify one or more wavelengths of light to be used for evaluation. Typical choices include:

633 nm	Bright, visible red — HeNe laser
660 nm	Visible red — solid state laser
800 nm	Near infrared — solid state laser
900 nm	Farther infrared — nonvisible wand

Guidelines are being developed for specifying the diameter of the measuring aperture as well. In the absence of a clear industry standard, the aperture and wavelength of the verifier should be approximately the same as those of the anticipated equipment. This will ensure that symbols which receive acceptable grades from the verifier will meet performance expectations in the scanning environment.

Following the ANSI guideline, bar code symbols are ranked according to the academic grades A, B, C, D, and F for a specific wavelength and aperture. For example, a particular symbol verified with a 5-mil aperture and 633 nm light might receive a B (good). If the aperture remained 10 mils, but the light changed to 900nm, the symbol could be rated F (failure). Symbol grade is only meaningful when the wavelength and aperture are stated.

Each time a verifier "looks" at a symbol, it obtains a scan reflectance profile which is evaluated according to eight attributes. The overall grade for the scan reflectance profile is the lowest grade for any of the eight attributes. Those symbols which receive a C (satisfactory) grade or better, can be expected to scan easily on virtually any well maintained equipment. Symbols which are graded D or F may scan easily on some equipment, but badly or not at all with others.

"Symbol contrast" is the first attribute which affects the grade of the profile. The blackest possible bars printed on the whitest possible surface would have a 100 percent contrast. Practical printing of bar code symbols results in less than 100 percent contrast. When the contrast becomes too slight, scanners have difficulty distinguishing the bars from the spaces.

"Minimum reflectance" is the second attribute by which a bar code is measured: The darkest bar must have a reflectance of less than half the background. The third attribute detects two types of printing defects: "voids" and "spots." Defects are undesirable because the scanner may become confused and think that a defect is an additional bar or space within the symbol. Each printing process is susceptible to its own kind of defects. For example, matrix printers develop visible voids within the bar, particularly as the ribbon ink becomes depleted.

Thermal and thermal transfer printers can produce bars containing vertical white streaks when the heat adjustment is too low. Ink jet and ion deposition printers have a tendency to put ink or toner spots on spaces. Equipment operators must be able to spot defects and take corrective action.

"Global threshold" is the fourth attribute. If the bar code does not have the correct number of bars and spaces, it is reported as a global threshold failure. Otherwise it is a "pass." Scanners can't see spaces when there is excessive bar growth due to ink spread or voids that appear as spaces. The fifth attribute is "modulation." This occurs when scanners and verifiers perceive narrow spaces to be less "white" than wide spaces. Similarly, but to a lesser extent, narrow bars "look" less black than wide bars. This diminished intensity of narrow elements, as compared with that of wide elements, is called modulation. With a little practice, printing problems caused by low modulation can be identified by examining the symbol with a 5- to 10-power magnifier or optical loupe. The narrow bars and spaces should appear to be approximately equal in width.

The sixth attribute is called "minimum edge contrast" and is graded on a pass/fail basis. A failing grade for minimum edge contrast will always be accompanied by low grades for symbol contrast and/or modulation. "Decode" is the seventh attribute. A verifier applies specific rules to the sequence of bars and spaces to decode them into a series of digits. When the verifier is unable to decode a symbol, and any internal check characters do not match, the decode fails. The eighth and final attribute, "decodability," is graded A through F. It measures how near the scan reflectance profile is to decode failure. Verifiers make this determination using standard published decode algorithms. One reason for low decodability grades is ragged, uneven bar edges, which can be caused by some of the coarser printing processes.

There is an ongoing debate about whether or not to verify printed bar code. As with other quality assurance tools, verification should be used with judgment and discretion.

RUGGED LABELS ■

Printing rugged duty labels subject to prolonged outdoor use or tolerant of caustic immersion and metal degreasing treatment requires special equipment. Lasers play a role in this process, too. High-power lasers can etch (burn away) metal, leaving a contrast between the normal metal surface and the etched area. Some scanner vendors will offer devices to read these markings, but success is not assured. Another approach to marking metal is to paint a label area with white paint and burn in black bars, using a laser, against the white background. This technique is generally successful, although the laser etching equipment is expensive and requires special safety protection. The next frontier of bar code expansion will be paced by the development of printing techniques to meet the requirements for special labels particular to dozens of rugged industrial processes.

■ SUMMARY

Printing advances are announced continuously and are often driven by broad applications in the word processing and desktop publishing markets. It usually takes only a year or two for a bar code printer vendor to translate new print technology into useful products. Higher-resolution printers will continue to appear, and printer costs will come down while effective print speeds rise. The broader use of 32-bit microprocessors and megabites of RAM memory available at ever lower prices will ensure this trend. Bar code users will continue to have more attractive printer choices to select from and, consequently, better labels to scan.

Part Two

COMPONENTS

Part One presented an in-depth description of bar code technology. Part Two describes how that technology has been incorporated into the components which comprise a functioning bar code system. Software, data entry terminals, and bar code labels are discussed along with guidelines to assist you in making the best choices from the available suppliers. There are software products, terminal choices, and label variations which can satisfy any bar code system requirement. In Part Two the authors use their insight and experience with components to make you aware of the role of each component in a bar code system.

Chapter 5

Software for Bar Code Systems

Chapter 5 covers a key component for success with a bar code application — software. The need to understand the role of software when designing a bar code system cannot be overemphasized, since software controls virtually every component of a bar code based data collection system. Our discussion of software includes sections on operating systems, programming languages, software sources, and databases. Although books on bar code generally gloss over the importance of software, a basic knowledge of this material is important when planning a bar code program.

Software to support bar code use has advanced dramatically in recent years. Early bar code systems were often an assembly of proprietary hardware linked with software written in obscure assembly languages for custom applications. For instance, users of portable data entry terminals were prompted through their data collection steps by a program tailored for each application by the device manufacturer using a unique programmable read only memory (PROM) chip. Gradually, bar code manufacturers came to realize that these early systems were too inflexible, unadaptable, and difficult to repair. Today, portable data entry terminal programs are created on personal computers for a wide range of manufacturing, retail, hospital, and other applications, with software written in higher-level languages. Many of these languages resemble BASIC or C.

In the past, many corporate bar code users developed their own application software using programming personnel from their management information services (MIS) or engineering staff. This practice is changing, as more "off-the-shelf" application software designed to run on PCs, minicomputers, and even mainframe processors becomes available.

Programs are developed by linking prewritten modules to create a system tailored to each user's individual requirements. Software, which at one time was the most expensive component of a bar code system, is now less expensive, and the development time has been substantially reduced.

■ OPERATING SYSTEMS

Operating systems are required for computers ranging in size from giant mainframes to small personal computers, as well as for the portable, hand-held data entry terminals that are used in some bar code systems. The operating system shapes the user's view of the computer and makes the hardware usable. As a resource manager, the operating system also

- schedules resources such as CPU access and memory access,
- facilitates input and output,
- provides recovery from hardware and software errors, and
- manages the sharing of data and hardware in a multiuser or multitasking environment.

If your supporting computer system for bar code data collection is a minicomputer or a mainframe, you seldom have a choice of operating systems. Your bar code applications must run under the operating system used for your traditional MIS programs.

PCs are increasingly preferred as the host in bar code data collection systems today, and even here some choices are possible. MS-DOS-based, IBM-compatible PCs are most popular for the following reasons:

- More bar code application software has been written under MS-DOS than any other operating system.
- MS-DOS supports advanced versions of high-level languages.
- A large pool of talented software engineers who are fluent in MS-DOS are available to develop, maintain, and customize bar code system software.

- New PC hardware architecture (80486-based systems with a 32-bit bus running at 50MHz) greatly increases PC processing speed, making it possible to run most time-critical bar code applications under MS-DOS.

Nevertheless, older PC architectures that are based on 80386 microprocessors are adequate for many bar code data collection systems — for example, fixed asset tracking or inventory control in small retail operations. In fact, it is not the number of scanners reporting to a PC that determines its power requirement but the frequency of transaction that is important.

If your system size and transaction volume drive you to a more powerful PC, there are three choices to consider: PC-OS/2, PC-Windows, and UNIX. Each of these operating systems can monitor multiple applications, which is a computer's ability to run two separate operations simultaneously, although real multi-tasking is only available with OS/2 or UNIX. For example, a shipping control system using bar code scanners should be able to record order shipment information and, at the same time, organize and print a shipping manifest for completed orders. In other bar code applications, it is sometimes necessary to query a PC database while bar code scanning continues in a separate location.

Both the PC-OS/2 and the PC-UNIX operating systems will support 32-megabyte address space, whereas PC-DOS is limited to one megabyte, due to its 16-bit mode. The additional memory is convenient or essential for bar code systems that use large databases or require fast access times and large, complex programs. Other OS/2 and UNIX features include clear interprocessor communications, fast I/O (input/output), memory protection, and memory management.

Bar code applications that may require a multitasking, high-speed processor include work in process (WIP) tracking in a large production environment and conveyor-belt scanning in a distribution center. The host computers controlling these applications receive a large volume of input data, and are expected to return control signals and operator instructions within milliseconds.

One advantage of using OS/2 over UNIX or Windows is that you can emulate a DOS-like environment with OS/2. This ability allows the user to continue to run application software previously developed for an MS-DOS-based system. This means that the large selection of software written for earlier PC processors can run on a 386 PC.

> **NOTE:**
>
> A PC industry battle over Windows versus OS/2 for dominance as the operating system of the future continues. Meanwhile, make your decision on a PC operating system based on your own bar code application requirements, your current PC environment, and your own insight into what the future holds.

This section has not discussed minicomputer or mainframe operating systems such as VMS for the DEC VAX, VM for IBM mainframes, or Wang VS. If a decision is made to base the bar code application on these systems, the user must seek information from individual scanner and software vendors regarding compatibilities within these architectures. In most cases, modification tailoring will be necessary.

■ PROGRAMMING LANGUAGES

As with other decisions faced in the design of a bar code system, several questions must be addressed when choosing a programming language for bar code applications. These questions include:

- *What programming language are you currently using?* The answer to this question is especially important if software will be written in-house. The exception to this rule would be a case in which existing application software is old and written in an outdated language (such as FORTRAN).

- *What programming language is most familiar to in-house software engineers?* This question should be a factor only if programmers use a modern, higher-level language like BASIC, C, C++, or a 4th Generation Language (4GL).

- *In what language is the off-the-shelf bar code application you are considering written?* If a "canned" package ideally suits your needs but is not developed using a familiar language, it may still be a good selection if no extensive tailoring is required.

NOTE:

In the past, it was generally believed that BASIC was only to be used for developing elementary programming skills or for simple applications. This is clearly no longer the case. New versions of BASIC can be as powerful as languages such as C, with advanced data structures and complex I/O routines, with the added advantages that it is a very popular language and easy to learn.

After considering these questions, take a last look at the C language. This popular, powerful language can be easily transported from a PC environment to a mainframe computer with minimal changes. This capability gives the user more flexibility when expanding or modifying any bar code application.

NOTE:

Whenever possible, acquire the application source code from the software supplier for the following reasons:

- Software suppliers can go out of business or abandon their support for your application.
- You may decide to modify or expand the scope of your application. Having the application source code will permit you to enlarge your bar code application and generate new benefits.
- If you have the source code, hooks to other programs can be added to your bar code application later by in-house programmers or other contractors.

SOFTWARE SOURCES ■

The three sources of software available for designing a bar code based data collection system are in-house programming, prewritten applications, and customized software.

Programming In-house

Many organizations with a strong software engineering staff choose to create their own custom bar code application software. Their decision usually is based on the following rationale:

- The in-house staff is totally familiar with the new bar code system environment.
- Integrating this new software with the existing database and related application software will be required.
- Out-of-pocket costs will be lower and under more control.
- The new bar code system will gain support and cooperation from the staff.

On the other hand, those who choose not to use in-house programmers to implement their bar code system cite these reasons:

- The programming staff has little or no experience with bar code systems and their unfamiliar timing and interface characteristics.
- Internal resources would be committed for extended periods of time, and other more traditional projects would suffer.

Purchasing Prewritten Applications

The second source of bar code application software is from the vendor that has already written a "canned" software package — that is, software designed and written to a general application description which fits the needs of many users. Successful bar code data collection can result from a decision to buy prewritten software when the following considerations are important:

- You have only a short time to implement your bar code data collection project.
- The budget rules out custom-written software.
- A tested and debugged program is more important than unique fit and tailoring.

Choosing prewritten software has certain disadvantages. For example, canned packages are not flexible. They cannot be tailored to a particular user, and they cannot be modified when the environment changes. With some programs, the user is locked into a single type or brand of scanning or printing hardware. Canned software may be written with such limited options that the user cannot even vary the bar code symbology or label field length.

Customized Software

The third general source of software is customized software developed by software suppliers and hardware manufacturers, or provided with bar code hardware and a host computer by a systems integrator. Bar code users will often choose this software source for these reasons:

- Software can be tailored to the exact bar code application required by each user.
- No limitations are placed on the choice of host computer, scanner supplier, or label design.
- Application changes and system expansion can be anticipated and provided for by the original software supplier.
- Bar code data handling speed can be optimized by the supplier for peak application efficiency.

The disadvantages of contracting for customized software applications fall into the following areas of complaint:

- The systems integrator was unfamiliar with bar code and never understood what was important with the application.
- The project took a long time because the contract had to be written around an exact description of the process.
- The software costs kept skyrocketing, even though the changes that were asked for were small.

> **NOTE:**
> Whenever software is to be written by outside suppliers, it is critical to evaluate the vendor's reputation for customer support. The evaluation should include the vendor's history of correcting "bugs" as well as responding to modifications in a timely and reasonable manner.

Frequently, bar code system users wind up with a combination of software sources. For instance, mainframe resident software might be developed in-house, while standard applications are solved with "canned" bar code software packages. Finally, the complex bar code applications with many scanning devices and time-critical data handling are often obtained as a customized project from a systems integration house.

With the increase in bar code popularity, more vendors have entered the software applications market, generating more sophisticated software programs. In addition, familiar control problems shared by many customers have reduced the cost of canned and customized software. Today, many sources of software for WIP tracking, retail POS management, inventory control, and several other applications for bar code are available. While some of these programs are rigid and inflexible, many others can be adapted to the user's needs by tailoring via menus or interactive prompting.

A new generation of systems integrators has come into the bar code software supply field with an intent to develop a market specialty. This trend gives bar code users many more software choices today than were available several years ago.

■ DATABASES

As an introduction to this section it would be worthwhile to review the basic components of a database management system (DBMS). Also, an understanding of database terminology is useful when considering system requirements for your bar code application.

NOTE:

Many bar code system vendors speak of "the database" when, in reality, they are referring to a simple data file. For some bar code applications, this distinction is not important. For other applications, where access times and the size of the records are considerations, a data file structure will not be adequate.

What, then, is a database? Simply put, a database is a repository for stored data that is to be integrated and shared. When we say "integrated," we mean that several potentially distinct data files have been combined, but with redundancies removed. Shared data means that several users not only have access to the data but also have more than one way to view the data.

A database management system usually denotes the layer of software which resides between the user and the database files. It allows the user to be unconcerned about hardware-level details and provides a user-friendly way to view the data in one or more combinations.

The three basic components of any database are the field, the record, and the file. The *field* is the actual value or message contained in each element of your database. These values can be quantitative, qualitative, or descriptive in nature. For example, the field could be a part number or the part's color, size, value, or location. The *record* is a collection of fields assembled as an associated message. For example, the above part number, along with the part's color and size, value, and location, is a record. The *file* is a group of records that are kept together for a sensible reason. For example, a file could be all the parts and their details that are required to build a toy wagon.

All database management systems can be placed into one of three categories: a relational, a hierarchical, or a network database.

Relational Database

The relational database appears to the user as a number of tables. An item appears on a table if it can be acted on or processed in the same way as all the other entries on the table. In other words, a relationship between entities must exist. This is by far the most popular database design. It builds around the concept of the relationship between an item and its attributes. Exhibit 5.1 contains three samples of relational database files.

The main advantage of a relational database is its simplicity and ease of understanding by the end user. Information appears to be arranged in a form that is logical to the human mind. In fact, the computer may not store the information in physical tables, but the user does not need to be concerned about that.

Exhibit 5.1

Sample Data in
Relational Form

Supplier #	Part #	QTY
S1	P1	100
S1	P2	50
S2	P1	200
S2	P4	400
S3	P2	150

(a) Shipment Table

Supplier #	Supplier Name	Supplier Address	Contact
S1	ACME	New York, NY	Smith
S2	NATIONAL	Kansas City, MO	Jones
S3	GENERAL	Boston, MA	McDonald
S4	UNITED	New York, NY	Clark

(b) Supplier Table

Part #	Part Name	Color	Weight
P1	nut	red	1
P2	bolt	black	1
P3	screw	silver	2
P4	wheel	black	20

(c) Parts Table

A relational database can support what is referred to as SQL (Structured Query Language) developed by IBM, or similar query languages developed by others. All questions asked of the database are accomplished through this "sublanguage."

These query commands can be used to assemble reports from the database. A user can do this from the keyboard of an on-line terminal, or the commands can be embedded in bar code application software programs. More important, the users of relational databases are able to write a custom program to report bar code information in a useful format.

Hierarchical Database

The hierarchical approach is implemented using nodes and branches. A node is an attribute which describes the entity. The highest node, called the root, is the entity being described. Every occurrence of a root node represents a database record. Exhibit 5.2 contains the same data previously presented in the relational database; now the data is represented in the hierarchical form.

Exhibit 5.2

Sample Data in Hierarchical Form

In this example, part information may be duplicated if it is available from more than one supplier.

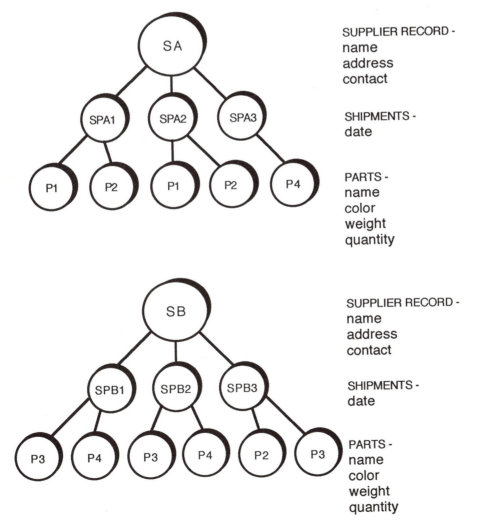

SUPPLIER RECORD -
name
address
contact

SHIPMENTS -
date

PARTS -
name
color
weight
quantity

SUPPLIER RECORD -
name
address
contact

SHIPMENTS -
date

PARTS -
name
color
weight
quantity

The main disadvantage of the hierarchical approach is that the same data might get stored more than once, which sometimes happens when many relationships exist between entities. In addition, operations such as adding and removing records or fields can be complicated. The strict structure of the database requires commands that are more procedural than practical.

Network Database

The network approach has a more general and at times a more confusing structure than the hierarchical model. Any entity may have many immediate "superiors." Exhibit 5.3 is again the same data that was represented in the relational and hierarchical database; now the data is in the network form. Note that some of the fields are related in some manner to several other fields.

The main advantage of the network approach is the ease with which "many-to-many" relationships can be represented without duplication of data.

Choosing a Database System Design

In general, most bar code application software utilizes a relational database. When purchasing a bar code system, whether custom written or off-the-shelf, it is important to determine the database source. Is it a "popular" product used in other application software such as *Oracle*, or *dBase*, or did the vendor develop a proprietary database optimized in some way for a bar code system? While there are valid reasons to go in either direction with your system design, do consider the following points:

- The "popular" database may be more thoroughly developed and debugged.
- Many "popular" databases support SQL or another widely used query language. (The features and benefits of this kind of "sublanguage" were discussed previously.)
- Bar code system software containing a "popular" database embedded should be delivered with all relevant DBMS documentation. This means the bar code software can be easily integrated with application software using this same database elsewhere in your operation.

Exhibit 5.3

Sample Data in the Network Form

In this example, parts have two "superiors": suppliers and shipments.

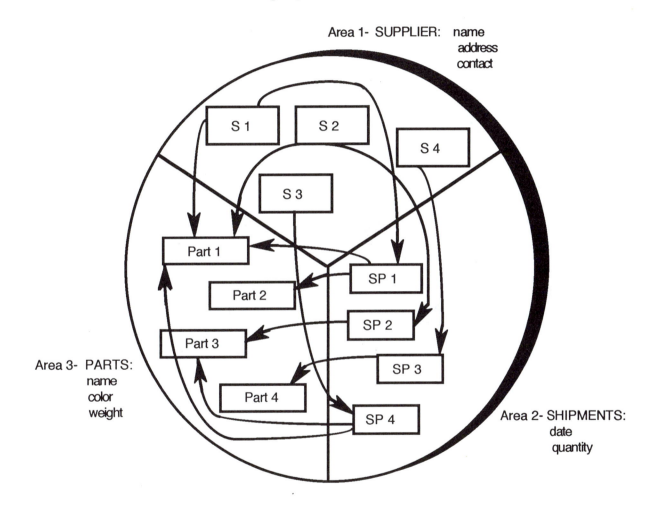

- A proprietary database often can be designed and optimized for a specific bar code application, thus leading to a more streamlined system with greater data throughput capability.

Many applications lend themselves to a direct and inexpensive solution. A simple program can be written to accept scanned data from a bar code terminal into a PC. Here the data is stored in a flat ASCII file which is then translated to a "popular" database such as *Oracle*, *Paradox*, or *dBase* for query and report generation. This systems approach is particularly appealing if you are already using the database for related applications. Inexpensive import software, which automatically takes data from ASCII files and translates it for compatibility with popular databases or integrated software packages such as *Symphony*, is available.

■ SUMMARY

While the sophistication of bar code scanning devices, printer products, and symbologies is continuing to advance, the rate of expansion of bar code data collection is more dependent on the availability of application software or refined software development tools than on any other factor. Today, suppliers to the industry are applying more of their development resources to software than to any other component of this technology.

The growing popularity of PCs and workstations running under multitasking operating systems will have a strong effect on the design of future bar code systems and will influence the programs that tailor these systems to your application. Despite the progress of the last several years in bringing prewritten application packages or customized software to the bar code data collection marketplace, the role of the systems integrator will continue to be important, too. Many progressive companies want to add the power of bar code to extensive corporate applications that have been operating under manual data input for some time. Blending bar code data collection into these processes will remain beyond the scope of prewritten software and will require a higher level of expertise for many years to come.

Chapter 6

Communication Components and Networks

Chapter 6 examines the two system elements closely related to software: communication components, including protocols and interfaces, and networks. The purpose of the following discussion is to strip away any misunderstanding of concepts or terms in the linkage between bar code terminal devices and a host computer. The principles that govern the connection of devices to terminals are not really complicated. It helps when you can understand the acronyms that vendors and experts who make this field their specialty use.

COMMUNICATION COMPONENTS OF BAR CODE SYSTEMS

In developing a system design, you will need to determine what data is to be collected, where and by what means that data will be collected, and how the collected data will be managed. The final step in this sequence is to decide on the communications method you will use to move the data from where it is collected to your computer. If this issue is not addressed correctly, you can lose much time in your system development or fail to get your system working at all.

Data Terminal and Data Communications Equipment

There are three distinct components to a communications "network":

1. Data terminal equipment (DTE), which is any digital device such as a display terminal, data entry terminal, or printer.
2. Data communications equipment (DCE), which includes devices such as a modem designed to manipulate the transmitted data.
3. The actual medium over which the signal is sent, such as radio frequency or cable.

Bar code terminals are usually designed to include DTE functions to simplify communication with a host computer. Bar code terminals can also include DCE features that permit easy interface with other digital devices such as printers or weigh scales. Exhibits 6.1, 6.2, and 6.3 are somewhat representative of typical network combinations.

Exhibit 6.1

Bar Code Terminals as DTEs

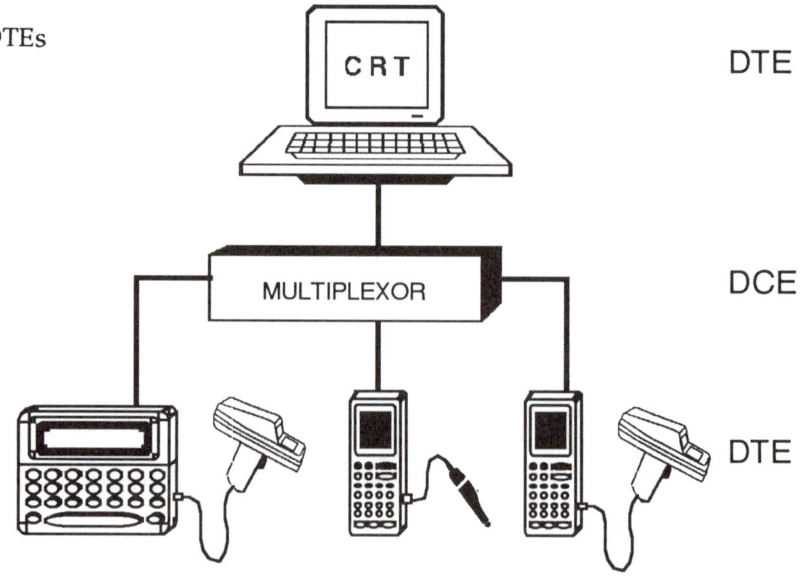

CRT — DTE

MULTIPLEXOR — DCE

DTE

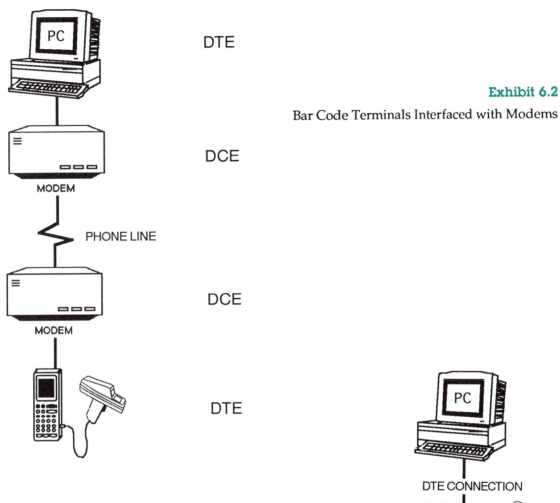

DTE

DCE

MODEM

PHONE LINE

DCE

MODEM

DTE

Exhibit 6.2

Bar Code Terminals Interfaced with Modems

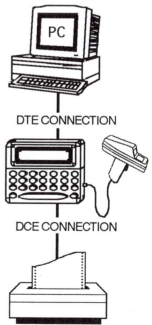

DTE CONNECTION

DCE CONNECTION

Exhibit 6.3

Bar Code Terminals as Both DTE and DCE

Transmission Codes

Two other terms used extensively when discussing data communications are EBCDIC and ASCII — the transmission codes most commonly used in data processing today.

EBCDIC (Extended Binary Coded Decimal Interchange Code) was developed by IBM and is used extensively in systems featuring IBM processors. Each character is represented by an 8-bit structure, with the capability of generating 256 characters. EBCDIC is used primarily for communication with byte-oriented computers.

ASCII (American Standard Code for Information Interchange), developed by the International Standards Organization (ISO), is the more widely used code for data communications. With this code, characters are represented with a 7-bit structure, permitting a total of 128 characters. An eighth bit is used for error checking or parity.

The ISO Model for Open Systems Interconnection

Some time ago the International Standards Organization saw the benefit in facilitating information exchange through data networks and authorized a standard model known as the Reference Model of Open Systems Interconnection (OSI). The OSI model has a seven-layer structure that is similar in some respects to a computer operating system. Each layer acts autonomously, performing clearly defined assignments. The model specifies the role each layer plays in data communications.

Interfaces define the relationships between the various layers operating within a device — that is, layer-to-layer communication. Protocols, on the other hand, define relationships between equivalent layers. Protocols define message formats and the rules for message exchange. Exhibit 6.4 graphically represents the ISO seven-layer model for OSI. Briefly, each layer performs in the following manner:

1. *Physical link layer*: defines the mechanical aspects of interfacing to a physical medium. It is responsible for setting up, maintaining, and disconnecting physical links. Included are software device drivers for each communications device and the interface devices themselves, such as modems and communications lines.

2. *Data link layer*: establishes the communications path, frames the message for transmission, guarantees proper sequence for data transmission, checks for errors in the received messages, and manages the access and use of the physical channel.

Exhibit 6.4
The ISO Seven-Layer Model for OSI

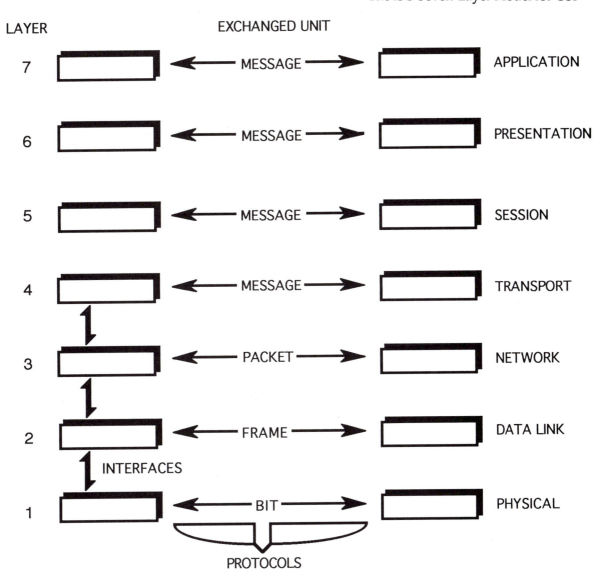

3. *Network control layer*: insures delivery of a message to the correct node by providing the network address, routing the message across nodes, and controlling the flow of the message between nodes.

4. *Transport layer*: provides end-to-end control of a "communication session" once a path has been established. This lowest level of the seven is totally independent of the type of devices that are communicating or their location.

5. *Session control layer*: controls the system-dependent aspects of the communications sessions. It also bridges the gap between services provided by the transport layer and the operating system.

6. *Presentation control layer*: translates received data into formats which can be understood and manipulated by the end user. An example of this would be the conversion of EBCDIC data to ASCII, or the deciphering of encrypted data.

7. *Application layer*: provides a standardized interface to the user's application programs. Examples of this function include file transfers and database management.

Different networking standards such as IBM's NetBIOS, TCP/IP, and SNA/3270, DEC's DECnet, and Novell's IPX/SPX protocols have attempted to work within the OSI model. However, hardware such as internetworking gateways is still needed for connecting dissimilar computer devices and networks.

Interfaces

Interfacing bar code equipment can be unnecessarily complex if communications requirements for each device are not understood. Many end users, particularly those purchasing equipment directly from a hardware supplier, find the terminal documentation confusing.

Two devices claiming to use a "standard" interface such as RS-232 will not always communicate the same way. Device suppliers may use different pin-outs for their connectors, which makes the plugs incompatible. Another problem deals with connector "gender." The end of the connector itself can be either "male" or "female" but cannot be connected to the same "sex." To complicate matters further, some terminals utilize a 9-pin as opposed to a 25-pin connection.

Voltage Interfaces

The most common type of interface between DCE and DTE equipment is described as a voltage interface. The Electronics Industry Association (EIA) has established various standards to provide compatibility between different brands of equipment, including the RS-232C standard and the RS-422/RS-485 standards.

- *RS-232C.* The most common physical interface is the RS-232C, established in 1969. The principal limitation is that connected equipment should be within 50 feet. This distance can be exceeded using slow data rates, provided that the environment is relatively "noise" free or if shielded cable is used for the connection. The maximum data

Pin Number	Description
1	Protective Ground
2	Transmitted Data
3	Received Data
4	Request to Send
5	Clear to Send
6	Data Set Ready
7	Signal Ground (Common Return)
8	Received Line Signal Detector
9	(Reserved for Data Set Testing)
10	(Reserved for Data Set Testing)
11	Unassigned
12	Secondary Received Line Signal Detector
13	Secondary Clear to Send
14	Secondary Transmitted Data
15	Transmission Signal Element Timing (DCE Source)
16	Secondary Received Data
17	Receiver Signal Element Timing (DCE Source)
18	Unassigned
19	Secondary Request to Send
20	Data Terminal Ready
21	Signal Quality Detector
22	Ring Indicator
23	Data Signal Rate Selector (DTE/DCE Source)
24	Transmit Signal Element Timing (DTE Source)
25	Unassigned

Exhibit 6.5

RS-232C Pin Assignments

transmission rate using RS-232C is 20 kilobits per second. This interface standard specifies the voltage of the signal, the normal pin-outs, and the control signals. Exhibit 6.5 represents the pin assignments of an RS-232C connection.

Among bar code data collection devices, RS-232C is by far the most prevalent interface for the reason that bar code scanners are usually located in close proximity to each other. This, however, may not be the case for your system.

- *RS-422/RS-485*. As networks of connected bar code scanners become more extended, devices are often located across distances exceeding 1000 feet. Bar code devices may also communicate with more than one controller, complicating network issues further. To address this situation, equipment manufacturers are now supporting RS-422 and RS-485, which are newer data signaling standards.

The RS-422 and RS-485 standards are significantly more immune to noise than signals sent via the RS-232C standard. Additionally, data can be transmitted reliably up to a distance of 4000 feet. A maximum

Exhibit 6.6

Data Collection Network Using RS-485 Interface

(Photo of Symbol's LS 7000II laser scanners and LL701 scanning network courtesy of Symbol Technologies, Inc. [Symbol MSI])

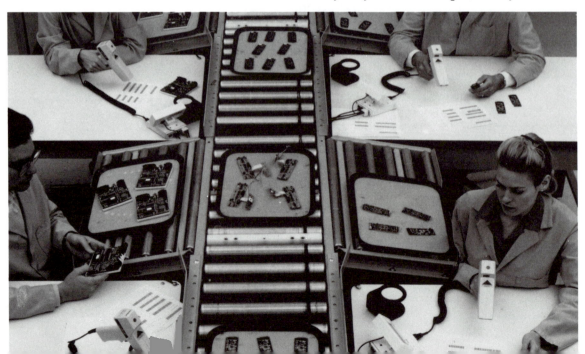

data rate of 10 megabits per second provides an additional advantage to bar code system applications. Also, the properties of the interface are such that several devices can share a single cable.

The major difference between RS-422 and RS-485 is that RS-422 supports one sender to multiple receivers, whereas RS-485 supports many senders and many receivers. With their high immunity to noise, these standards are well suited to the normal industrial environment. Exhibit 6.6 represents a bar code data collection network which uses the RS-485 interface.

Current Loop

The current loop interface is seldom used today, but it does warrant a brief description. A 20-milliampere loop (20mA current loop) is used for binary serial asynchronous data transmission. This standard requires a four-wire interface and supports a data rate of 1200 bits per second. Any 20-milliampere transmission loop must have an active transmitter sending to a passive receiver or vice versa. Historically, 20mA current loop was used to connect processors and printers in the earlier days of data processing. The two advantages to choosing this interface are economy and simplicity. Two disadvantages are that this interface has low noise immunity and that there is a low level of standardization in practice.

Transmission Methods and Protocols

Transmission codes were discussed earlier. Now let's turn to the components of data transmission — that is, the actual methods and protocols. These constitute the "rules of the road" governing data communication, ensuring that data sent is accurately received.

Data can be transferred as "serial" bits over a single line, or as "parallel" bits over several lines at once. Message transfers may be "synchronous," meaning that the arrival and departure intervals of transmitted bits are predictable. Message transfers can also be "asynchronous," meaning that data is transferred at irregular intervals.

Parallel and Serial Transmission

With parallel transmission, each bit, or the set of bits constituting a byte, is sent on its own wire. An additional wire, called the clock, notifies the receiver that all the bits are present and ready to be sampled. Parallel transmission is commonly used when the sending and receiving devices are in close physical proximity. As distances increase, the cost of the wire becomes a consideration, and the complexity of line drivers and receivers increases.

With serial transmission, the group of bits that represent a byte, or character, are sent down a single wire in serial procession. Serial transmission of bar code collected data is more common than parallel transmission.

Asynchronous Transmission

Asynchronous transmission, sometimes referred to as "start/stop" transmission, employs a technique to ensure that the receiving DTE is ready to receive the stream of data, coordinated at the correct character break. Within the transmitting DTE, start and stop bits are attached to every character telling the receiving DTE when each byte begins and ends. Data synchronization, then, is reestablished every time a start bit is detected.

Asynchronous transmission is most often used with unsophisticated terminals in simple bar code system designs. Asynchronous terminals cannot be polled, cannot acknowledge errors, and have no memory. On the other hand, the advantages of asynchronous transmission are that it allows for variable speed transmission, it regains synchronization quickly if it is lost, and it is less expensive to implement. Asynchronous transmission is somewhat inefficient because the start and stop bits, plus the idle time between characters, slow down the transmission rate.

Synchronous Transmission

Synchronous transmission does not require any special control bits. It does, however, require either a separate clock lead from the transmission point to the reception point, or a modem that includes clock information in the modulation process which encodes the data.

Synchronous operation is frequently used in polled or multipoint networks where many terminals share the same line. It can be used in point-to-point networks as well. Synchronous transmission permits higher transmission speeds and can employ sophisticated data error protection, which increases data integrity. Rather than transmitting individual characters framed by start and stop bits, entire blocks of data can be sent from a transmitter's data buffer. Balancing these advantages are higher costs, due to the sophistication of the equipment required.

There are several popular synchronous protocols. Binary Synchronous Communication Protocol (BISYNC) represents an early, widely used technique. Developed by IBM in the mid-1960s, BISYNC supports both ASCII and EBCDIC transmission codes and is character-oriented. Certain special characters, such as start of text (STX) to indicate the beginning of a message, and end text block (ETB) to indicate the end of a block of text, are employed for data integrity purposes.

Digital Data Communication Message Protocol (DDCMP), developed by Digital Equipment Corporation, is a byte-oriented synchronous protocol. All data are sent with a header which indicates the number of characters in the data block, together with certain control information. DDCMP is a general-purpose protocol which can be used on synchronous or asynchronous, point-to-point or multipoint, and serial or parallel systems.

High-Level Data Link Control (HDLC) procedures were developed in an attempt to improve on BISYNC. HDLC is a bit-oriented protocol that delineates which bits constitute messages by separating messages with a special flag character. Synchronous Data Link Control (SDLC) is the most well known expression of this standard. Other examples include American National Standards Institute (ANSI) and CCITT Recommendation X.25.

The bar code systems designer who is planning to integrate bar code scanning devices directly to a mainframe should have a thorough knowledge of the more elaborate communications protocols. The most common interface to bar code scanning devices is RS-232C asynchronous serial ASCII communication. Generally, data entry devices do not support any of the advanced protocols which mainframe computers require.

To work around this limitation the bar code system designer has three approaches to consider. One possibility is to utilize the PC as an intermediary device between the scanning hardware and the mainframe computer. This PC can be configured to emulate the protocol required to send data to the mainframe.

A second option would be to purchase a dedicated control unit to reside between the mainframe host and the bar code data collection devices. Exhibit 6.7 is one example of this approach. The control unit not only performs the communication role to the host, but also does local data management, as well as data validation and temporary storage. These controllers support communications such as BISYNC and SDLC.

A third approach would be to attach a bar code data collection device (or several through a controller) to the RS-232C port on the mainframe host if distance limitations permit.

Exhibit 6.7

Communication to Host Using
System Controller

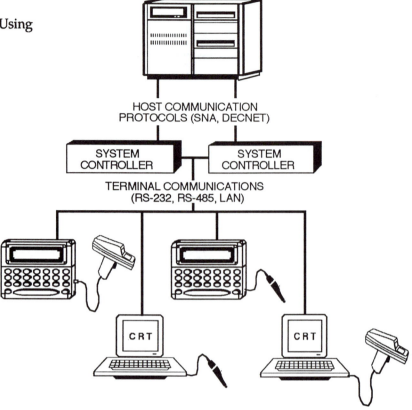

HOST COMMUNICATION
PROTOCOLS (SNA, DECNET)

SYSTEM
CONTROLLER

SYSTEM
CONTROLLER

TERMINAL COMMUNICATIONS
(RS-232, RS-485, LAN)

NOTE:

Many vendors make claims of compatibility to mainframe computers.
The buyer must be cautious! Sometimes the only protocol supported
is asynchronous, serial transmission. Higher-level protocols would
have to be supported through custom software, at additional expense.

■ DATA NETWORKS

Many of the bar code systems in use today include a network. A
network is an interconnected assembly of autonomous devices, usually
including a computer and two or more related digital devices. This
collection of devices is assembled to contribute to a related task.

Bar code data collection systems can be assembled around "popular" networks frequently used for traditional data collection or communication tasks. Alternatively, bar code device suppliers may provide proprietary single-use network designs that promise a high level of data efficiency. Regardless of the particular network's architecture, networks are an integral part of any bar code system that requires many scanning devices, printers, and dedicated controllers.

Bar Code System Architectures

The architecture of a system defines not only the components used, but how these components are configured. There are three system paths to consider in the design stage of your data collection project: PC-based architectures, mainframe-based architectures, and hybrid architectures. In addition, there is a variation of hybrid architecture to consider called redundant architecture.

PC-Based Architectures

Exhibit 6.8 represents a PC-based data collection system. The scanning devices can be controlled through a board connected to an empty PC slot or via an external terminal controller. Data residing on a PC can be uploaded to a mainframe on an as-needed basis. The advantages of this system design path include the following:

- Data collection will be performed independently from the mainframe. At times, when the mainframe is unavailable to support data collection, the application continues.
- The system design is relatively simple. Applications can be tested and modified easily without mainframe complications. Also, the user can clone an application to another location easily.
- System cost is usually lower and more predictable than when bar code data collection is controlled directly by a mainframe.
- The user generally experiences greater departmental control of the application. This advantage translates into better user training and acceptance.

PC-based architectures do have certain disadvantages, which fall into the following categories:

- PC and mainframe database coordination has to be thought through carefully. Initial database structural imbalance or poor database "housekeeping" could lead to troublesome mismatched records.

- Mainframe files will not be updated in realtime. Batch file refreshment is the rule here, although batch intervals may be very short.

- Over time, departmental independence with data collection may result in a drift away from a corporate plan or standardization.

Exhibit 6.8
PC-Based Bar Code Network

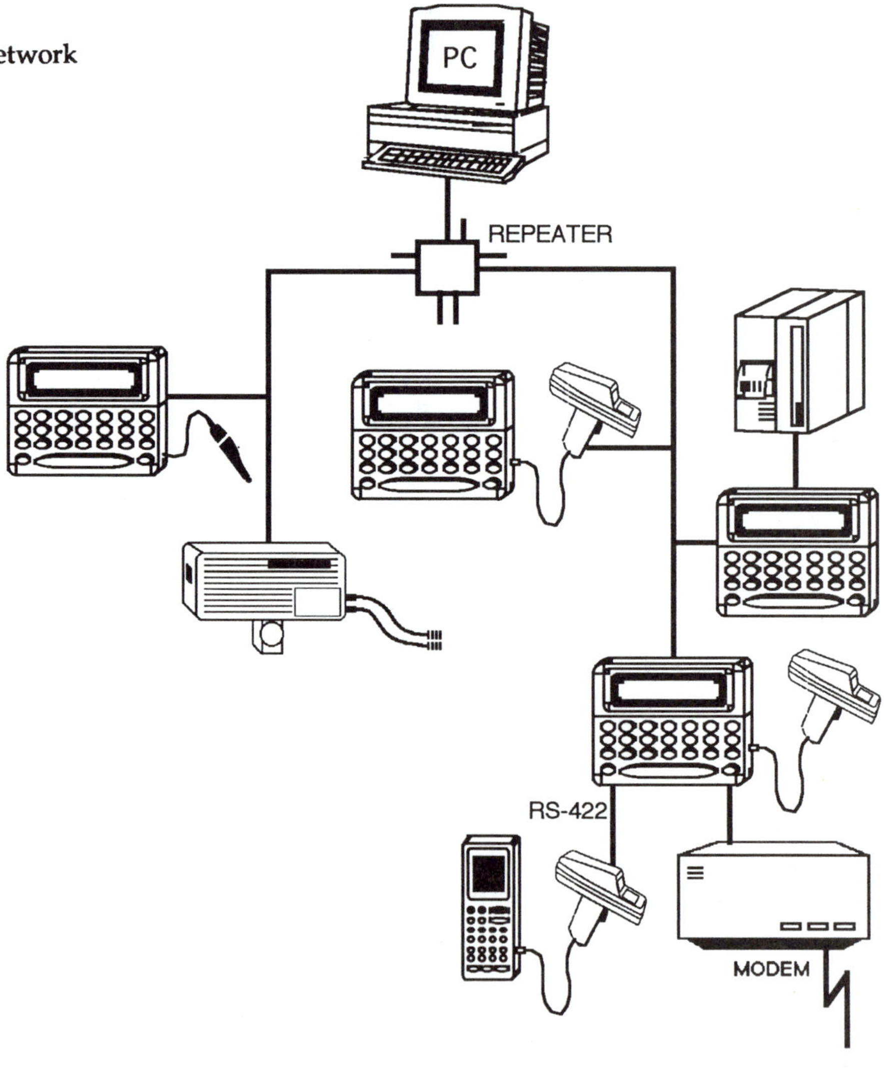

PC-based networks have been used in every type of bar code system. In large operations, they have been networked together for distributed control, or attached to a mainframe, thus allowing data to be shared throughout the entire organization.

Mainframe-Based Architectures

Exhibit 6.7 (p. 116) illustrates a mainframe-based bar code system. This is a common architecture for large production or manufacturing control systems. A mainframe computer also serves as the network controller. Bar code devices attached to a LAN communicate to the host via a front-end processor. Operators can also enter data through wedges attached to system terminals. Advantages of this architecture include the following:

- Data is controlled from a single point, minimizing file duplication and avoiding complex file transfer requirements.
- Data can be updated to master files in realtime. This is a prime requirement in bar code driven systems where recorded events are eligible for immediate query from a system terminal. Also, some bar code systems deal with information which requires mainframe resident validation before the scanner user can continue.
- System developers may wish to avoid expanding their mainframe-based architecture. In this case wedge scanners are the most easily integrated.

Mainframe-based bar code control systems do have a number of disadvantages, including the following:

- System overload may result from the quantity of local bar code devices the mainframe must now support. In addition, the frequency of data received may increase beyond the mainframe's available response time.
- The system design can become complex rapidly. As a result, you may experience escalating expense in support of development and implementation.
- System application development and task responsibility assignment are more difficult to manage. With data collection performed off site from the mainframe, user supervision and discipline require more attention.

- System integrity may suffer over time. Users of scanning devices cannot "see" the successful transfer of their work to the remote mainframe files. If data integrity begins to decay, finger pointing between data source and destination is common and the problem is costly to correct.

Hybrid Architecture

The third bar code architecture to consider is actually a hybrid of the two earlier approaches and is illustrated by Exhibit 6.9. Bar code data collection occurs prior to the involvement of the PC. Both the PC and mainframe next play their role. Initial data validation and record assembly usually take place in the PC. Then a realtime transfer of this message to the mainframe takes place for immediate database update.

Exhibit 6.9
Hybrid Network Architecture

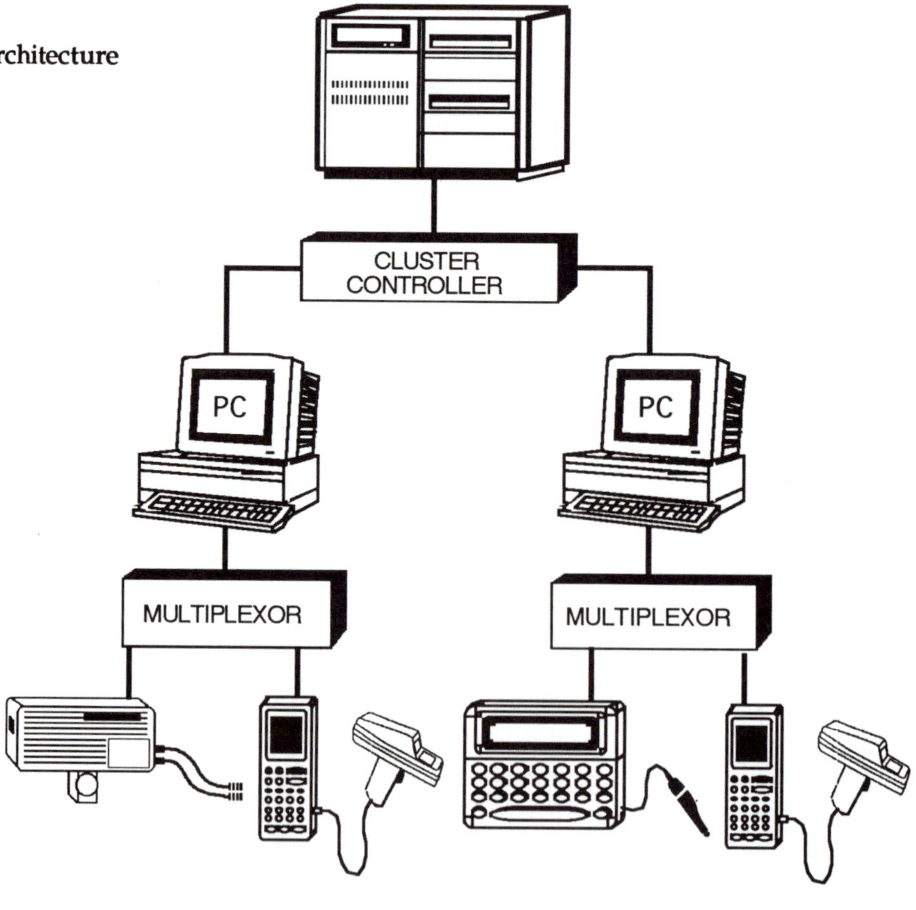

Users choosing a hybrid bar code system may find this system a complex one to implement. While the intent is to off-load local edit tasks to a PC while updating a mainframe in realtime, results can prove unpredictable in practice. Total time intervals from scan to total data capture may vary widely. The demand on the PC from many devices becomes a factor in response time. Additionally, the mainframe will vary in its responsiveness due to differing workloads of contending applications with varying priority assignments.

Another consideration before selecting a hybrid approach is the complexity of the system architecture itself. Due to the number of connection points and data buffering and manipulation locations, the source of a "bug" may prove difficult to locate.

On the other hand, when operating changes occur in the user's environment, resulting software changes can be implemented fairly easily on the PC. This may prove more practical than attempting software changes at the mainframe.

Redundant Architecture

A variation of hybrid architecture is termed a "redundant system." In this design, all data processing normally occurs at the mainframe. A PC simply acts as a pass-through mechanism in normal operation.

If the host "goes down" and becomes unable to receive and process data, the PC takes over, performing basic mainframe data collection and processing functions. When the mainframe comes back on-line, the PC transmits the processed data and the mainframe files are restored.

This system design approach can be very expensive. It may be an expense worth incurring when the environment cannot tolerate downtime. A case for employing this architecture can be made in production or process control situations where computer failure during a complex process could cause irreparable damage to many items.

NOTE:

A less expensive alternative to the redundant hybrid system could be the combination of two PCs, thus avoiding use of a mainframe altogether. These PCs can be located side by side, with a quick switchover of files and connections to scanners.

Local Area Networks

A local area network (LAN) is a privately owned network providing high-speed data communications, interconnecting data collection, and processing equipment in a limited geographic area (from 25 feet to 25 miles). Data transmission rates vary from 100 thousand to 10 million bits per second. LANs are characterized by their topology, signaling method, cabling type, and control method.

Topology

The four LAN topologies are referred to as star, ring, bus, and tree. Certain topologies require a particular control method and cabling type. The topology determines if control of the network is to be centralized or distributed. Exhibit 6.10 represents these four topologies.

■ *Star Topology.* In a star topology, which is centrally controlled, all nodes are joined at a single point. Point-to-point lines connect the central and outlying nodes, eliminating the need for complex link and control mechanisms. This type of network is suited to environments where traffic between the central and outlying nodes is minimal. The size and capacity of the network are direct functions of the power of the central node. This topology is used most commonly in bar code systems. If the central node should become overloaded, another PC or central node may be added for attaching additional bar code terminals. These central nodes may then be networked.

■ *Ring Topology.* The distinguishing feature of ring topology is that each node is connected to two other nodes and arranged to form a closed loop. Each node must be able to recognize its own address in order to accept messages and serve as an active repeater, retransmitting messages addressed to other nodes. This type of topology is rarely used in bar code systems because of the linking and control mechanisms that must be present at each node.

■ *Bus Topology.* The bus topology, frequently used for distributed control in LANs, is characterized by a single line, shared by a number of nodes. Since messages are broadcast to all nodes, each node must recognize its own address and is not required to repeat and forward messages addressed to other nodes. Because of this passive role in transmission, network operation will continue in the event of node failures, making bus networks resistant to single-point failure.

- *Tree Topology*. Tree topology is a bus which allows "branches" off the single cable, providing expansion flexibility.

Exhibit 6.10
LAN Topologies

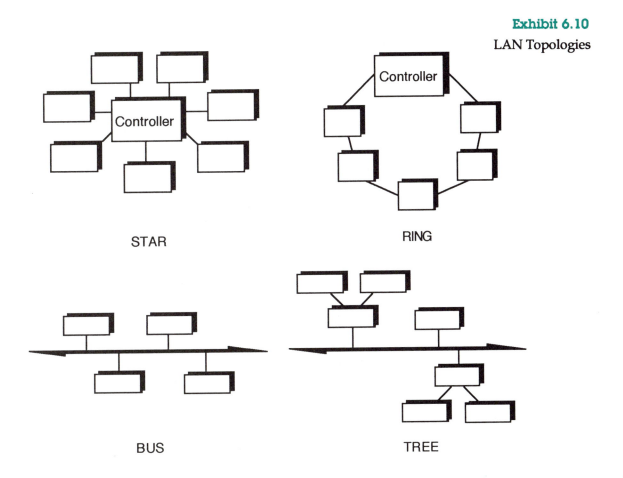

STAR

RING

BUS

TREE

Signaling Method

The two forms of signaling used in LANs are called baseband and broadband. In general, baseband is less costly, while broadband uses the cable more efficiently by sending and receiving on different frequencies.

Signaling in baseband is digital, where voltage is modified to represent the binary ones and zeros. Broadband uses analog transmission, where binary ones and zeros are represented by different signal frequencies.

Cabling Type

Transmission media provide the physical channel used to connect nodes in a network. Bounded media include wires, cables, and optical fibers. Unbounded media include radio, microwave, and infrared broadcast. Twisted pair, one of the original wire type cables used, is still the most popular. It is usually the least expensive but has the disadvantages of limiting data transmission speed and being most prone to error.

Coaxial cable allows for higher transmission rates and is more reliable. It is more expensive — a significant factor when used over long distances. Fiber optics provide the highest transmission speeds as well as the best immunity to noise. Their two major drawbacks are expense and installation complexity. Fiber optics are utilized primarily internetwork as opposed to intranetwork.

Control Methods

Three control protocols are in prominent use today: CSMA/CD, token passing, and polling. These protocols can be distinguished by whether or not communication between devices is managed by a "master." Systems with masters are usually simpler and have lower connection costs. Masterless systems, where the control of the network is passed from device to device, are much more complex. The protocols are elaborate, and the implementation costs are greater.

- *CSMA/CD.* The most common masterless protocol is Carrier Sense Multiple Access/Collision Detection (CSMA/CD). Ethernet, a popular local area network, uses this protocol. The IEEE Standard 802.3 is the definitive document describing this protocol.

Carrier sense is the ability of each node to detect any traffic on the channel. Multiple access lets any node send a message immediately upon sensing that the channel is free. The collision detect feature is the ability of the transmitting node to sense a collision of two messages on the channel. In this case a re-transmission of the message must occur. CSMA/CD is the protocol of choice when messages are long and fewer in number.

■ *Token Passing*. Token passing is most often associated with the ring topologies described earlier, although it has been applied to bus networks as well. This is a masterless system in which each node, in a predetermined order, receives and passes on the right to use the channel. The passing of control of the network is called the token. Possession of the token gives a node exclusive access to the channel, thus avoiding collisions with other messages. Although the average transmission delay may be longer using this protocol, it is generally more predictable in systems controlled by a master. One problem associated with this protocol is that the system must be able to recover from lost tokens that were sent to failed nodes. The IEEE Standard 802.5 specifies the token ring scheme and 802.4 specifies the token bus scheme.

■ *Polling*. The third control protocol is polling. This technique determines the order in which a node has access to the channel, so that direct conflict between nodes is prevented. The most common form of polling is centralized. One node acts as the master, controlling all other nodes' channel access.

Distributed polling is accomplished by each node containing an internal timing mechanism synchronized with all other nodes. Each node owns an exclusive slot of time in which it has access to the channel. Collisions are prevented and transmission delays can be accurately estimated. Both token passing and polling can lead to inefficient use of the channel by requiring a terminal to wait for a token or poll, even when the network is free.

The Ethernet Network

The Ethernet Local Area Network was developed jointly in 1980 by Digital Equipment Corporation, Xerox Corporation, and Intel Corporation. Standard Ethernet specifies the lowest two levels of the OSI seven-layer model. The topology is bus, in the shape of a tree. Shielded coaxial cable is used with a transmission rate of approximately 10 million bits per second. Network control follows the CSMA/CD

Exhibit 6.11

Network Data Collection
Using Ethernet

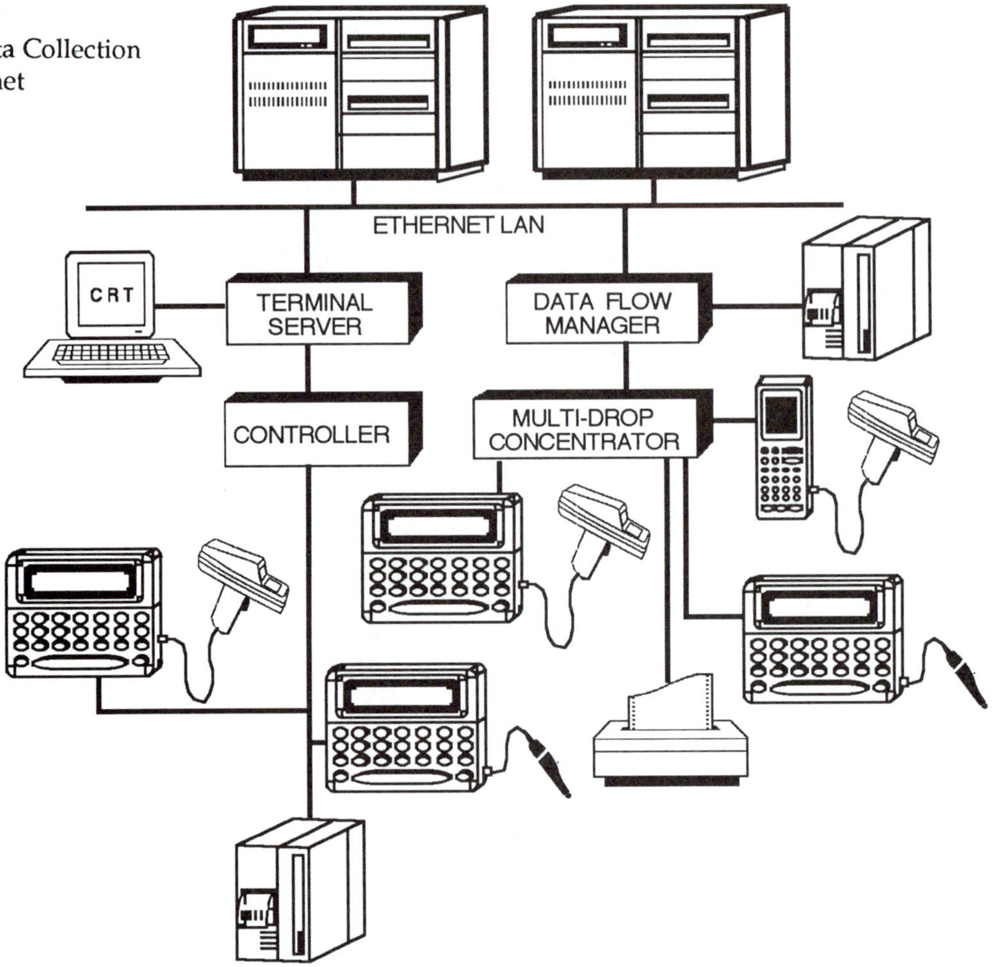

protocol. Ethernet is a very popular network with literally millions of applications. Exhibit 6.11 illustrates a network architecture for a complex application using Ethernet.

The MAP Network

The Manufacturing Automation Protocol (MAP) network is OSI-compatible. It was developed originally by General Motors to integrate computers in their manufacturing plants. MAP specifies all seven layers of the OSI model. The topology is bus, using a token passing control protocol. Coaxial cable provides data transmission rates of 10 million bits per second. The network can cover a distance of 25 miles with 1000 nodes attached.

Recognizing that various applications require different functional and performance characteristics, MAP has defined three protocol configurations: Mini-MAP, EPA MAP, and full MAP. A bar code system designer might be particularly interested in Mini-MAP, a configuration where only OSI layers one, two, and seven (physical, data link, and application) are provided.

Mini-MAP is intended for connection of low-cost, low-complexity devices, such as terminals and bar code readers. As a result of bypassing the middle layers of OSI, Mini-MAP reduces protocol overhead, providing optimum performance needed for realtime systems. There are restrictions, however, including these two:

- All transmissions are restricted to a single network. No internetwork transmission is provided.
- Message length is restricted by the packet size of the data link layer, because the transport's layer of packet assembly and sequencing is not present.

MAP is still evolving, with new versions being released frequently. Unfortunately, some of these versions provoke changes in programs that interface with MAP, while other changes involve only refinements and optional services.

The IBM Token Ring Network

The IBM Token Ring Network supports PCs, Systems 36 and 38, and 3725 mainframes. IEEE 802.5 Token Ring Standard is used for OSI layers one and two (physical and data link layers). Layers three through seven use IBM's System Network Architecture with twisted pair cabling. Data transmission rates stand at 4 million bits per second. Up to 260 nodes can be connected over an area of 1000 feet.

Because SNA is not compatible with the OSI model, other networks wishing to communicate with the IBM token ring must be interfaced above the application layer (layer seven).

Cableless Networks

A fairly new development in the world of LANs is the "cableless" network, which utilizes AC electrical wiring as its carrier. The advantages to this architecture are universal access and reduced installation time. PCs are networked by plugging into a network communication module board.

Scanners, printers, and modems can, in turn, be interconnected using specialized hardware. Data transmission occurs at a speed of 19 kilobits per second. These networks can be configured as master/slave or token bus, or a combination of the two, with up to 255 nodes attached. However, the system designer should be concerned with the error control mechanism and the access protocol developed by the supplier.   Exhibit 6.12 represents a possible system design for a cableless network.

Exhibit 6.12
Cableless Network

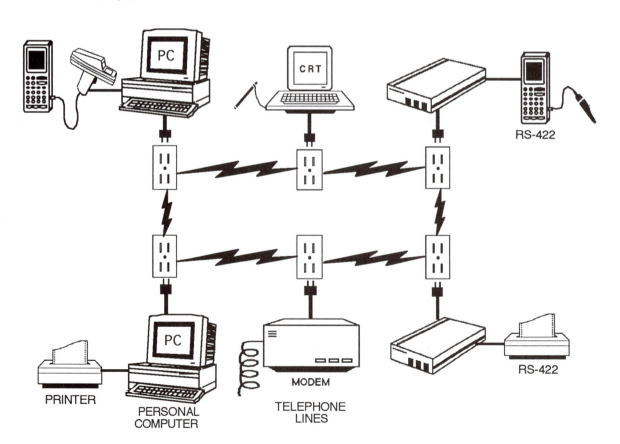

RS-422

RS-422

PRINTER

PERSONAL
COMPUTER

MODEM

TELEPHONE
LINES

Proprietary Networks

Many manufacturers develop their own variations of network architecture and access control protocols which are optimized for bar code data collection and related applications. Interfacing to these networks can occur at different layers of the OSI model, although it usually occurs at the application layer. As a system designer there is no reason to be biased against proprietary LANS. However, you must consider your long-term interfacing requirements to ensure compatibility. In addition, remember the requirement to obtain software source codes and complete network documentation.

Radio Frequency Network

The use of radio frequency in identification and control systems appears in two distinct roles. Radio frequency identification (RFID) is data collection technology where a miniature radio transmitter is used as a label and a radio transmitter/receiver is used to scan for an encapsulated message. Discussion of this technology can be found in Chapter 14. On the other hand, radio frequency used for data collection from bar code systems (RFDC) has a very important place in this book as a network to consider in bar code system design.

RFDC is the network technology which transmits data collected by bar code scanning devices over licensed radio frequencies rather than through a wire network. Exhibit 6.13 represents a simple RF-based data collection network.

A typical RF network system is comprised of the following elements:

- Bar code scanning devices similar to those covered in Chapter 3, with the addition of radio transmitter and receiver functions.
- A master radio transmitter and receiver (RF base station) capable of intelligently formatting messages and polling the scanning devices.
- A host computer controlling the RF base station. This host receives data from each scanning device and sends prompt messages (if appropriate) back to each scanning device through the base station.

Exhibit 6.13
RF-Based Data Collection Network

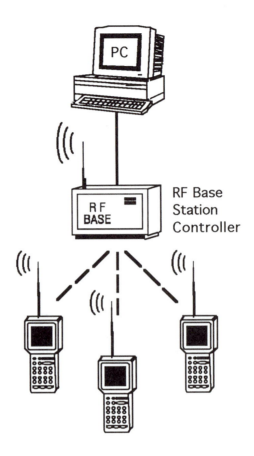

Exhibit 6.14 represents the scanning device and portable RF data entry terminal in a retail setting.

Host application software remains in contact with bar code terminals that are often battery powered and hand held. These features permit free-roaming users, but data collected can be immediately verified and acted upon.

In an RF network, the base station performs the following tasks:

- Acts as a modem, converting the radio signals to digital data on message receipt. It plays the reverse role when sending verifying or exception messages back to the RF scan station.

- Acts as the network multiplexer, controlling the flow of data (the message traffic) between the RF-equipped scanners and the host computer. RF data collection systems generally rely on two different protocols: polling and contention. The multiplexor polling rules are often more elaborate than wire-

Exhibit 6.14

Radio Data
Network Equipment

(Courtesy of Norand Corporation, Cedar Rapids, IA)

based systems. In contention systems, each terminal attempts to transmit at its own timing. If another terminal is occupying the network channel, the device tries to retransmit after a randomly set delay. A polling protocol is usually chosen if there are few terminals, each with approximately the same transaction rate. If there are many terminals, with a small number having high transaction rates, then the contention protocol should be chosen. In either case, the goal is to have a consistent response rate. The RF base station will usually perform error-checking tasks and network diagnosis, and track data terminal status.

The RFDC network design is now widely accepted due to improved reliability and high performance. In the past, RF-based systems required site licensing by the FCC. Now, however, most companies are using spread spectrum technology, which literally spreads the signal over a wider frequency band at a lower transmission power. The impact of spread-spectrum has been both positive and negative. Benefits of this technology are increased data rates of up to 244,000 bits per second (BPS), up from an average of 9,600 BPS, two-way simultaneous real-time communication, and less interference. On the negative side, system design requires more base stations.

A well-functioning system includes the following benefits:

- Bar code driven data collection terminals can be installed in areas where a "hardwired" terminal would be inappropriate. Fork-lift trucks in warehouses cannot be hardwired to a computer, for example, but are vital to many bar code data collection tasks and have benefited from RFDC.

- Data reaches the host in realtime, frequently permitting better database refinement in extended operations. Data reporting discrepancies detected by the host may be immediately corrected by on-site personnel.

- Operations can become more efficient. In a conveyorized order-picking environment, for instance, stock can be selected continually from incoming orders. The host computer knows the status of the work plan and can continually and efficiently add new assignments for employees.

RFDC applications have successfully performed many bar code data collection tasks. You might particularly consider this network technology for the following tasks:

- *Warehouse picking operations*. The host application software determines the most efficient route for the picker to take and issues instructions after each location has been serviced.

- *Retail stock control*. In each store, clerks can use RF-equipped bar code terminals to perform price checking and to update received inventory. In the distribution center, order picking, location updating, and cycle counting are performed.

- *Distribution center control*. RF-equipped bar code scanning terminals can efficiently verify stock location, perform cycle counts, and direct an order picker to alternate stock locations if necessary.

- *Authorized material returns*. Items are scanned on arrival, checked for return authorization, and immediately assigned a disposition status.

When choosing an RFDC system, an important consideration in your system design will be its response time. We encourage system designers to configure their hardware and applications software in such a way as to ensure that average bar code driven transactions can be completed in 1 to 2 seconds. Designers of RFDC networks must take a number of factors which influence response rates into consideration. Antenna efficiency, band width, data rate, and noise can be affected by choices the system designer makes. Two other factors are generally out of a system designer's control. They are:

- *Hardware overhead*. Each time the data encounters RF-linked hardware, the system response time increases. Converting network signals from digital to RF, and RF to digital, again increases response time.
- *Protocol overhead*. Establishing an RF connection with every active device on the network during polling adds to data delays.

Some rules of thumb should be observed for greatest efficiency. For instance, the fewer terminals connected to each RF base station, the more quickly the message will get to the host. Also, to keep response time to a minimum with RFDC systems, be sure that the message length over the RF link is short. This advice applies to the collected bar code data as well as the host reply.

System designers choosing RFDC networks for their bar code data collection application should choose a vendor after the careful evaluation of similar applications by other customers. Then a vendor survey should be conducted and vendor advice sought and followed.

SUMMARY ■

The material presented in Chapter 6 can appear overwhelming in scope and complexity. Although the system designer may not need to have a complete knowledge of all the information presented here, an overall appreciation of this subject matter is necessary for the development of a realistic project plan and schedule.

If an outside systems integrator is not called upon, it will become your project manager's responsibility to choose a bar code system architecture. Ordering the correct components and tying them together successfully requires perspective and some self-education.

Chapter 7

Data Entry Terminals

Chapter 3 explained how a scanner "reads" a bar code, decoding the black and white stripes into the data message which computers or printers can interpret. The physical scanning of a bar code, however, is only part of the process of automatic data collection. Next, the data message must be sent to a host computer or printer so it can be processed or examined. Data entry terminals provide the link between the scan function in data collection and the subsequent steps of message processing. This chapter describes the basic elements of a data entry terminal, presents the most popular terminal features offered in the marketplace, and makes distinctions about classes of terminals you might choose from. Recommendations concerning the most important features in different applications are included to assist you in system design.

Bar code data entry terminals have evolved significantly in recent years. The earliest bar code terminals were hardwired hardware configurations with transistor logic and relay-based processors and switches. Later manufacturers adopted commercial microprocessors and created PROM resident set-up and application programs to provide users with terminal adaptability. Next, terminals appeared, with user setup provided through a CRT keyboard or downloaded from a PC, with more elaborate application-level prompting and data validation capabilities. Today, data entry terminals range from simple to sophisticated. In other words, you can apply as little processing power and feature choices as you wish to pay for at the terminal junction of your design, or you can choose terminals with powerful microprocessors and extensive local RAM memory. Auxiliary hardware choices, such as keyboards and displays used in connection with the scan terminals, give you ideal system design flexibility.

■ ELEMENTS OF A DATA ENTRY TERMINAL

All bar code data entry terminals today share the following three common elements:

1. *Firmware*. Firmware has the same characteristics as software, except that it cannot be modified by the user. In terminal firmware you will find the operating system, the communications protocol commands, and the decoding algorithm. Firmware accepts and stores in memory the user application program entered from a keypad or downloaded from a PC.

2. *Software*. Software for a terminal is written by the user, or for the user's application by the software department of the device manufacturer, a consultant, or a systems integrator. This application software usually performs some or all of the following functions: prompts the user, accepts the data input, displays data or prompts, verifies the data, formats the verified data, stores the data, and manages the transmission of the data to a host computer.

3. *Communication ports*. Most data entry terminals have several input and output ports to provide the communications capability with other system components. Scanners (light pens, laser guns, etc.), printers, scales, and host computers can all be attached to a data entry terminal. Some data entry terminals can also be "daisy chained" together for inexpensive shared communications to a host.

Understanding the nature of these elements is important when you are comparing devices from different vendors or laying out your design architecture. Exhibits 7.1 and 7.2 present two worksheets you will find useful when configuring a bar code system. Because so many product choices are available in the bar code marketplace, it is essential that you choose equipment that will be consistent with other components, and at the same time, provide the highest performance without wasteful feature duplication.

Exhibit 7.1
Interface Specification Worksheet

INTERFACE SPECIFICATION WORKSHEET

DEVICE A

Name: _____

Model Number: _____

Specification Notes Page: _____

connected to

DEVICE B

Name: _____

Model Number: _____

Specification Notes Page: _____

adapter(s) required:* _____

	available device A	available device B	choice
baud rate			
data bits (7 or 8)			
parity			
stop bits			
XON/XOFF			
RTS/CTS			
start of text char			
end of text char			
host echo			
timeout			
transmit delay			
field delimeters			

Message Notes: _____

Signal Notes: _____

* refer to Device/Cable Pin-Out Worksheet

Exhibit 7.2
Device/Cable Pin-out Worksheet

DEVICE/CABLE PIN-OUT WORKSHEET

Device A

male _____ female _____   25 pin _____ 9pin _____

Device B

male _____ female _____   25 pin _____ 9pin _____

Connecting Cable

male _____ female _____   25 pin _____ 9 pin _____

Signal	Color	Device A ←	Adapter ←	Connecting cable	→ Adapter	→ Device B			
GND	green	1	1	1	1	1	1	1	1
TX	black	2	2	2	2	2	2	2	2
RX	red	3	3	3	3	3	3	3	3
RTS		4	4	4	4	4	4	4	4
CTS		5	5	5	5	5	5	5	5
DSR		6	6	6	6	6	6	6	6
SGND	white	7	7	7	7	7	7	7	7
DCR		8	8	8	8	8	8	8	8
		9	9	9	9	9	9	9	9
DTR		20	20	20	20	20	20	20	20

in most cases

DEVICE A pin 1 ⟶ 1 DEVICE B
DEVICE A pin 2 ⟶ 3 DEVICE B
DEVICE A pin 3 ⟶ 2 DEVICE B
DEVICE A pin 4 ⟶ 8 DEVICE B
DEVICE A pin 5 ⟶ 6 DEVICE B
DEVICE A pin 6 ⟶ 5 DEVICE B
DEVICE A pin 7 ⟶ 7 DEVICE B
DEVICE A pin 8 ⟶ 4 DEVICE B
DEVICE A pin 20 jumpered with 6

DATA ENTRY TERMINAL FEATURES ■

To present every combination of features and options offered by bar code terminal manufacturers today is beyond the scope of this book. This section discusses the general features of terminals and the most important options to consider for your design. Recommendations are offered wherever appropriate.

Operating System

Bar code data entry terminals usually have a proprietary operating system installed as firmware, although some manufacturers are using an MS-DOS-related operating system due to the widespread popularity of PCs. The chief advantage to offering MS-DOS is to provide the user with the ability to program a terminal in a familiar programming language such as C or BASIC. Otherwise, you must learn a terminal programming language unique to your manufacturer's terminal family. Usually this is not difficult and can be performed by nontechnical personnel. On the one hand, MS-DOS-based software can be more powerful, essentially putting more functions in the hands of your data collection personnel. On the other hand, such sophistication can represent overkill for many traditional data collection applications and may prove costly or unnecessarily elaborate. In most data collection designs, you should reserve your complex processing of bar code data for the host computer and perform only simple data verification and formatting at the terminal level. Proprietary operating systems are designed specifically for bar code data entry. They are usually quite efficient for this task compared with MS-DOS; they also use less on-board memory, which can translate into lower energy consumption with battery-powered terminals.

> **NOTE:**
> Although there is some attraction to using MS-DOS, be aware that total compatibility may not exist. You may find that your program will not run on a given terminal, or that the program runs slowly, producing unacceptable response times. You may also find there is not enough memory available to store the collected data.

A bar code data collection terminal, with an efficient proprietary operating system but which supports program development on a PC, is often the best choice for applications needing a fast, compact prompt-and-edit program.

Programming Languages

There are pros and cons to a MS-DOS-based data entry terminal. One advantage to working under MS-DOS is the ability to program in C, Pascal, or other popular languages. However, you should not be too concerned about using a proprietary terminal programming language. In most instances, these are very similar to the BASIC programming language and can be easily mastered, especially to the degree needed when you are writing short programs. Useful controls to which terminal programming languages frequently give you access include the following:

- Beeper and LED commands — beep, buzz, set green, set red, signal
- Input/output commands — get character, put, set COM port, set symbology, define key
- Character string manipulation commands — copy, pack, unpack, edit
- Numeric functions — length, position, value
- File manipulation commands — create, open, close, read, write, find, purge
- System commands — set time and date, pause, wait, alarm

Almost every terminal manufacturer now offers a PC-based programming development system, which includes a programmer's guide, editor, compiler, and the ability to download the applications program to the data terminal. For terminals running the same application, cable program transfer is provided, which allows any program to be "cloned" from one device to another. These features are especially helpful when a number of data terminals must be updated with new programs. In addition, the data collection host PC can be instructed to download a new or refreshed terminal program to all on-line addressable terminals individually.

Communications

The communication features offered with bar code data entry terminals can differ on the basis of communications standards supported and capacity. Terminals differ in the following ways:

1. *The number of physical "ports" or hardware connectors available on the terminal.* Terminals have a minimum of two connectors — one for the bar code scanner and another for external communication. Generally, the external connection is linked to a host computer and supports serial asynchronous transmission. Sophisticated terminals can have several input and output connections accepting interfaces from bar code and magnetic stripe scanners for input, and supporting RS-232C, RS-422, or radio frequency transmissions for external communications. Other terminals have input ports for sensing states of external switches such as photoeyes and gates, or for accepting digital input from scales and measurement gauges. Most terminals can drive a printer through the serial port. Portable data collection terminals are generally less sophisticated, offering the minimum requirement of two ports, or one port if the terminal has an integrated scan function.

2. *The number of communication protocols the terminal supports.* Depending on the sophistication of the device, one or more of the following protocols will be supported: XON/XOFF (character mode), RTS/CTS (ready-to-send, clear-to-send), ACK/NAK (acknowledge/negative acknowledge), Monitor Mode, Polling, and Multidrop Mode. Radio frequency-based terminals (RFDC) provide an antenna for external communications and may support DECNET, BISYNC, or SNA-SDLC protocols.

3. *The transmission parameter choices offered.* The ability to select the following transmission parameters is common: baud rate, parity, message prefix/suffix, and several other formatting options. The most popular baud rate used in bar code networks is 9600 baud, but terminals usually support rates from 300 to 19,200. Parity is user-programmable for even, odd, or none, with one or no stop bits. Other user-programmable parameters may be word length, block length, or intercharacter delay.

Review Exhibits 7.1 and 7.2 before you attempt to establish your communication requirements. With the exception of baud rate, the selection of other parameters rarely impacts system performance. The most important consideration is compatibility, and terminal devices will seem like they are broken if even a single parameter value is set incorrectly.

Devices that employ radio frequency communication must be approached differently as described in Chapter 6. In addition to the factors which influence RF system performance, each manufacturer of RF portable data entry devices has developed its own proprietary terminal-to-base-station communications protocols. The base station is frequently equipped with firmware to support network communications or terminal emulation, however.

> **NOTE:**
>
> When your bar code system is put in service, be sure that you record and store in a safe place all terminal setup values and programming codes. Later, when a device is added, or a repaired unit is put back on the network, the reconnection will be orderly and immediate. Too often this information is misplaced after a system has been running successfully, and you will have to conduct a time-consuming and costly redevelopment of terminal protocols and programs.

Data Buffers

The amount of memory for data storage is an important consideration for portable, hand-held units and for on-line terminals in certain applications. Most organizations would like to have the capacity to collect and maintain one complete day's or shift's data in a unit before it has to be uploaded. There are portable terminals available today that contain as little as 2 kilobytes of RAM to as much as 2 megabytes of memory. For most applications, 32K to 128K bytes are adequate. There is always a risk of losing data held in portable terminals for any length of time due to damage, the effects of static electricity, or certain low battery conditions. You should provide for frequent (hourly) data upload to a host when designing a portable terminal based on bar code technology. Not only is this a sound operating philosophy, but the cost of the terminals will be significantly reduced.

On-line data collection terminals can also be equipped with RAM memory used as data buffers. Some application programs are designed to continue vital data collection even when the link to the host, or the host itself, is down. A microprocessor in the terminal can continue with local prompting and data verification indefinitely, while the terminal data buffer holds the collected information until the link is reestablished and the data is uploaded again.

Keyboard

Although very basic data entry terminals do not support a keyboard, most portable and many on-line units do. You can choose a simple numeric keyboard, a numeric keyboard with assignable function keys, an alphanumeric keyboard, or an alphanumeric keyboard with function keys. If an alphanumeric keyboard is required, you have a choice between the standard QWERTY layout or an ABCDE layout. If the terminal will be located in a manufacturing or warehouse operation, the ABCDE keyboard is appropriate. For an office setting where users may have some key entry skills, the QWERTY keyboard makes more sense. Other options to consider when choosing a keyboard include the following:

- *Key size.* Device suppliers can go overboard in miniaturization, and the gloved hand, or even a large man's fingers, may not navigate a small keyboard easily.
- *Dual function keys.* Devices can be smaller or less costly if fewer keys are used. To give full alphanumeric capability to a small keyboard set, device manufacturers sometimes use shift keys to combine two or three values per key. This compromise may limit the terminal's usefulness.
- *Special function keys.* These should be programmable and easy to mark with the function's purpose.

A bar-coded menu card can be a practical substitute for a keyboard when data of short message length is to be entered manually on a frequent basis. These menus can be custom designed and can often eliminate all key entry. Exhibit 7.3 is an example of this.

Making the correct trade-off among all these features may be a challenge. Put yourself in the place of the terminal user and imagine each step in a normal, and unusual, transaction. Then decide what features are required to keep every operation effective but simple.

Exhibit 7.3

Data Entry Terminal
with Light Pen and
Bar-Coded Menu

(Courtesy of LINX Data Terminals, Inc.)

Display

The messages you would typically display on a terminal would be
an operator prompt, a data entry error message, or the echo of scanned
data. The supplier community offers many different display technologies: LED (light-emitting diode), LCD (liquid crystal display), VFD
(vacuum fluorescent display), and CRT (cathode ray tube). Each offers
different features at varying costs. When making your decision, you
must consider the angle and distance from which the display will be
read, as well as the ambient light. Unless you are close to the terminal
and are viewing the display head-on, LCD displays can be difficult to
read. Backlighting the LCD display will improve the readability
somewhat. LED displays are not practical when used in sunlight. The
issue of display effectiveness can be very difficult to evaluate from

specification sheets, and borrowing demonstration units from several suppliers is a sensible path to take before you finalize your decision.

Other display variables include the number of characters that can be displayed and the size of the character. Most portable terminals have more limited display choices, governed by the terminal package, which is typically small and of limited battery capacity. Exhibit 7.4 illustrates a data terminal with a clear and easy-to-read LCD display.

NOTE:

If your application has alphanumeric data and you are considering an LCD display, make sure you can easily distinguish numbers from letters. For example, in a seven-segment LCD display, a "5" looks identical to an "S" and a "2" can be confused with a "Z." Dot matrix LCD displays do not have this limitation.

Exhibit 7.4

Data Entry Terminal with LCD Display and ABCDE Keyboard Layout

(Courtesy of International Business Machines Corporation)

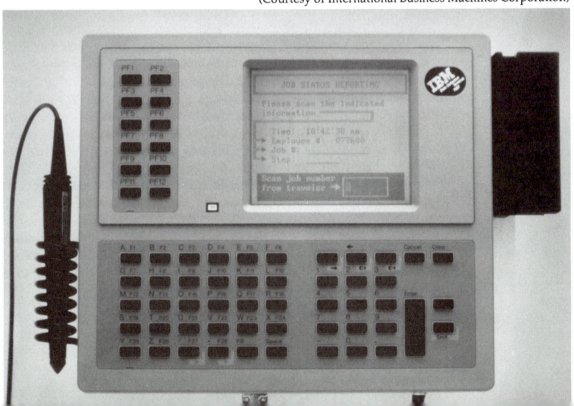

Symbology Decoding Options

Data entry terminals today should be able to read all of the symbologies described in Chapter 2, and perhaps one or two more. The minimum should be Interleaved 2of5, Code 39, Code 128, UPC, EAN, and Codabar. Frequently, manufacturers will offer you the choice of Code 93 or Plessey Code, or perhaps one or two others. Your terminal should be able to autodiscriminate among a number of symbologies, which means that you can intermix, say, Code 128 labels and Code 39 labels without making any system or terminal modifications, after your initial terminal setup has been made. In addition, you should be able to set up your terminal to ignore selected symbologies. For example, you could tell a terminal to only accept UPC labels and ignore all others. With certain symbologies, such as Interleaved 2of5, additional set-up instructions are necessary such as label or message length. With Interleaved 2of5, you should read one message length only in any application.

While the label symbology standard published by AIM provides a valid symbology decoding algorithm, certain manufacturers of terminals have chosen to use their own proprietary algorithm. Some of these are superior to the AIM decode algorithm, but some are disappointing. For this reason, you should borrow several demonstration terminals and test the decoding ability of each against samples of your label to satisfy yourself that the combined performance is good.

> **NOTE:**
> In conducting this test of decoding algorithm and label, be sure to vary the scanning instruments you use to eliminate that factor. A terminal should be able to perform with a high read rate using a wand, several types of laser guns, and a CCD scanner.

Indicator Lights

Most on-line terminals come equipped with several display indicators (LEDs) to display such conditions as power on, line connect, successful scan, and data send. There may be other lights indicating other functional modes if there are additional capabilities with the unit. Some designs offer one or more user-programmable lights in different colors, such as red, green, or yellow. These can be set to indicate certain conditions such as data buffer full, transmission errors, receipt of input from a scale, or providing a signal to a relay.

> **NOTE:**
> The simpler terminals are more dependent on lights to alert an operator about conditions of interest. Terminals can be designed to nest in a PC slot, and certain suppliers offer this feature. Unfortunately, if you adopt this terminal approach, you lose the assistance of the display lights, which are missing or out of sight.

Beepers

Although lights are useful in indicating the various conditions of the terminal, most applications benefit from a beeper as well. After scanning a label, the operator is typically looking at the item, not the terminal, and an audible beep is a helpful assist in indicating a successful scan. A well-designed terminal will allow you to vary the beeper volume in your set-up procedure or disable the beeper if you desire. You will find these considerations are important once you begin to apply the devices to the shop floor environment.

> **NOTE:**
> If your environment is noisy, even a loud beep may not be satisfactory. In an environment with many scan stations and with high ambient noise, trying to distinguish the beeper of one terminal from another becomes very difficult. Sometimes operators are fitted with an earphone wired to the terminal or linked by infrared energy.

The use of the beeper in a bar code data collection system of any complexity can be a great operator assist, or a source of confusion. The terminal beeper should be addressable by the host computer. If you want to use this device to prompt the operator, then you may decide to suppress the "read" beep and trigger a "message accepted" beep from the host when all record checks for that label have been processed. Beyond this step, you may wish to trigger a multiple beep sequence from the host for an unaccepted message sequence, and have the scan steps repeated, or have the operator go to a display station for detailed instructions.

Clock/Calendar

Most portable data entry terminals are equipped with a realtime clock. A few of these track time in relation to when the unit was powered on. More commonly, a traditional time and date sequence is generated by the microprocessor clock and is available to append to data messages as they are collected. This information is useful in almost every bar code application. A time stamp permits a more complete audit trail of activities and provides detail for productivity or job-costing analysis. Also, in the event of some data loss, time and date information can permit a well-targeted and efficient data recapture exercise.

> **NOTE:**
> Even though on-line terminals may have a time stamp capability, it is only needed when records are being written to a terminal buffer while the terminal is off-line. More typically, the host time stamps transactions in on-line networks.

Power Source

On-line data entry terminals require 5 to 12 Vdc for operation, depending somewhat on the type of scanning device attached. These devices are usually connected to an AC/DC converter plugged into a standard 117Vac outlet. The more sophisticated terminals, which are capable of running their own local programs backed with RAM memory, must also be provided with battery back-up to minimize the risk of data loss during primary power disconnect.

Hand-held portable terminals are usually powered by rechargeable NiCad (nickel cadmium) batteries. Some units are equipped with a "battery low" indicator to warn the user when to stop collecting data and recharge the batteries immediately. Portable units have a lithium battery or capacitor for program and data protection, as well. A strict procedure must be established and followed regarding the use and recharging of battery-powered portable terminals in order to avoid data loss.

> **NOTE:**
>
> Rechargeable NiCad batteries have a use-charge "memory." If the unit is used for short intervals between charges, then the battery will need charging at similarly short, or shorter, intervals. If this should happen to your equipment, each unit should be "deep discharged," erasing the NiCad "memory," and then fully recharged. More advanced manufacturers have designed this deep discharge cycle mode into their charger design for you.

Ruggedness

Industrial data entry terminals are frequently installed in a harsh environment or in a location where abuse may occur. Some terminal suppliers offer a heavy industrial version of their terminal line. Enclosures can be sealed against wind-blown dust, moisture, and toxic gases. Special environmental precautions can be taken against extreme cold and hot temperature as well. Sealed membrane keypads should be considered, even if the unit will not be exposed to extreme conditions. Open keyboards are particularly sensitive to water and moisture and should only be chosen for light-duty office applications.

If you choose bar code portable terminals for your application, you should examine the supplier's "drop test" data for your terminal. Units should be able to function after a repeated drop of 3 feet onto a concrete floor. The same resistance to drop damage should apply to your scanning device as well. The industrial environment is the natural habitat of bar code terminals, and there should not be any fragile enclosure or components supplied with a well-designed product. On the other hand, common sense says that the user must train supervisory personnel in the proper handling of equipment and take pains in installation to minimize equipment abuse and cable strain.

Size and Weight

The size and weight of portable data entry terminals are particularly important for hand-held portable units. As electronic packaging technology improves, these devices have been getting smaller and lighter. Many designs incorporate scanning, key entry, and display in a single package. Exhibits 7.5 and 7.6 present examples of compact, hand-held terminals.

Some portable units can be attached to fork-lift trucks, placed in a holster around the user's waist, or outfitted with a lanyard or strap that slips around the operator's neck. These mounting arrangements can leave one hand available for scanning and one hand free for driving or for manipulating the item to be scanned.

Bar code data collection terminals used on-line are typically bench, wall, or table mounted, and your supplier should be able to provide bracketing suitable for any of these arrangements. The proper mounting of a terminal and the readability of the display (if chosen) are, of course, related. When you run your display comparisons between terminal devices, be sure the terminal is positioned in the final mounting location. Scanners are usually connected to terminals with a strain-relieved coil cord for ruggedness and user flexibility. Some terminals come with a laser scanner or wand holder to further minimize the risk of instrument abuse.

Exhibit 7.5

Compact Portable Data
Entry Device with
Integrated Scanner
and RF Communication

(Courtesy of LXE, Inc.)

Exhibit 7.6
Integrated Portable
Data Entry Device

(Laser-Wand is a registered trademark of
Hand Held Products, Inc.)

DATA ENTRY DEVICES ■

After becoming knowledgeable about the terminal features currently
available from bar code suppliers, you should review the environment
where you plan to locate the terminals in your project. Then, make a
list of the features you need for effective collection of the necessary data
at each location. The remainder of this chapter describes the normal

choice of devices with which the bar code supply community will present you. There are combinations of features and options, packaged in distinguishable designs, which can complement your data collection architecture.

On-Line Data Entry Devices

These terminals are also referred to as "hardwired." This terminal type is directly connected to a host computer and, as a minimum, provides symbology decoding and interface connectivity. Three types of on-line data entry devices — wedges, decoders, and full data entry terminals — are described in the following sections.

Wedges

Bar code wedge devices provide the decoding and interface functions while physically "wedged" between the keyboard and terminal or PC unit they are supporting — hence the name. These devices accept scan signals, decode them into messages, and send the messages to the PC or terminal as though the information were entered through the keyboard. This is accomplished by sending signals that exactly emulate the equivalent key signal for each character decoded and transmitted. The PC or terminal literally cannot distinguish the wedge message from a series of keystroke characters. This produces a terminal design simplicity which permits the conversion of a traditional PC or key entry terminal into a bar code data collection station, with no new software or communications required.

Manufacturers offer a wide range of options in their wedge product lines. Data formatting to attach message preamble or postscript characters is a common feature. A wedge device can usually be set up via a bar code menu, or downloaded from the PC or terminal it is supporting. An input port is included to support bar code scanners such as wands, CCD, and laser guns. In addition, magnetic stripe readers or OCR (optical character recognition) readers can be added on some units, making them suitable for POS use where multi-identification media is the rule. An auxiliary serial port is desirable on a wedge to permit portable terminal uploading of data to a host computer. This feature may raise the price a bit, but it gives you a valuable gateway for data collected in batches via bar code.

There are three different types of bar code wedges: the self-packaged wedge, the plug-in wedge or printed circuit card nested in your terminal bus, and the software wedge. A typical self-packaged wedge is illustrated in Exhibit 7.7. The model shown has three communication ports. One cable connects from the wedge to the keyboard connector on the PC, one cable receives the cable from the PC keyboard, and one port is available for the bar code scanner. The wedge unit's power is usually provided by the terminal or PC through the keyboard cable port when used with low-power scan devices. However, if you were to connect a helium-neon laser scanner to the wedge, you would have to add a supplemental 12Vdc external supply.

Exhibit 7.7
Bar Code Wedge
Data Entry Device

(Courtesy of Bear Rock Technologies Corporation)

The plug-in wedge is shown in Exhibit 7.8. This wedge design uses no desk space and has no external cables except, of course, the scanner cable. This wedge variety must be used for PCs or terminals with nondetachable keyboards. They may be chosen for traditional PCs as well. A disadvantage of this wedge type is its use of a slot in the machine nest, which might be needed for additional memory, a modem, or other accessory. Here, the decoding processor resides on the printed circuit board, and the bar code scanner is connected to the board by a 9- or 25-pin connector at the back of the PC or terminal. Plug-in wedges can transfer bar code messages to the keyboard buffer, or directly to the PC processor, where they are controlled by a modified application program. These wedges are usually much faster than self-powered wedges, but the operator loses the assistance of the LED visual prompts described earlier in this chapter.

Exhibit 7.8

Plug-in Wedge

This plug-in wedge is able to autodistinguish
both bar codes and optical characters.   (Courtesy of Opto Wand Inc.)

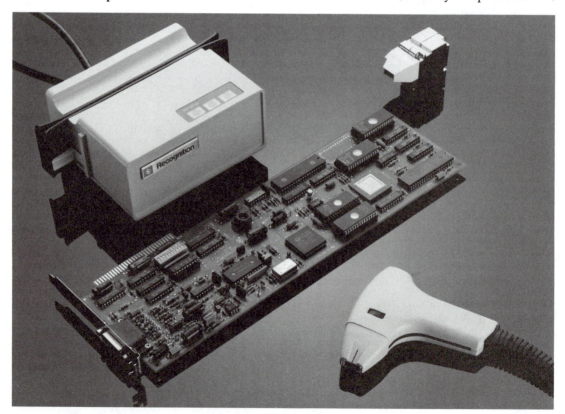

The software wedge is a utility residing on the PC which accepts input from any RS-232-compatible device attached to either the COM1 or COM2 serial port of the PC. Incoming data is then placed in the keyboard buffer. Decoding is done outside the PC; the software does not perform the decoding. Typically, the software instructs the PC to accumulate data until the end of a character string or bar code message is reached. Then the message can be displayed on the screen and acted on by an application program.

The advantages of using wedges in your bar code architecture are many. Ease of installation, low cost per scan station, and data integration without new software are the three reasons most frequently cited by users of wedges. When you use bar code wedges with PCs or on-line terminals running complex MRP II or distribution center control software, you can scan enter volumes of data and use the scanner to control screen selection and cursor position, eliminating substantial operator training.

The use of separate wedge hardware is steadily declining. One of the reasons for the decline is the software wedge as described above; however, a greater influence is development of the integrated scanner which has the decoding logic and communications firmware built in. Light pens, laser scanners, and CCD scanners are available with this option. Drawbacks to these products include the increased cost and the reduced flexibility in switching scanner types. Advantages include the elimination of a piece of equipment that will require maintenance and use valuable space at the data entry station.

> **NOTE:**
> If you intend to use bar code wedges to drive multiscreen software, you should use Code 128 symbology for your menu messages. This powerful code contains all ASCII characters and will permit you to embed all keyboard control characters in bar code, thus simplifying operator training.

Decoders

Decoding terminals are easily described: primarily, they decode scanned bar code messages and convert this data into a serial ASCII character stream. They also provide power to the scanning device and give an indication of a successful scan, usually with a beep. Most simple

Exhibit 7.9

Bar Code Decoder Terminal

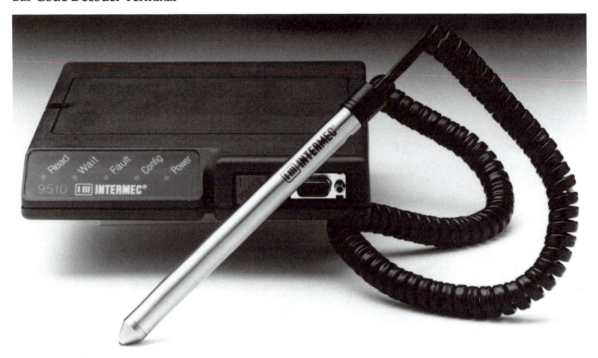

(Courtesy of Intermec Corporation)

decoders have several input ports and one output port, usually RS-232C, or RS-422. This architecture allows many decoders to be "daisy chained" together to form a low-cost network. Exhibit 7.9 illustrates a simple decoding terminal.

These units can be programmed by scanning a set-up menu, or downloaded with set-up instructions from the host PC or terminal. Once programmed, parameters are stored in nonvolatile memory, so that these devices can be removed from use or repositioned without losing their setup. Simple decoders are often used at work stations where there is no need for complex user prompting, because bar code transactions have been simplified.

Full Data Entry Terminals

Full data entry terminals are on-line interactive devices with decoding, keyboard, and display as standard features. These terminals can be classified as either "intelligent" or "dumb." Dumb terminals cannot perform any independent processing of bar code messages. In this case, all prompt messages must be created by the host computer and broadcast to the terminal. A dumb terminal can service only one host, and, if networked, must be polled and directed by an intelligent controller.

Intelligent terminals can be programmed with sophisticated routines and can communicate with a host in realtime or batch mode. They can be taught to validate and verify bar code data and to arrange several data entries into records. These units can generate and display error messages and activate indicator lights and beep sequences. Many intelligent terminal designs have their own RAM memory and offer multiple input and output ports. Input ports would accept all bar code scanner types, usually at 5 to 12 Vdc. In addition, magnetic stripe readers, OCR readers, and digital scales or other measuring instruments can provide input. Multiple output ports provide a wide range of ASCII-compatible data communications, and can also set relays or drive current loop communications. Intelligent terminals can transmit to and receive from more than one master, which permits the development of a powerful and efficient data collection system.

Before deciding which type of terminal is best for your project, consider the following questions:

- How many terminals will provide input to a host?
- Is realtime response to your input needed from the host?
- Will a series of visual display prompts increase the operator's performance?
- Will the host or communications network be unavailable for record upload during the work period?

Because of the many features full data entry terminals can contain, these units are significantly more expensive than wedges or simple decoders. Bar code data collection systems can be assembled with a wide range of terminal types, often intermixed. You can use a full terminal where the task requires it, and simpler, less expensive terminals elsewhere, to hold down overall system cost.

Portable Data Entry Terminals

Portable, hand-held data entry terminals experience a product redesign by their manufacturers about every two years. Through this process the marketplace has seen a rapid product evolution in microprocessor power, available memory capacity, more display capacity, and smaller packaging. Portable terminals are very popular bar code data collection devices and are used extensively in warehouse and retail applications, as well as many tracking projects. Portable bar code terminals can be viewed as falling into two categories: integrated and nonintegrated packages.

Integrated designs have the scanner function incorporated into the terminal package. Nonintegrated terminals are equipped with a cable-connected scanner which can be removed for key entry only use. An advantage of the nonintegrated scanner is its ability to mix scanner types while keeping a constant portable terminal design. Exhibits 7.10 and 7.11 are examples of two portable data entry terminals. Exhibit 7.11 also shows an alternative to having a cable connect between the

Exhibit 7.11

RF Portable Data Terminal with Integrated Scanner

Exhibit 7.10

Portable Data Entry Terminal

(Courtesy of The Peak Technologies Group, Inc.)

(Courtesy of The Peak Technologies Group, Inc.)

portable terminal and the port for transmission of records to the host. This portable unit uses radio frequency transmission to transfer data and download resident software.

Depending on the application, you may find one of the above approaches more satisfying than the other. An integrated unit frees one

Exhibit 7.12

Integrated Portable
Data Entry Terminal
and CCD Scanner

(Courtesy of Densei)

hand, which gives the operator more flexibility in many data collection tasks. However, you are limited to a single type of scanner for each portable model. An integrated unit may require higher service costs, since the entire system will have to be replaced or repaired if damaged, rather than the scanner unit or terminal unit alone. Exhibit 7.12 represents an integrated portable data entry terminal.

Bar code information can be easily and accurately collected with modern, hand-held portable data collection terminals. Remember, though, unless your terminal is RF-based, you must upload the information you have collected frequently — ideally every hour. Until this data has reached the host computer or has been put in hardened media locally, you should consider the information to be very fragile. Also, portable terminals should never be used when an on-line terminal could be installed instead. Since bar code data collection systems are most valuable when information is received and processed instantaneously, or in realtime, limit your use of non-RF portable terminals to applications which require operator mobility and where data is not extremely time critical.

■   SUMMARY

Although the use of intelligent data entry terminals appears to be the trend these days, you should be cautious and maintain system balance. As a first principle, bar code data entry terminals should be simple and easy to use, speeding the data collection process — not slowing it down. Often, using a dedicated host PC, programmed to collect data from simple terminals and providing prompts or edits as needed, will cost less than using the more intelligent and powerful terminals with local prompting and memory backup. Whatever data collection architecture you choose to follow, you can be sure that terminal devices are available from experienced bar code suppliers offering features to support any mainstream application reliably.

Chapter 8

Labels

Successful integration of bar code data collection systems requires thoughtful development of the various labels that carry the bar code messages. The labels are the data bearing medium particular to this technology; they must meet technical symbology standards and follow strict presentation guidelines. The label material has to be suited to the environment and length of service expected for each application. Finally, the label is frequently the bridge between the automatic data collection process being introduced into an operation and the previous manual data collection system, which may continue to function as a back-up technique.

Chapter 8 begins with a discussion of the steps to take in creating labels, including the choice of in-house versus off-site label printing. A review of available label materials and software for printing labels will answer many questions about how to get started efficiently with these vital system components. The design of the bar code label is the single most important step to take in unlocking a design solution to most bar code applications.

BAR CODE LABEL CREATION ■

The following five steps in creating an effective bar code label are presented as a helpful guide. If you fail to go through these steps early in your bar code planning, you could run into costly corrective changes in your program later on. Worse, you may find that your system design objective is out of reach, due to label limitations that could have been anticipated and avoided. Neglecting label design can lead to costly consequences.

1. Choose your bar code symbology (or symbologies).
2. Decide on your label content, including the following:
    - number of data characters
    - content of the human readable label information
    - graphic label enhancements
    - the exact layout of all label elements
3. Choose the print method (or methods) and printer locations.
4. Decide the label printing frequency. Will you print labels once a day, once a week, once a month, or on demand?
5. Choose your "label team" — that is, the individuals responsible for producing labels when needed and controlling all label changes.

While these steps should all be carried out for effective label creation, they need not always be followed in exactly this order. Since several of these steps are interdependent, it may well happen that taking one step will lead to several related decisions.

Choosing a Bar Code Symbology

Chapter 2 described the five most popular bar code symbologies. The historical significance, data encoding capabilities, and relative message density of each code were discussed in some detail. All of these factors should be considered before changing an existing bar code symbology or choosing a symbology for a new application. For example, if your message includes alphabetic characters, you cannot consider Code I 2of5, Codabar, or UPC. If the label area available for the bar code is limited, or if ASCII symbols are necessary in your bar code, Code 128 would be a sensible choice. Stacked bar codes like Code 16K or Code 49 should be considered for applications that have severe space constraints but require many data characters. Tracking the use of medication in hospitals and recording data from printed circuit boards in electronics assembly are applications that are likely candidates for using stacked bar codes.

> **NOTE:**
> Try to choose a symbology that offers flexibility, while using the least amount of label space, or "real-estate." If your bar code data content should increase in the future, then your label will not require a costly redesign.

In some situations, there may be no choice regarding the symbology or label design. Interindustry groups such as the Uniform Code Council (UCC) and the Automotive Industry Action Group (AIAG) have chosen their members' symbology and published standards for label design. If you must adhere to certain label standards in final product packaging, you may still have a symbology choice to make for internal data collection. Chapter 13 contains more information about bar code standards organizations and their role in defining labels.

With the development of scanners that can autodistinguish several symbologies, many companies are using two or more symbologies on the same label. You may also choose to phase out an early symbology to take advantage of more dense codes. This may mean scanning early labels of the old symbology, intermixed with new labels employing a more modern symbology, for a short time. Exhibit 8.1 is an example of a label containing bar code data in both Code 128 and UPC. Code 128 carries serial number information, while UPC fulfills the point-of-sale data requirement.

The Code 128 bar code is read within the manufacturing plant, and the UPC bar code is read at the retail point of sale. Substantial cost savings can be realized when two requirements are satisfied with one label.

Exhibit 8.1

Multisymbology Label

(Courtesy of Lotus Development Corporation)

Deciding on Label Content

Based on the results of your bar code system design analysis, you will make a decision on the data message that must appear in bar code on the label or tag. The size of the label will depend on the data message, the symbology chosen, the "X" dimension, and the bar code height. Human readable information and graphic enhancements must be added. The available surface of the item on which the label will be attached is the final label size determinant. The worksheet in Exhibit 8.2 can be helpful when designing a label.

Retail applications frequently require that only a small amount of information be in bar code. Exhibit 8.3 gives several examples of retail labels. Note that the labels and tags contain only one bar code. Price, SKU, and size information are in human readable OCR font.

Industrial bar code applications identifying case or pallet information often require large labels that might contain a product identity code, a serial number, product quantity, shipping information, and date or weight information. Tracking labels used for file control, video-tape circulation management, and fixed asset tracking usually contain a single bar code data message with human readable interpretation below the bar code.

NOTE:

Unless there are security issues related to a bar code label, the bar code message should also be interpreted in human readable form below the bar code.

After you have decided on the data message, you must carefully position the bar code within the label to be sure it can be easily scanned. If several bar codes are placed close together, an operator may accidentally scan the wrong bar code, especially when using a laser gun. Alternating horizontal and vertical bar codes within your label may minimize label scanning errors. Application Identifiers (AIs) used at the beginning of a message can also permit bar code message editing at the data terminal level or at the host processor. (Refer to Chapter 14 for more information on Application Identifiers.) Some sophisticated users have incorporated creative graphics to aid operators in identifying a particular bar code related to a certain operation.

Exhibit 8.2

Label Design Worksheet

LABEL DESIGN WORKSHEET

Considerations:

Maximum size of label: _____ x _____
Dimensions of item surface where label is applied: _____ x _____
Expected life: _____
Environment: _____
Quantity required: _____

To be scanned at:
location 1 _____ location 2 _____ location 3 _____
scanner type _____ scanner type _____ scanner type _____

Conveyor scanning: yes __ no __   Distance between labels: _____
Conveyor speed at read point: _____ Distance between boxes: _____

Required data:

Bar coded				Human Readable	
Alpha/numeric	Length	Variable	Data	Variable Data	Fixed Data

Solution: Label layout

Size of label: _____ x _____
On/off-site printing: _____
_____

Printer type: _____
_____

(adjust to scale or actual size)

Exhibit 8.3

Bar Code Retail Labels and Tags

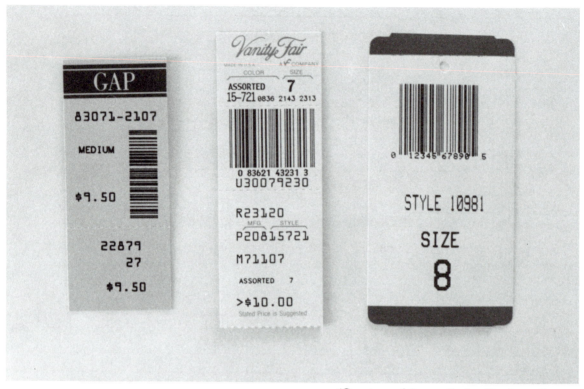

(Courtesy of Avery, Soabar Products Group)

Color coding labels can further enhance your bar code system if more than one label is utilized. When using label stock other than white, keep away from colors with blue content. Pink or yellow background colors are the safest choices. Recent developments in thermal transfer printing permit the use of color enhancements for bar code labels. Colors can be used to box in bar code label zones or for other graphic enhancement; however, each bar code should be printed in carbon black against white stock. This will assure the highest scanner "first-read rate."

Consider the following guidelines when creating the bar code field:

- The aspect ratio (height vs. length) of the bar code should be as close to 1:1, or square, as possible. If the bar code is long and the height is very short, the label will be difficult to scan with wands or laser guns. When scanning with a wand, the natural tendency is to scan across the bar code with an arc pattern as your hand rotates around your elbow. If the bar code is long and narrow, the wand will run off the label before the stop character has been reached, causing a "no read."

- The "X" dimension, or narrowest bar element, controls the bar code length and the distance from which it can be read. For sound label design, choose a large "X," preferably 20 mils or greater.

- Labels should not permit the quiet zone to be encroached upon with printed information. If the bar code is placed too close to the edge of the label, a minor misalignment in the paper travel path through the printer could eliminate a vital portion of the quiet zone.

- Labels with multiple bar codes should be laid out so that only one bar code can be read at a time. This means that bar codes should not be placed side by side if hand laser guns are used.

NOTE:

The best test of a label's design is to review it with the data collection scanner operators in the actual bar code application environment. Let your users comment on the label's clarity and friendliness. Also, you can borrow vendor demonstration scanners to simulate readability.

Choosing a Print Method

Considerations that influence the choice of a print method include the symbology's "X" dimension, desired label life, cost per label, quantity of labels required, and the environment in which the label will be used. Chapter 4 describes mainstream bar code printing methods, including technical strengths and limitations of print technology. Reviewing that chapter at the beginning of your label design should help narrow the printing choices.

Deciding how to source your label is another consideration. If labels are to be generated in-house, the purchase of printers, supplies, and bar code software requires a capital budget, personnel, and training. The advantage of printing in-house labels is to bring this important assignment under direct project control.

Labels may also be purchased from an off-site bar code label printing vendor. Companies expert in this field can supply labels from an extensive product catalogue, or they can design and supply a unique label tailored exactly to your application. The better suppliers of bar code labels can provide messages in any symbology, created through a choice of several print engines, and any label medium, with adhesive and durability characteristics matched to the project's requirements. The better bar code label vendors will maintain the serial number database for their customers and fill routine label requirements in 24 hours from purchase orders transmitted electronically using electronic data interchange.

> **NOTE:**
>
> Sometimes companies choose to have labels printed off site during the start-up phase of an extensive bar code application. Later, after the "kinks" are worked out of the data collection portion of the system, they then examine the option of producing labels in-house with similar printing standards.

In-House versus Off-Site Printing

Several factors should be weighed before a final decision is made concerning the printing method and source. Applications involving fixed asset tracking and personnel security badges are enhanced by label technology developed by vendors with proprietary material. Applications that can benefit from copyproof bar code labels, or labels that self-destruct when tampered with, may depend on outside vendor printing. However, some off-site printers will license or sell complete bar code print shops to their larger customers, training personnel and transferring all relevant knowledge for a reasonable "know-how" fee.

The following list of factors will influence your choice of in-house or off-site printing:

1. *The content of the label.* If information that is to appear in bar code on the label is derived from last-minute events, such as item weight, date and time of production, production line conditions, or unique customer order details, you will have to print labels in-house.

2. *The "X" dimension.* The smallest "X" dimension reproducible by on-site printers is approximately 6 mils. If you have an application

Exhibit 8.4

Board Label
Printed Circuit

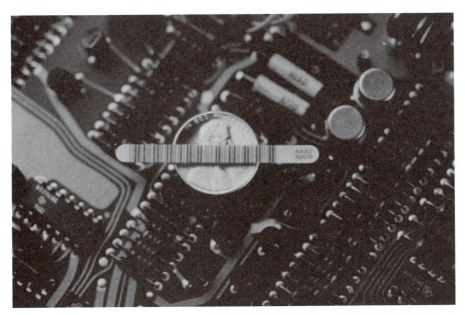

(Courtesy of Watson Label Products)

dependent on smaller bars, photocomposed labels should be created off site. Exhibit 8.4 illustrates a small label developed especially for use on printed circuit boards.

3.   *The label substrate*. Off-site printing processes usually have few limitations on the type of substrate or adhesive employed.

4.   *Continuous form printing*. Most low- to mid-range laser printers do not support continuous form label stock. Some bar code label requirements, such as those on automated production lines, require labels supplied on roll stock. In this situation, the purchase of a dedicated thermal-transfer printer is recommended. Another alternative would be off-site printing of laser-generated labels.

5.   *Printing speed*. Applications that require large numbers of labels may not be efficiently serviced with an on-site printing capability. For example, the total daily consumption of overnight shipment tracing labels and the number of locations where they are used combine to require that this label printing task be assigned to one or more high-capacity, off-site label printing vendors.

Even if the factors listed above are not present in your bar code environment, consider these additional issues before making a final print site determination:

1. *Total cost.* If you require large quantities of special labels, off-site printing may be less expensive than the combined cost of the printer, software, supplies, and trained personnel. The worksheet shown in Exhibit 8.5 is useful when trying to compare the cost of labels produced in-house with the cost of label printing off site.

2. *Personnel expertise.* The operator responsible for producing bar code labels must become familiar with the bar code printing device and also take responsibility for maintaining serial number integrity, replenishing label stock, generating labels as needed, and maintaining the printers. This comprehensive job description may extend beyond the capabilities of available personnel.

3. *Implementation time.* If labels are required quickly, there may not be sufficient time to research and purchase printer hardware, adapt or create label-generating software, order label stock, and organize a project team for label printing on site.

> **NOTE:**
>
> The "implementation time factor" is less important if labels are simple in design, of average size, and will not be subjected to a harsh environment. A printer salesperson may be able to adapt label software for you and supply label stock and print ribbons quickly.

4. *Quality control.* Off-site printing vendors that offer offset, ion deposition, high-speed laser, and photocomposition printing can provide very high quality labels consistently. When alternate off-site printing techniques are used, procedures such as ribbon changing or print head cleaning must be strictly followed. You should require your off-site label vendor to sample-verify bar code labels continually for message composition and symbology tolerances.

> **NOTE:**
>
> Most companies that have bar code labels printed off site maintain a limited capability to print labels in-house. This is important if your off-site printer is temporarily unable to fill an order, or if special conditions require labels sooner than the normal order-filling cycle.

Exhibit 8.5
Label Production Cost Worksheet

LABEL PRODUCTION COST COMPARISON WORKSHEET

	ON SITE	OFF SITE
Cost/label	* _____	_____
Inventory cost	_____	_____
Plates and film master	_____	_____
Production/management labor	_____	_____
Q. C. labor	_____	
Q. A. labor	_____	N/A
Software cost	_____	N/A
Printer cost	_____	N/A
Equipment maintenance cost	_____	N/A
Ink/ribbon	_____	N/A
TOTAL	_____	_____

* Add 10% for scrap.

Note: Many companies make a decision to purchase a back-up system
to the offsite printing.

If you decide to print labels in-house, be sure you understand and
anticipate the normal time between printer failures, and make provi-
sion for some back-up labels. Having a demand print requirement will
normally require the purchase of a spare printer. If your vendor is close
by and stocked with rental or back-up units to loan, you may be able
to avoid the expense of a second printer.

Choosing the Printer Locations

After you have chosen your printing technology and have decided to print the labels in-house, you must decide how many printers will be needed and where they should be located. The following factors will influence printer location:

- *Quantity.* If many labels are required, you may need several printers working in parallel to keep up with the demand.

- *Label type.* If more than one label format is needed, and at several locations, you may decide to equip each labeling site with a print station for local control and to produce demand information such as time, date, and product weight. On the other hand, this distribution of print locations may create a weakness in maintaining strict serialization control, since two different printer databases could generate the same serial number twice.

- *The environment.* Some locations that would otherwise be suitable for a printer station may experience extreme heat, cold, or dust, which could cause exceptional printer maintenance problems.

- *Demand vs. batch.* A bar code application where batch labels are required gives users more flexibility when selecting printer sites. Even if labels need to be produced each day, an overnight print routine performed centrally for many different bar code applications may provide tight label control inexpensively. Maintaining control over many demand printers in different sites can require elaborate database coordination.

- *Noise.* Some print methods may produce more noise or require more space than the application can adapt to. Matrix impact printers may not be suitable for certain office or hospital sites, for example, unless allowances are made for special enclosures.

Many company policies require centralized control of all label printing. If security would be compromised by local printing, or if product serialization control would be weakened with department print stations, then perhaps the bar code label printing function should be developed into an autonomous department serving a broad corporate user base.

Determining Label Printing Frequency

A label production schedule must be developed regardless of whether you chose in-house or off-site printing. With internally created labels, intervals between printing can be hourly, daily, weekly, or monthly for batch printing. Labels created on demand are event dependent, and once a system is set up, labels are created automatically. Off-site label vendors usually establish a schedule with you for weekly or monthly resupply. Daily label printing would not be the norm, although some print houses will support special overnight requests.

Printing frequency in production applications is typically derived from the production schedule cycle. In some companies, schedules are planned for an entire month, while different demand forecasting requires other companies to plan weekly. The grocery industry established vendor source marking of bar code data at the inception of retail scanning. General merchandise applications are currently divided on this matter, with some source marking by vendors, some retailer marking at the distribution center (DC), and some bar code labeling in the store.

Your data system architecture may also play a role in print scheduling if you print bar code labels in-house. Some company information systems relegate printing to several off-peak hours each day to permit high mainframe availability for on-line activities during normal work hours. However, a dedicated printing host would not subject your bar code projects to this artificial constraint. From the beginning of the bar code system planning phase, you should be prepared to modify any constraining company regulations to assure that exacting labels are available when and where they are to be applied, from the most reliable source.

Creating a Label Team

People are key to the success of a bar code project, and instituting broad personnel involvement in bar code label design and production decisions will avoid costly mistakes. Although choosing a label team is listed earlier in this chapter as the fifth step in label development, you should organize a label team early in the bar code project. The scope of label design decisions is very broad and touches many departments in a company. The label team should work throughout the company and with outsiders, such as trading partners, who will eventually be scanning labels for their data collection needs. Some companies choose to volunteer a bar code label team member to an industry standards committee to help coordinate interindustry label uses.

If labels are to be generated in-house, you must perform the following tasks under your label team's direction before the bar code project can go on-line:

- Purchase printer hardware, label stock and other related supplies, and set up a supplies agreement with a reliable provider.
- Purchase, write, or customize label printing software.
- Establish a documentation library for bar code printers and print software. Also, develop a back-up plan to cover printer failure episodes. This usually requires an on-site spare printer and a return-to-distributor or -manufacturer service agreement.
- Run periodic quality control inspections on selected production labels.
- Take any organizational steps necessary to assure consistent, on-time production and distribution of labels. Your bar code label will be carrying vital operating control data and cannot take a back seat to any administrative barrier.

The entire bar code label team should be committed to the success of the bar code project and have a clear understanding of its goals. They should have the collective skills to plan carefully and execute details accurately. Diplomacy is useful, too, since a complete bar code data collection program will usually encroach on intradepartmental traditions. This includes new requirements for label space to print bar code messages and procedures to assure accuracy in data input to the print software.

■ LABEL STOCK CHOICES

The options to choose from in bar code label stock are too numerous to cover here in detail. As the label designer, you may select one option within each of the following categories:

- *Putup*: roll form, fan-fold, sheets, single labels, or continuous pin feed.
- *Face stock*: paper or tag, vinyl, polyester, cloth, or metal.
- *Adhesive*: permanent, pressure-sensitive, high- and low-temperature resistant.
- *Topcoat*: laminating, varnish.
- *Special features*: tinted labels, jointed pairs, double adhesive, or multipart.

Label stock should be chosen after considering environmental conditions such as temperature and humidity before and after application, and toxins, grease, and dirt. Additional factors to consider in label stock are shelf life and resistance to abrasion. Double adhesive labels are useful if a bar code is used in two distinct applications, such as warranty registration after earlier serving in production control. Exhibit 8.1 on page 163 illustrates a double adhesive label. The right-hand portion of the label is removed by the owner and applied to a return warranty registration card. Through this bar code label, manufacturers can track an item from production assembly through to the final product purchaser, producing useful future marketing information.

Capital asset tracking and other security-related bar code applications often require tamper-proof labels that self-destruct when tampered with or removed. Surface laminates are recommended for bar code labels that may be subjected to chemicals or repeated scanning by contact wands or slot scanners. The choice of a suitable label adhesive is important for labels that are permanently affixed to items that are expected to have a long shelf or service life.

Exhibits 8.6 through 8.8 illustrate several label stock options. Virtually any label design can be created by quality label media vendors. Your label design team should enlist the support of vendor experts and seek examples of designs used by other progressive bar code users. While there seems to be no limit to combinations of label stock, adhesives, and laminates, cost is always a design influence and must be closely matched to the useful life and multiple roles of labels.

We urge readers with unusual label requirements to gain support of technical specialists from label media and forms supply vendors if the labels are to be produced in-house. If you obtain finished bar code labels from print houses, their technical staff should take the lead in educating you regarding special label considerations and illustrating examples of other bar code users they supply with similar products.

Exhibit 8.6

Capital Asset Label

Exhibit 8.7

Label with Graphic
Enhancement

(Exhibit 8.6 and 8.7 Courtesy of Screenprint/Dow)

Exhibit 8.8

Multi-part Label
for Lab Specimens

(Courtesy of Computype, Inc.)

BAR CODE PRINTING SOFTWARE ■

Label printing software is a subject that should be addressed in the early planning stages of a bar code data collection program. Two questions need to be examined at the beginning. First, is additional bar code generating software required for your printer to print bar codes easily and accurately, or is that ability provided with the printer? Second, how will the printer interface with its host computer?

If bar code generating software is required to give your printer this functionality, it is available in three categories. You can select a totally prewritten package for average or standard bar code labels, you can customize a label design using templates and tools, or you can write a unique bar code label program entirely from new code. The remainder of this chapter will describe and discuss these choices.

Prewritten or "Canned" Bar Code Label Software

There are two methods of providing "canned" bar code label printing capability: it can be software supplied to run on a generic PC host, or a vendor can provide a proprietary hardware package with this functionality. At this time more choices of the former kind are available in the marketplace than the special hardware packages.

Prewritten packages should support all the bar code symbologies described in Chapter 2, although you should be sure that Code 128 is optimized for density before you purchase any package. All software packages do not print every symbology with equal accuracy and efficiency. You should insist on a sample label printout from the printer you intend to use as a proof of symbology exactness. The most common host for printer software is the PC, but popular packages are also available to run on Macintosh, DEC minicomputers, and IBM mainframes. Exhibits 8.9 through 8.11 illustrate examples of bar code label printing packages. Exhibit 8.11 is a hardware-based label generating system, although label formats can also be downloaded from a PC or created at the terminal.

Some options available with prewritten or canned packages include the following:

- *Industry standard labels.* A user library contains AIAG, UCC/ EAN-128, UPC, LOGMARS labels, and others.

Exhibit 8.9

PC-Based Bar Code Label Printing Software

(Courtesy of The Peak Technologies Group, Inc.)

- *Bar code document production.* Create forms, such as shipping documents with multiple fields and multiple bar codes inserted.

- *Interface.* Many drivers should be offered for popular printers, with revisions available when new printers appear on the market.

- *Automatic serialization.* Selected label data fields can be driven by a controlled, serialized database.

Exhibit 8.10

Total System — Scans and Records Data, Prints Label

(Courtesy of Integrated Software Design, Inc.)

- *Graphic enhancement.* Graphic enhancement can be provided through graphic tools under software control, or with imported graphics such as corporate logos.
- *Import data.* Through ASCII files, data can be imported to, and inserted in, selected label fields.
- *Network communication.* Mainframe or PC communication protocols are often provided for uploading or downloading of files.

Exhibit 8.11

Hardware-Based Label Printing System

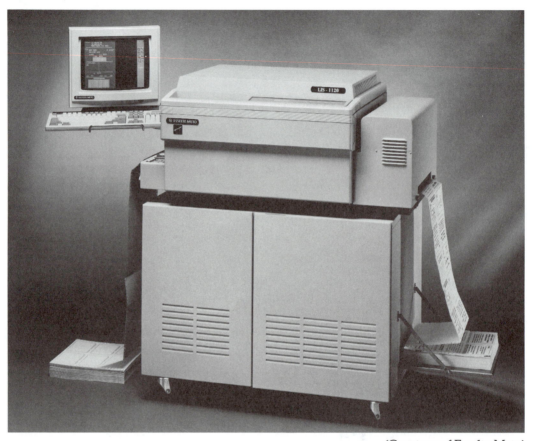

(Courtesy of Esselte Meto)

Most of the canned packages are reasonably friendly and can be mastered by personnel without a software background. Exhibits 8.12 and 8.13 illustrate an Apple Macintosh® based software package. Using user friendly icons and WYSIWYG (what you see is what you get) screens, these programs require only a brief learning process. Canned packages can reduce the time and cost of getting a bar code system up and running, compared with using customized or user-originated bar code printing software. However, you may need to compromise the design of your labels in order to adapt to a prewritten format.

Exhibit 8.12

Macintosh Bar Code Label Software

 File **Edit** Bar Codes Fonts Style Labels Grid Viewing

	AI	Data Field	Variable?
Serial Shipping Container			
Shipping Container Code	00	123456789123456	☐
Batch or Lot Number			
Production Date	234	2398	☒
Packaging Date			
Sell By Date	30	144	☒
Safety Expiration Date			☐
Product Varient			
Serial Number			☐
HIBCC			
Lot Number			☐
Quantity			
Net Weight (Kilograms)			

[**Continue**]   [Cancel]

Bar Code Data

(Courtesy of The Mac-Barcode Company)

Exhibit 8.13

Barcode Label Printing
Software for the
Macintosh Computer

(Courtesy of The Mac-Barcode Company)

Customized Bar Code Label Printing Software

If you are unable to find a canned software package to suit your label or computer environment needs, the next option is to create a customized label using tools that have been popular for ten years. These are printer resident graphic image controllers that employ a resident bar code and graphics-generating programming language. This powerful label design and production package can make the task of printing your bar code quite straightforward.

Graphic controllers are usually packaged as a printed circuit board installed within the printer, though they may also be provided as an external box. With their own microprocessors, they perform the following three functions:

1. Accept and control the flow of label data from the host computer.
2. Process the label data and equivalent graphic elements (including symbologies) into printable "dots."
3. Control the mechanical operation of the printer.

The user communicates to the graphic controller in two stages: first, to set the printer's functional parameters and operating conditions; second, to direct the bar code or other graphic image printing. Several popular graphic controller programming languages have been developed by QMS, Inc., and Printronix, Inc. These languages may be used alone in small macro-type programs, or they may be embedded in a larger document printing program, written in C, Pascal, or other high-level languages. You may need professional programming talent to generate labels and forms if they are very complex. The commands of these languages allow you to specify the symbology, orientation, size (ratio and density), content, and location of the bar code. They also provide the ability to auto-increment certain fields, draw lines, incorporate custom graphics, and control page feed.

This method of printing bar code labels and forms has been popular for many years. Not only can graphic controllers convert many traditional mainframe-driven printers to bar code form and label printers, but host level programming to accomplish this is very modest, and host processing time should not increase noticeably. Since graphic controllers have been developed for many different printers, the languages to instruct them, once learned, will allow you to drive different printers from your host with a common command set.

Writing Your Own Bar Code Printing Software

This third approach to bar code label generation is the most costly and complex to implement. For these reasons it is not normal for a user to take this path. The programmer responsible for developing a label printing system must have in-depth knowledge of the printer, printer interfaces, bit mapping, and the published standards for the chosen symbology. Acquiring this knowledge, writing the software, putting together the components, and testing the labels is a substantial undertaking.

This solution to your bar code label printing is not recommended unless there are strong influences that justify this complexity. Developing a proprietary label printing package to be used in hundreds of company or customer locations where processor and memory efficiency are paramount might be an example. Otherwise, select the bar code printing tools most easily learned and adapted to the host or printer you prefer from the assortment of commercial products on the market. The complex graphic generation of bar code has been mastered by many vendors and is available for data expression easily, in quality label format.

SUMMARY ■

Expressing a bar code message in label form is the beginning of an effective data collection program. Surprisingly, the detailed analysis of your program labels and the development of printing administration often take more time and resources than the development of the label printing software. This reflects the highly developed state of bar code printing tools available. A comprehensive label design cannot be rushed, even in the simplest applications. However, using an off-site printing vendor or choosing modern tools for in-house printing can convert your label design into reality very quickly. Following the label design steps covered in this chapter, and selecting qualified vendors of media, label development tools, or outside label production capability can simplify the creation and quality reproduction of bar code labels throughout all your different bar code applications.

Part Three

SOLUTIONS

Part Three contains design suggestions for three bar code systems: inventory control, retail management, and physical tracking. Our purpose is to present illustrative solutions to problems that are frequently and successfully solved through bar code technology.

The general systems approach presented in these chapters can frequently be adapted to other somewhat related applications. Each of these chapters discusses issues such as design considerations, bar code scanner choices, bar code label and printer choices, and software requirements.

Chapter 9

Inventory Control Systems

Bar code control systems have been successfully applied to the improvement of warehouse operations for a long time. The earliest fixed-position laser scanners were developed for routing cases of finished products more rapidly and accurately through warehouses and distribution centers.

Viewed in the simplest manner, a warehouse is a temporary location for products or material between one stage in manufacturing and the next. Knowing what is contained in a warehouse may be viewed as remembering what was taken in and subtracting what was taken out. In the real world, warehouse management is a complex and challenging task due to the volume and mix of different items to record and track. Item status such as age, cost, lot number, and originating source are required for operating and accounting reasons. Tying all the relevant data together for warehouse management planning may require the capabilities of large mainframe processors.

When data collection mistakes are made at any stage of warehouse transaction reporting, the problem is often multiplied before it is corrected. For any item incorrectly recorded as appearing to be in a certain location, another item is really at that location, unreported.

Not surprisingly, many bar code suppliers currently offer a broad selection of devices and systems designed to maintain accurate inventory control on a perpetual basis. These range in complexity from simple location and count programs to warehouse management systems that are totally integrated with plant operations.

To discuss the details of a complete warehouse bar code control system is beyond the scope of this book. Instead, we offer an insight into effective inventory control using bar code, which is usually an early and rewarding warehouse control application.

■ DESIGN CONSIDERATIONS

Chapter 9 contains two different design approaches to an inventory application. The first approach is an economical solution that can be implemented quickly. The second approach is an integrated solution, which includes many advanced features you may wish to consider.

In considering a system design that will fit your needs, you should seek the answers to several questions before choosing your solution path. The answers to these questions will help determine which solution to pursue and lead you toward software, as well as scanner and printer decisions. How, for example, would you answer the following questions:

- Is continuous communication from each scanner to the host required? Would periodic batch data collection be sufficient?

- Must scanning be performed continuously, or only at certain times during the day? What is the total amount of data per day to be collected?

- How many users will want access to the system at one time to enter data? How many users will want to access the database for inquiries or reports, and how frequently?

- How will physical locations in the warehouse be labeled? (See Exhibit 9.1 for an example of a location label reduced 75 percent.)

- Where, when, and by whom are the bar code labels on items to be applied? (Exhibit 9.2 illustrates a case label, and Exhibit 9.3 illustrates a pallet label created and applied by the manufacturer before transfer to the warehouse.)

- Will the labels be scanned by another user after leaving the warehouse?

Exhibit 9.1

Warehouse
Location Label

LOCATION
1A0157

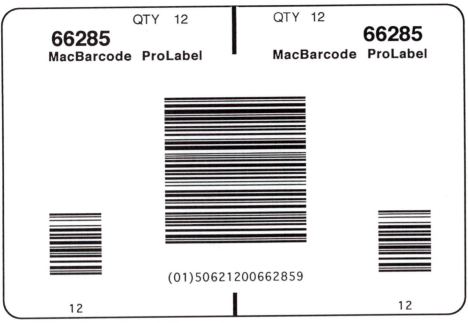

(Courtesy of The Mac-Barcode Company)

Exhibit 9.2
Carton Label

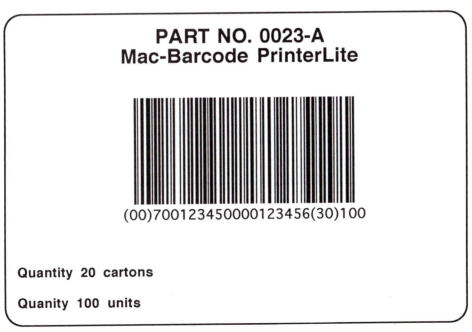

(Courtesy of The Mac-Barcode Company)

Exhibit 9.3
Pallet Label

> **NOTE:**
> Here are some additional issues to consider:
> - What are the ability and motivation of your bar code entry clerks? The answer to this question will influence your selection of the scanner design, as well as any requirement for data validation that may be necessary. Data terminals may be used simply for data entry or with prompted message reply from the host computer.
> - Does your warehouse have suitable lighting, and do you have any extreme noise or temperature considerations?
> - Will your bar code entry clerks be carrying a hand scanner for a long duration? If so, weight and battery power may limit your choice of equipment.

The following discussion outlines two approaches to developing a bar code driven inventory control system. We will cover a functional description of the problem to be solved and then suggest software, hardware, and printer and label elements for each design path.

■ THE ECONOMICAL SOLUTION

Functional Description

The ability to verify inventory quantities and locations in the warehouse is crucial to accurate inventory control. If all item placements and withdrawals in the warehouse were done according to a plan, the role for bar code control would be limited. Unfortunately, in the real world of warehouse operations, not every transaction is performed according to plan.

The economical bar code control system allows for daily item and bin location reporting. In addition, the system will support periodic inventory cycle counts of specified sections of the warehouse.

Although the architecture described next was developed for inventory control, it can prove useful in application requirements for stock checking in retail operations and for open stock supplies replenishment on hospital floors. Exhibit 9.4 shows the system architecture of the economical solution.

Exhibit 9.4

Inventory Control Architecture

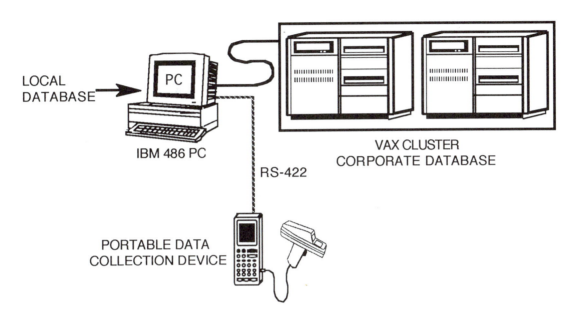

As often as data replenishment needs dictate, a bar code data collection clerk, using a hand-held bar code scanner, sequentially scans a bin or storage location in the warehouse and the part number located at that specific location. After that, a physical item count is taken and key-entered into the keyboard of the hand-held scanner. Clerks repeat this procedure throughout the warehouse. Then they bring the hand-held scanners to the PC host computer and upload their data to a PC file. This current inventory record is compared with the existing stock location records. Inventory discrepancies are reported via a program in the PC. If significant discrepancies are reported from the recent scan cycle, the records will be updated to reflect the current facts.

Software

The advantages of this system design are its simplicity and low implementation cost. Software to control inventory resides partly on the hand-held terminal, partly on the PC host computer, and partly on the corporate mainframe. The software that resides on the hand-held terminal prompts the user through local data collection routines. Prompt software for portable data collection terminals is often created in BASIC, or in a BASIC-like language, and requires very little programming experience.

The prompt program in Exhibit 9.5 guides the inventory clerk in the operations to be performed. Key-entering the letter "C "starts the data input program. All data is verified through the use of match strings and format requirements. Later, when data collection is complete, key-

Exhibit 9.5

"BASIC-like" Program for a Hand-Held Terminal

```
!CYCLE COUNT
10 PROMPT "\024(C)YCLE OR (D)MP"        34 STORE
INPUT USER
GOTO 30, IFMATCH, "C"'YCLE'              35 PROMPT "024\QUANTITY:\013\010"
GOTO 51, IFMATCH, "D"'MP'                INPUT USER
GOTO 511, IFMATCH, "QUIT"               GOTO 36, IFMATCH, Nnnnnn
PROMPT "\024INVALID OPTION\022", DISPLAY, 3   PROMPT "\024DATA ERROR\022",
GOTO 10                                 DISPLAY, 3
                                         GOTO 35
20 STORE                                36 STORE
TRANSMIT BUFFERED %\013\010
UNSTORE                                 37 TRANSMIT BUFFERED
GOTO 10                                 %\013\010%\013\010%\013\010

!CYCLE COUNT SELECTED                   39 UNSTORE
                                        GOTO 30
30 PROMPT "\024LOCATION:\013\010"
INPUT USER                              51 DEFINE 1PORT,Y, "2120100"
GOTO 20, IFMATCH, "STOP"                PROMPT "\024XMIT STARTING\013\010" ,
GOTO32,IFMATCH, DDDDDDD                 DISPLAY
PROMPT "\024DATA ERROR\022", DISPLAY, 3  PROMPT "DATA TRANSMISSION START
GOTO 30                                 NOW\013\010",1PORT, 1

32 STORE                                PROMPT "\024XMIT DONE", DISPLAY, 3
                                        DEFINE 1PORT N
33 PROMPT "\024PART NUMBER:\013\010"    GOTO 10
INPUT USER
GOTO 34, IFMATCH, DDDDDDDDDddddd        511 PROMPT "\024LEAVING CYCLE",
PROMPT "\024DATA ERROR\022", DISPLAY,3      DISPLAY, 3
GOTO 33
```

entering the letter "D" initiates data transmission to the PC host. This data is then displayed on the PC screen during upload. If an error is seen on the screen during upload, the transmission can be reinitiated.

The system software on the PC host computer has a "popular," non-bar code specific database. This particular application was developed to report through *Symphony*, an integrated software package, including an embedded database, spreadsheet, and communications module. A three-field database was created to accept data records from the terminal. To simplify the system, these fields have been given the same names as those used in the portable terminal.

Input synchronization of data records is assured through the execution of a macro within *Symphony*, which continuously searches for the start data marker and terminates when "STOP" is encountered. The inventory clerk or supervisor then follows macro-generated menu commands and screen instructions to sort and examine the data and to print reports. Exhibit 9.6 is a partial sample of the *Symphony* macros created to accept inventory data from a hand-held bar code terminal.

Once data is in the *Symphony* database, the macro can be expanded to initiate a file transfer to the corporate mainframe. One of the macros in Exhibit 9.6 indicates a PC-to-mainframe connection through the KERMIT protocol. However, many different communications protocols could also perform these file transfers.

The software residing on the mainframe includes the corporate database. Costly software modifications are not required to blend this inventory control application with existing programs and files. Inventory variations can be explored by comparing the data collected through bar code terminals with item locations and counts stored on the mainframe.

A valuable feature of this software architecture is the easy expandability of its functions. For instance, the program on the portable terminal can be modified to prompt the clerk to enter additional data fields. Clerk identity and inventory tag-number fields can be appended to the original prompt program to automate collection of the annual physical inventory. Date and time can be added to collected records, either from the portable terminal or the PC host system software.

None of these expanded functions requires changes to mainframe software. Relatively small changes would be made to the hand-held terminal prompt software and to the *Symphony* macro. Mainframe software independence permits a continuing refinement of collected data without a major impact on headquarters' resources.

Exhibit 9.6

Symphony Macro for Inventory Data Collection

```
THIS IS THE MACRO TO UPLOAD DATA FROM THE PORTABLE TERMINAL TO THE PC
COMM_CAP:{WIND MESSAGE}{s}wi{WIND CAPTURE}{WOFF}{POFF}{TYPE}S~E$A
            $1..I..$8192~{GOTO}$A$1~{TYOE}C{m}snr{esc}{esc}c:\SERIAL\INPUT.CCF~q
            {WON}{WIND MESSAGE}
        {blank MESSAGES}{let MSG1,"Connect a reader to COM1 and press RETURN. "}~{?}
        {let MSG2, "Press the 'D' function key  on the reader."}{let MSG3,"Wait for transfer
                to finish and menu to appear. "}{WOFF}{POFF}{WIND CAPTURE}{TYPE}C~
        {M}SCR$A$1..%I$8192~Q{capture}ry{WON}{handshake "","\003",600}{ERROR
                4}{restart}{branch START}
        {capture}{rn{blank MESSAGES}{WIND MESSAGE}{let MSG1, "To transfer again,
                press 'Y', otherwise 'N'"}~{PON}{get CAP_AGAIN}{if CAP_AGAIN="y"#or
                #CAP_AGAIN="Y"}{blank CAP_AGAIN}{branch COMM_CAP}
        {blank CAP_AGAIN}
        {blank MESSAGES}{let MSG1,"Transfer of data complete."}{PRN_FILE}
        {blank MESSAGES}
        {WIND MESSAGE}{s}wi{blank MESSAGES}{down}{up}{let MSG1,"You May Now Choose
                Another Option"}~{WON}{PON}
        {return}


THIS IS THE MACRO USED TO LOG ON TO THE VAX
LOGIN: {TYPE}C{M} SNRVAX~A{m}ph{handshake "\030\030\013","BRIDGE >",3}{ERROR 7}
        {handshake "C VAX!\013","VAX1",20}
        (WAIT @NOW+@TIME(0,0,5)}
        {handshake "\013\013\013\013",{Username:",15}{ERROR 7}
        {handshake "INV\013","Password:",20}{ERROR 7}
        {handshake "PASSWORD\013","$",30}{ERROR 7}
        {return}


THIS IS THE MACRO TO TRANSMIT DATA TO THE VAX-USING KERMIT
MAN_TRANS: {handshake "KERMIT SERVER\013","on your local machine.",6}{ERROR 1}
        {s}aidos~command/c kermit send C:\SERIAL\INVEN.DAT~ exit
        {s}aidos~command/c kermit finish~{handshake "\013","$",7}{ERROR 5}
        {S}aidos~command/c exit~
        {handshake "\013\013","$",5}
        MAIL/SUBJ="SUCCESSUL UPLOAD OF INVENTORY DATA" NL:J. DOE,M.SMITH~
        {WAIT @NOW+@TIME(0,0,10)}
        {handshake "\013\013","$",90}{ERROR 6}
        {handshake "LO\013","BRIDGE >",5}
        {handshake "\030\030\013","BRIDGE >", 10}{ERROR 6}
        {s}aidos~command/c copy c:\SERIAL\*.dat c:\SERIAL\ARCHIVE\*.DAT~
        {return}
```

Hardware

The hardware required to support this bar code data collection architecture is basic and can be simply configured. Portable bar code scanning terminals are employed here as batch data collection stations. Since inventory transactions and mainframe files are running under batch update software, RFDC terminals with realtime PC host connectivity would not increase the value of the information collected.

These portable terminals need only a minimum feature list and data storage capability. A 2-line-by-16-character display for bar code data presentation and program prompting is sufficient. A keypad is required for entering item quantity information, and 32K bytes of file memory are capable of storing batch data from the time of data collection until PC host data transfer.

The portable terminals may support a wand scanner or laser gun or both. In addition, an RS-232C asynchronous serial ASCII interface port for two-way communication to the PC host is required. Portable terminal prompt programs are downloaded from the PC, and collected data is uploaded through this connector.

The host for the collected data in this system is a 386 PC running 25MHz. A 40-megabyte hard disk, with a floppy diskette drive for file back-up and an available RS-232C serial port, is adequate. As warehouse operations expand, more hand-held terminals can be added. Collected data is uploaded periodically through the PC, but this procedure should only take several minutes. Attention to scheduling would assure that the PC would not need duplication or expansion, even if operations increase greatly.

Labels and Printers

Several label types are required in an economical bar code system. The location or bin label, along with the item or product label, is needed to provide "what and where" inventory information. You will have to decide how to apply the product label, however. It may be applied to the unit package, carton, pallet, or all of these.

If the additional bar code driven data collection features suggested for annual physical inventory are added to this application, employee bar code badges and inventory bar-coded tag numbers will also be scanned. Refer to the earlier chapters to review symbology choices, printer considerations, and label design.

You may wish to consider an off-site label source for your bin labels. The following are some typical features of bin labels:

- Large "X" dimension bar code to provide greater depth-of-field scanning if laser guns are employed. This label should use 40- or 50-mil bar widths.
- Aggressive adhesive label backing for nonpeel application to a wide variety of bin and shelf materials.
- Abrasion-resistant label overlay so scanning wands do not reduce label life.
- Graphic enhancements, such as large type faces for human readable information and arrows to designate bin positions.

Product labels are usually applied as a final step in the product assembly or packaging process. A decision must be made regarding what packaging level to bar code. You may bar code the unit package, carton, pallet, or even a universal shipping container. Since we have described an economical inventory solution here, begin by bar coding the product package level currently used for existing stock-picking purposes — usually a carton.

Your bar code should express the following information:

- Item identification by standard product number.
- Carton serial number keyed to date of production.
- Quantity of items per carton.

Be sure that the above information is also expressed in human readable form in a clear, easily understood format. The label may contain additional information on product detail or identification for manual warehouse handling. Exhibit 9.7 shows a portable RF data collection terminal being used in a warehouse setting.

NOTE:

Modern laser scanners can read bar code labels at distances of up to several feet. Some care must be taken in carton label design to simplify the warehouse clerk's task of identifying and isolating the correct bar code to scan for valid data collection.

Exhibit 9.7

Portable Data Collection in Warehouse

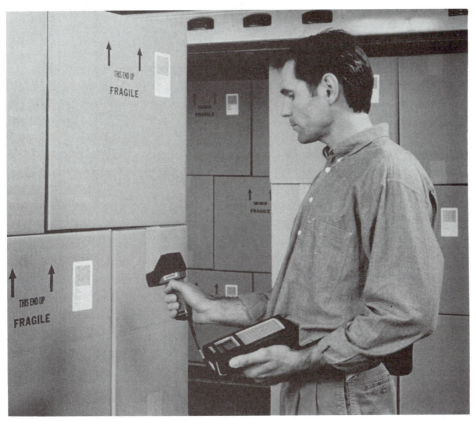

(Courtesy of Symbol Technologies, Inc.)

Summary of the Economical Solution

We have presented the advantages to using design simplicity in bar code data collection applications from the point of view of cost to implement and future system flexibility. Other advantages are often seen at the user level. Middle-management supervisors and warehouse personnel are more likely to embrace a new technology when they completely understand how it works and what their role is in keeping it effective. Exhibit 9.8 presents the cost schedule for our economical solution. Note that the cost can be significantly less if the PC and *Symphony* database have already been purchased for another application.

Exhibit 9.8

Cost Schedule for the Economical Warehouse Design

COMPONENT	PURPOSE	UNIT COST	QTY	OPERATING COSTS	TOTAL TO INSTALL
PC (or PC compatible) 80486 processor 4 MB RAM VGA monitor 1 Serial Port 120 MB Hard Disk 1.2 MB Diskette Windows,DOS or OS/2	Host computer receieves scanned data	$1,500.00 [a]	1	maintenance agreement diskettes	$1,500.00
Printers letter quality thermal transfer	generates reports finished goods labels	$400.00 $1,500.00	1 1	paper label stock	$400.00 $1,500.00
Hand-held terminals	collects on-floor data	$1,500.00	3	maintenance agreement	$4,500.00
Laser Scanners		$1,000.00	3		$3,000.00
Software *Symphony* Database hand-held units *Symphony* macro mainframe software interface (optional)	accepts scanned data prompts user for input data processes data integrates with corporate database	$400.00 [a] $00.00 [b]	1		$400.00
Labels shelf	printed offsite	$500.00/1000			$500.00
a Cost for these items can be shared with other applications using same hardware and software.					$11,800.00
b All software can be developed in-house.					

THE INTEGRATED SOLUTION ■

Suppliers providing integrated inventory control systems have taken three product design paths. Looking at the market today, you can find a number of "canned" inventory control software packages, with little or no customization available to the user. Or, you could contract with a systems integrator who will provide turnkey customized inventory control packages that will conform to your exact system description. Between these two extremes is a third choice to consider: Some vendors are offering a package of software with a common base program, along with a significant degree of customization to better fit each customer's unique business methods and procedures. This customization covers:

- application integration with existing system software
- communication with preexisting computer hardware
- customized data collection and reporting routines

Many successful bar code data collection systems have been developed and executed by a PC running under DOS. Other software developers have chosen OS/2 or Windows platforms. Increasingly, similar systems have employed the UNIX operating system on Digital, Hewlett-Packard, Data General, or IBM workstations, as well as 32-bit PCs. UNIX-based bar code systems offer an assortment of advanced features, including:

- Enhanced ability to follow bar-coded raw material from receiving, through inventory, and onto the production floor.
- Visibility of material, through RFDC bar code terminals throughout a warehouse. Items can be directed and monitored under fork-lift movement, recording location placement for real-time inventory updating under "random" placement philosophy.
- Supervisor report generation while data collection takes place.
- Continuous inventory monitoring and automatic stock replenishment report generation.
- Automatic generation of detailed activity and exception reports tailored to the user's requirements.

- Ability to customize data collection routines and reports through menus or WYSIWYG screens.

When considering a bar code system, a group representing all departments affected by that system should be formed to assure completeness and coordination. For inventory management, this might include the raw materials supervisor, the production supervisor, the finished goods inventory manager, and the shipping supervisor. Additional committee representation would include MIS and communications staff. A delegation of "hands-on" users should also be included in some of the discussions.

Consider a familiar company inventory management scenario. Controlling each step in this range of material responsibilities is within the scope of bar code application packages today. Available, or slightly tailored, commercial pieces of this integrated solution are discussed next.

Functional Description

In our scenario, an inventory clerk is using software which presents a menu of valid operations.

When material arrives at the receiving dock, the following sequence takes place:

1. The bar coded case or pallet label of raw material is scanned. Raw material that is not bar coded is assigned a bar code tracking label. This label is printed on demand by a local printer driven by a PC running a bar code serializing program. Data for the label may also be received via EDI transmissions.

2. The raw material is sent to an open bin for storage. Then, the item label and the bin label are scanned by a portable bar code reader used in batch data collection mode. A clerk enters the material quantity to complete the putaway record. The portable record is uploaded to the computer putaway file.

3. When material is selected for use in the production area, related bar codes are scanned, adjusting the raw goods inventory.

4. When finished goods have been produced, a new label containing part identity and serial number is created by a

local bar code printer. This label will be scanned by a fixed-position laser scanner adjacent to the take-away conveyor. The data will flow to the computer for finished goods recording.

5. On receipt of an order for finished goods, an order entry program, interfaced to a warehouse control program, generates an order pick list. Now, an order-picking clerk, carrying an RFDC bar code terminal, will be directed to the location of the item ordered by the terminal display screen. The item is scanned as it is picked, and this data is then transmitted to the computer adjusting the count in the finished goods database.

6. Further integration of data files with a bar code driven shipping verification system allows the contents of each order to be verified as the order is shipped.

All scanned information should be appended with each clerk's employee number, in addition to the time and date of each transaction. Exhibit 9.9 illustrates the composition of this integrated system.

The design of this system can also support the following additional applications:

- inventory cycle count, with reconciliation of discrepancies
- inventory transfers
- material scrap transactions
- audit trace for all material transactions
- increased security functions to inhibit unauthorized database tampering
- report printing on demand

Software

The entire system in our scenario is driven by the software which resides on a single host computer. Through its multitasking operating system, the following functions are performed simultaneously :

- communication to all bar code scanning stations, including RFDC
- batch data upload from portable data terminals

Exhibit 9.9
Integrated Warehouse Management

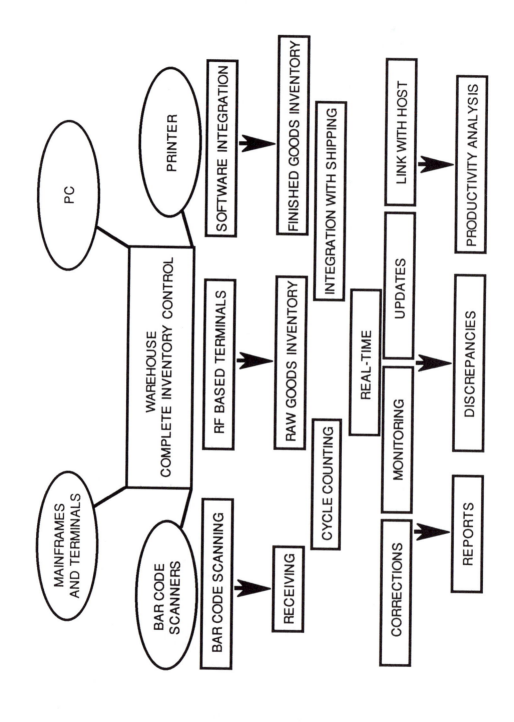

- continuous data exchange with a mainframe computer
- continuous report generation

All software is written in C.   Using this popular programming language gives the user more options for implementing minor changes. As the system grows in size and processing scope, the originally chosen host computer may become overloaded, making it necessary to port the software to a more powerful mini- or mainframe computer.

Software residing in bar code data collection terminals should be supported by the vendor through friendly program generation procedures, and be easily modified. Software residing on the host should buffer the corporate database from application-specific involvement. Mainframe software should accommodate the bar code system without alteration.

Hardware

Exhibit 9.10 illustrates the bar code scanner hardware required to implement this system. Portable, hand-held terminals with laser guns or wand scanners are used for putaway and raw material picking. A simple, two-line display prompts the user through the appropriate data collection steps.   Data from batch portable scanners should be uploaded on a regular basis so that production and shipping schedules can be integrated.   Similar terminals will also be used for finished goods inventory and cycle counts.

Hardwired data collection terminals are used on the production line. These terminals include a keypad and a 160-character display for more interactive communication. Laser guns, wand scanners, or fixed scanners monitoring a conveyor may be used to scan items within or at the end of the production line. These terminals may also be used to record damaged and scrapped raw material, as well as unused material being returned to inventory. Because the terminals are hardwired, the finished goods inventory database on the host and mainframe remains current, providing timely information throughout the entire production process.

Radio frequency bar code terminals are used for order picking. As shown in Exhibit 9.11, when orders involve pallets, the terminals can be installed on fork-lift trucks. For small unit orders, they would be hand carried.

Exhibit 9.10

Architecture for an Integrated Inventory System

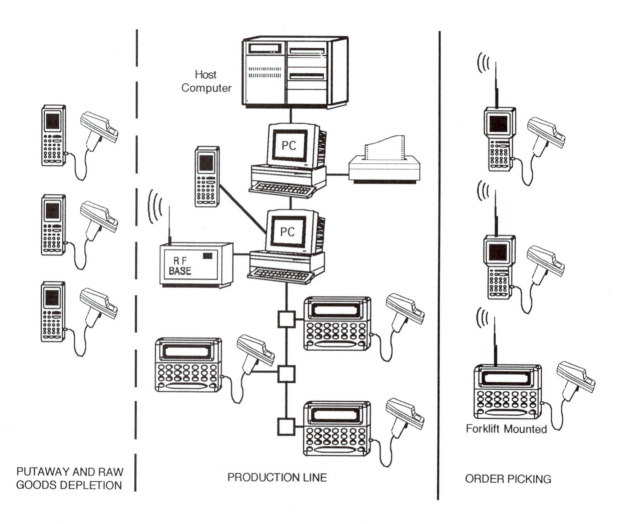

Host
Computer

PC

PC

R F
BASE

Forklift Mounted

PUTAWAY AND RAW
GOODS DEPLETION

PRODUCTION LINE

ORDER PICKING

Exhibit 9.11
Portable Data Collection Device Mounted on Fork Lift

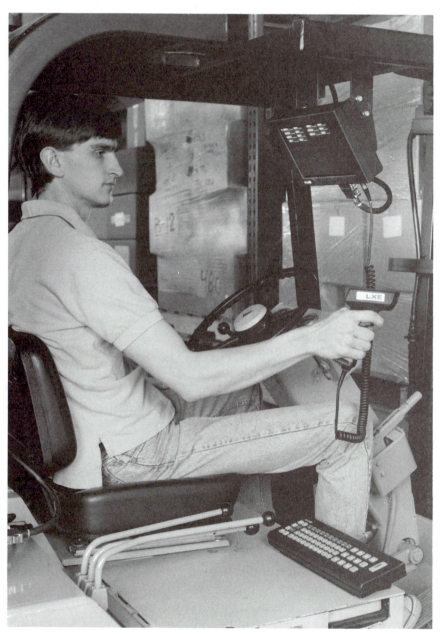

(Courtesy of LXE, Inc.)

.   A 486-based PC, equivalent minicomputer, or workstation is needed to handle the high volume of transactions efficiently. The UNIX or comparable multitasking operating system supports transactions to the RF-based units, hand-held terminals, fixed terminals, and mainframes, simultaneously.

> **NOTE:**
>
> While a multitasking operating system can adequately exchange data to support several applications, a premium must be placed on servicing the bar code scanners. Software which performs the data collection and prompt functions should complete those cycles in 1 to 2 seconds, or operator resistance will be encountered.

In a small company, all the applications just described could be run on a single host. However, for moderate to large operations, another UNIX-based PC or minicomputer would need to be added in order to support the shipping portion of this bar code control system. All system hosts would then reside on a local network.

In the example provided, periodic communication to the mainframe provides updates to the corporate database. The mainframe host does not need to be modified for this application, except for a communications link to the PC. For smaller operations, this system could be implemented without using a mainframe host. All picking orders and exception reports would be generated directly from another PC or from a minicomputer. A viable alternative would be to connect two or more PCs throughout a plant with a network server and shared data files.

Labels and Printers

The question of when and where to create labels presents several options. Raw material receiving labels can be generated on site when the purchase order is generated or the shipment arrives. (A review of Chapter 4 and Chapter 8 would be in order here.) Another option is to require the manufacturer to apply standardized labels to raw material before shipment.

Finished product labels can be generated on or off site. On-site labels can be generated on demand with the printer attached to the mainframe or local application host. If an off-site label vendor is chosen, labels can be ordered as needed to parallel the production schedule. As a guide to selecting print source and method, the questions to consider are these:

- How long must the labels survive in their intended use?
- Will finished product labels be scanned after the product is shipped?
- What environmental extremes will the labels on raw and finished goods encounter in storage?

Exhibit 9.10 represents one suggested system architecture. Remember, many companies will decide to implement a system of this complexity in stages. Perhaps production labels might be printed off site initially, and produced in-house later as system integration tasks subside.

Finally, data encoded in finished product labels has broad uses. Manufacturers must consider current or impending industry standards or advisories from trade associations here. If a bar code label can serve double duty — that is, aiding data accuracy in your operations as well as serving your customers — a competitive market advantage may result.

Summary of the Integrated Solution

Once bar codes have been implemented in one area of operation, several other applications become very logical extensions to bar code control, which is one of the reasons behind bar code popularity. Bar code labels that can serve many departments or several companies produce substantial economic benefits.

Exhibit 9.12 presents a cost schedule for our hypothetical integrated inventory system. Final costs for your system may be greater or less than this model, depending largely on subtle variations you require in application refinement.

Exhibit 9.12

Cost Schedule for the Automated Warehouse

COMPONENT	PURPOSE	UNIT COST	QTY	OPERATING COSTS	TOTAL TO INSTALL
PC (or PC compatible) 80486 processor 4 MB RAM VGA monitor 1 Serial Port 120 MB Hard Disk 1.2 MB Diskette Windows,DOS or OS/2 Network Controller Board	Host computer receieves scanned data communicates to mainframe	$1,500.00 $1,000.00	1 1	maintenance agreement diskettes	$1,500.00 $1,000.00

Printers [a]
letter quality
  thermal transfer
dot matrix
	generates reports
	  finished goods labels
	raw goods labels
		$400.00 [b]
		$2,000.00
		$2,000.00
			1
			1
			1
				paper
				label stock
				label stock
					$400.00
					$2,000.00
					$2,000.00

Hand-held terminals Laser guns (RS-485 interface)	collects on-floor data	$2,500.00	3	maintenance agreement	$7,500.00
Fixed Data Entry Terminals Laser guns or Light Pens (RS-484 interface)	collects production data	$1,200.00 or $200.00	3 3	maintenance	$3,600.00 (or $600.00)
RF Network Hand-held Terminals Laser Guns Base Station Multiplexor Fork-lift mount RF based Terminal Laser Gun	for order picking for order picking pallets	$1,500.00 $1,000.00 $1,300.00 $1,200.00 $100.00 $1,500.00 $1,000.00	2 2 1 1 1 1 1	maintenance maintenance	$3,000.00 $2,000.00 $1,300.00 $1,200.00 $100.00 $1,500.00 $1,000.00
Software hand-held units PC-based software label generation software mainframe software interface (optional)	prompts user for input data processes data comm to mainframe comm to RF terminals performs network control integrates with corporate database	$00.00 [c] $30,000.00 $1,000.00 $00.00 [c]	1 1		$00.00 $30,000.00 $1,000.00 $00.00

[a] One time cost of printing shelf labels must be added.

[b] Cost for these items can be shared with other applications using same hardware and software.

[c] All software can be developed in-house.

$59,100.00
($56,100.00)

Chapter 10

Retail Application Solution

The use of bar code to control retail operations has been an early, productive, and very visible application for this technology. As early as 1973, bar code has been the industry standard of price look-up and inventory management in grocery stores, where high sales volume and low profit margins require fast, efficient customer check-out.

Bar code systems have now been installed throughout retailing, from airport gift shops to the largest chains of discount merchandise. Product labeling standards, which have been established by the Uniform Code Council (UCC), made this expansion possible. The most prevalent bar code symbologies used in retail operations are UPC-A for vendor item marking, Code I 2of5, and Code UCC/EAN-128 for vendor shipping container marking.

Even small stores find scanning is practical and manageable because it speeds up check-out, assures pricing accuracy, and provides a way to track stock turnover. The problem of retrofitting bar code scanners with pre-bar code cash registers has been solved with the use of bar code wedge scanners. These devices scan bar code labels and translate their symbology into data the cash register can interpret.

Retailers currently implementing bar code systems are faced with literally hundreds of system choices, each with pros and cons. The challenge is to choose a system approach that best fits your current and future needs. To do this you must first analyze your business and then decide which features of the hardware and software offered by the market are of greatest importance to you. Talking with fellow retailers is always a good place to begin.

Chapter 10 covers two major segments of retail management: point-of-sale (POS) transactions and direct store delivery (DSD). Design considerations covering software and hardware, as well as label and printer issues, are also discussed. In addition, sample system designs are offered for possible consideration. A final section of this chapter touches on other retail applications that have proven successful under bar code control.

■ POINT-OF-SALE TRANSACTIONS

Many retailers, faced with a shrinking or unstable labor pool, have installed bar code driven cash registers. The more modern of these point-of-sale systems — currently the most popular bar code application among retailers — feature simplified clerical training and on-line prompting to guide the operator through the necessary steps and branches of item check-out.

A POS system generally has four elements:

- *Terminal.* Located on the sales floor, the terminal is the primary element of a POS system. Many of the newer terminals use 80386-based microprocessors for information management, running under a multitasking operating system.

- *Store controllers.* Micro- or minicomputers collect information from each POS station, as well as from other connected terminals, and provide data interface with a remote central computer. Price look-up is often provided from the store controller.

- *Central computer.* This mini- or mainframe computer is typically located at the company's headquarters and performs routine batch data processing applications, including stock ordering, traditional accounting, and personnel time and attendance reporting.

- *Network.* The network includes the physical wiring and the software to manage data exchange between all terminal devices and the store controllers, and between store controllers and the central computer. The most common network method used in this industry is a star configuration, although ring topologies are implemented occasionally.

Design Considerations

State-of-the-art registers are equipped with a full screen CRT, bar code scanning device, automatic credit authorization, and network link to the store's host computer. Exhibit 10.1 shows a typical POS terminal. Exhibit 10.2 shows an alternate setup for a bar code scanner at the POS. The full screen CRT not only prompts the terminal operator for each transaction step, but also displays the following information:

- On-line help to assist the user perform complex operations.
- Clerk prompting for lists of items that complement the purchase.
- Information regarding current and future availability of a particular item.
- Off-line price look-up.

Exhibit 10.1
State-of-the-Art POS Terminal

Exhibit 10.2

Bar Code Scanner Setup for the POS

(Courtesy of Spectra-Physics Scanning Systems, Inc.)

NOTE:

Occasionally the media print reports about the "inaccuracies" of bar code scanning in the retail setting. These stories give the false impression that the actual bar code scanner is not "reading" the bar code correctly. This is not true. Bar code scanners are nearly 100 percent accurate. The problem arises when there is a discrepancy between the unit price shown on a shelf label and the unit price which has been entered into a store's price look-up table. Care must be taken to assure that prices displayed on store shelves match price tables in the current product database. Best practice today requires daily shelf price audits.

One important consideration when choosing a POS system is the fault tolerance of the terminals and the local controller. The severity of potential loss if sales transactions cannot be performed due to failed equipment has driven many stores to specify system redundancies, even to the extent of providing standby power generation.

The investment required to adopt new POS terminals is high, and large national chains plan these system-upgrade steps as part of a multiyear store improvement program. However, bar code scanning can be added inexpensively to many existing POS terminals without replacing existing hardware. Bar code scanner manufacturers offer devices that can interface with most existing cash registers. They also have developed software that can network a number of POS registers. Exhibit 10.3 represents a typical bar code wedge device in this application.

Exhibit 10.3

Point-of-Sale Bar Code Interface

MSR stands for Magnetic Stripe Reader.

(Courtesy of Welch Allyn Retail Systems)

Most older registers do not have a display screen. If new software requires a display, an inexpensive "dummy" terminal, consisting of a display monitor and a keyboard, is installed next to the existing register. The main disadvantage of this configuration is the loss of valuable counter space.

Most bar code vendors to the retail POS market supply not only the network and terminals, but also the store controller and resident software. Exhibit 10.4 represents one solution to the problem of stores with older registers that lack display screens. The diagram shows older register equipment mixed with new style terminals that were purchased with the bar code system. The software running on the PC not only communicates to the new sales terminals, but also to the "dummy" terminals, and on up to the central or mainframe computer. A printer has been attached to the store controller to print store reports and provide audit trails.

Exhibit 10.5 shows how this configuration can be expanded to link

Exhibit 10.4

Mixed Hardware Configuration

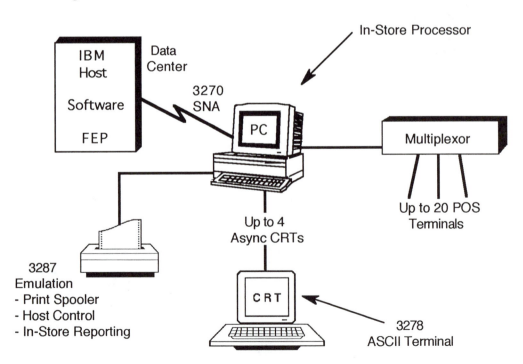

Exhibit 10.5

National Retail Communications Network

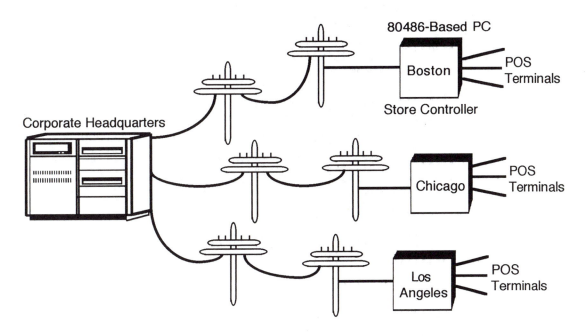

stores across the country. Here, the store controllers communicate to the central computer via phone lines and modems. For high-volume, around-the-clock transactions, leased lines or fiber optic cables are recommended.

NOTE:

If you intend to use existing hardware with new communications software, be sure to specify that the software must also be compatible with any new equipment you may be purchasing from major POS vendors. This gives you additional time to decide on new registers and extends the life of your system.

Choosing an efficient, accurate POS system that presents a lasting, favorable impression with customers should be your goal. Take the time to examine system design alternatives so that you can achieve that goal.

Software

The minimum POS software package should perform price look-up (PLU), add tax where applicable, tabulate the total sale, and handle various methods of payment (e.g., cash, check, credit card, store credit). Other desirable features which may be incorporated into the software include the ability to:

- Customize the system through user-modified displays and prompts.
- Accept keyed or scanned data for any input.
- Suspend and then recall a sale in progress.
- Handle refunds and exchanges.
- Manage multiple-payment-type transactions.
- Track layaways and custom order deposits.
- Perform credit checks and alert cashiers when they have a customer with a bad check or charge history.
- Communicate to other systems and mainframes.

Some system developers also supply software that will reside on the central computer, processing data sent from the store controller. Inventory adjustments, personnel tracking, and sales volume analysis are frequently derived from the sales data collected.

Hardware

In addition to choosing the POS terminal, the terminal controller, and the corporate mainframe, the retailer must also decide what type of bar code scanners to use. The retailer should consider the following questions prior to meeting with scanner vendors:

- What is the size of the price ticket/bar code label? What additional information can be scanned on the ticket or item?
- Will the scanner operator need to touch or hold the ticket while scanning?
- How much space does the cashier have to work within? How will items that cannot be placed on the counter be scanned?
- To what degree does the human factor (turnover, level of ability, and so forth) influence the scanner requirements?

Several scanner options are available, and although Chapter 3 covers scanners in some detail, consider the following points:

- Wand scanners or light pens have low cost, small size, and light weight as their main advantages. Possible disadvantages include the need to make direct label contact, a low scan rate, and awkwardness in use with uneven surfaces.
- Fixed laser scanners can be recessed into the check-out counter or lane and will scan an item label moving overhead. A variation of this option is a scanner mounted on edge with a small counter footprint scanning across the counter. A third choice is a hand laser gun mounted in a bracket facing down, so it will record labels passed beneath it. This option permits the clerk to lift the scanner off its mount and reach for a distant target, like a bar code on a heavy item in a cart. In any of these choices, noncontact scanning at a distance of 2 to 6 inches from the scanner is the norm. These devices may cost as much as ten times the cost of a wand scanner, but they can scan at speeds of up to 60 scans per second.

NOTE:

Care must be taken with noncontact laser scanners to be sure that the correct label is read in the proper sequence. If labels are close together, the laser beam may read a label not intended to be read.

- Hand-held laser scanners combine some of the features of wand scanners with the speed of fixed laser scanners. They weigh "ounces" and are coil-cord connected to the terminal. While they are available with visible laser or infrared laser energy, only the visible laser design should be considered.
- CCD scanners, which are proximate noncontact scanners, are held about 1 inch from the label in normal use. These devices can read labels on curved or irregular surfaces better than wand scanners. However, the CCD scanning array is fixed in length, and cannot read long labels such as those on cartons, or other labels with a large "X" dimension. These devices do not have a high scan rate and are priced about halfway between wands and hand-held laser guns.

> **NOTE:**
> The National Retail Merchants Association (NRMA) recommended OCR-A human readable font for scanning general merchandise tickets during the 1970s. Some difficulty was experienced by users of OCR-A labels in scannability, and NRMA now encourages bar code. However, some vendors offer combined OCR-A and bar code wand readers, which may give the retailer an opportunity to scan additional information at the POS or in back-room data collection.

Except for the in-counter scanners employed by supermarkets, there is not a clear trend in retailing for choosing one type of scanner over another. Your decision should be based entirely on the scanning environment, overall cost, and the quality of the labels to be scanned. If the bar code labels are high quality, and the number of transactions per customer is small, it is hard to beat the price and performance results of a wand scanner. Remember, you can use different types of scanners at different locations within the store, tailored to your departmental conditions.

Labels and Printers

The supermarket industry adopted a common bar code label (UPC) for unit package identification twenty years ago. Since then, POS data collection has evolved very little. Since only 2 percent of product coupons are currently redeemed, there is a trend toward printing them at the point-of-purchase location. Stores can then target customers to encourage coupons on a return shopping trip to that store. Large retailers are now encouraging customers to adopt identification cards with bar code labels, in order to gain insight into demographic buying habits. There is growing pressure to accept products packaged overseas and marked with the European Article Numbering (EAN) bar code, but this expansion has gone slowly due to the risk of having an installed base of scanning equipment become obsolete.

Many new retail applications are able to be tailored to the store's style of service, existing data system, or inclination of the user to be as creative as today's technology permits. Decisions involving item labels have to be made first, and analysis of your situation is the place to begin.

Many non-grocery retail product labels now include UPC bar code. Any system design should accommodate these pre-existing labels, eliminating the need for in-store labeling. If items are not normally bar coded, your first step will be to apply labels to the product upon receipt. Providing a local in-store printer would be necessary, but the symbology used here could vary from the premarked labels if auto discrimination scanners were used.

> **NOTE:**
> Using more than one label symbology within a store should not create a problem in selecting a scanner. However, if a different label length with different message content is intermixed, your software would have to manage this combination. Ideally, the user should have the ability to modify the system to accept some mix of label messages and symbologies.

If you decide to adopt a unique bar code driven POS system, you will first have to design your label. Then you will have to create a label for each item sold. Finally, you will have to apply each label with your own personnel. If labels are too big to fit certain small items or if certain items are not otherwise suited to a bar code label, then your clerk can open to the page of a store catalogue and scan the bar code relating to that item to complete the transaction.

After deciding on label content, you will have to print labels. A review of Chapter 4 and Chapter 8 may be in order here. Simply stated, though, you have the following options:

- Produce your tags with high-speed, medium-resolution dot matrix printers.
- Employ high-print-quality laser printers to generate sheets of pressure-sensitive labels.
- Use thermal or thermal transfer printers. Thermal printers are now available in hand-held models that print and apply tickets to items on the store floor.
- Order labels from an off-site printing company.

So far, there is no overwhelming trend in label choices. One factor that may affect your decision is whether you require hang tags or self-adhesive labels. Many retailers use both. An advantage to choosing a dot matrix printer is its ability to print forms and reports when it is not engaged in tag or label printing. Other questions you should raise in the printing issue are these:

- How many different label formats and mediums do you require?
- Have you considered label volume, variety, printing frequency, and lead time?
- How about the "X" dimension of the bar code itself? How far away will the label have to scanned? What is the smallest item the label will be applied to? Some bar code print technologies hold bar code specifications better than others, which affects the label first-read rate.
- Do you need to create labeled forms?
- Will the label printer be integrated with a data network or used as a batch printer off-line?
- Would one high-speed printer serve all your print needs? Or should you have two lower-speed printers, with one as a back-up in case the other fails?
- What capability exists for off-site printing in your area? Is the printer service oriented?

Decisions concerning the information to be placed on the labels can be guided by individual retail needs and any applicable industry standards. Retailers who sell very small items can apply a short numeric bar code to all but the most diminutive items. However, most small items of any value are packaged in a larger breakage- or theft-resistant container, which usually permits an adequate label application area.

Exhibit 10.6 shows the vertical ticket label design proposed by VICS (Voluntary Interindustry Communications Standards). The retailer can choose any of the available fields. Eventually, the VICS proposal may become a standard label format in some applications.

Items that do not contain a bar code when received by a retailer are labeled prior to being placed on the sales floor. Large, influential retailers may require supplier tagging of unit-packed items prior to shipment to the distribution center or retail store. This procedure can shift the labeling burden to the manufacturing site, saving the retailer a great deal of local cost and resulting in greater marking accuracy.

Zone 1 - Merchandise Identification
Zone 2 - Vendor Information
Zone 3 - UPC Version A Symbol
Zone 4 - Consumer Information
Zone 5 - Size/Dimension
Zone 6 - Space for Retail Price
Zone 7 - Manufacturer's
       Suggested Price

Key

Required
Optional

Exhibit 10.6

VICS Vertical Ticket
Format

NOTE:

Whatever the final decision concerning the basic source for bar code labels — on or off site — most retailers use an on-site printer to some degree. This provides a method for filling short-term gaps in label delivery and store-level flexibility for price adjustments or returns remarking.

Summary of Point-of-Sale Systems

Point-of-sale bar code systems have provided retail efficiencies and cost savings for many years. Grocery check-out systems paved the way for department stores and smaller retailers to install successful systems tailored to their particular environment. There should be no more mystery or anxiety associated with bar code use in retail operations. However, a careful design and planning effort is needed to ensure the best results. Exhibit 10.7 presents an estimate of a low-cost, point-of-sale budget.

Exhibit 10.7 Cost Schedule for a Low End Point-of-Sale System

COMPONENT	PURPOSE	UNIT COST	QTY	OPERATING COSTS	TOTAL TO INSTALL
PC (or PC compatible) 80486 processor 4 MB RAM VGA monitor 1 Serial Port 120 MB Hard Disk 1.2 MB Diskette Windows, DOS or OS/2 Multiplexor	Host computer receieves scanned data	$1,500.00 [a] $1,000.00	1	maintenance agreement diskettes	$1,500.00 $1,000.00
Printer letter quality	generates reports	$400.00	1	paper	$400.00
POSTerminal		$5,000.00	3	maintenance	$15,000.00
Laser Scanner with internal decoder and RS-232 interface [a] optional Hand-held terminal with laser gun	used for inventory, receiving, and price auditing	$1,200.00 ($2,500.00)	3 1	maintenance	$3,600.00 ($2,500.00)
Scanner Interface		$200.00	3	maintenance	$600.00
Software POS terminal resident PC-based	prompts user for input data performs PLU performs network control performs data back-up	$15,000.00			$15,000.00
					$39,600.00 (37,100.00)

a Cost for these items can be shared with other applications using same hardware and software.

DIRECT STORE DELIVERY ■

The second most popular bar code application among retailers is direct store delivery (DSD). A modern retailer must receive multiple vendor deliveries efficiently. In addition, the retailer may be returning damaged or out-of-date goods. Orders received with incorrect quantities or other purchase order irregularities can often go undetected, creating billing and inventory problems. Using a bar code scanner to record all items received, and then comparing this record against the purchase order, will permit you not only to detect errors at the start of your sell cycle but also to eliminate many costs down the line.

Other benefits of bar code driven DSD include:

- A reduction in future store delivery mistakes due to immediate vendor notification.
- A reduction of back-room shrinkage, since supervisors and key employees have immediate and dependable material receipt records.
- Better shelf or floor inventory management, with item restocking driven by integrated POS sales and back-room stock status reports.
- An elimination of staff time required to perform material receipt reports and to key records for accounts payable records.

The payback for a DSD system can be very rapid. The UCC and NRMA have both taken an aggressive role in facilitating bar code driven DSD by holding orientation seminars and workshops and through the publication of documents and videocassette user guides.

Design Considerations

Let's begin with a list of features which your DSD system may include:

- Time and date stamp on all transactions for audit purposes.
- Data link to the store's host computer and accounts payable program.
- User-modifiable report generator.

- Up-to-date item price file, including costs, deposits, allowances, margins, and cost changes.
- Credits and returns file to assure correct payment.

System features you may select in your DSD system are in large part influenced by whether you have implemented electronic data interchange (EDI) and whether your system supports DEX/UCS (Direct Exchange/Uniform Communication Standard).

DEX/UCS links the computers of the supplier and the retailer at the receiving dock. It takes automated DSD one step further by eliminating the need to scan each item as it is received. DEX/UCS specifies a direct method for connecting a supplier's portable terminal to the retailer's computer at the time of delivery. Delivery information is then uploaded directly into the store's host computer. The direct connect method, tested and operational in many retail settings, is supported by numerous bar code vendors.

The benefits afforded by DEX/UCS include:

- Improved receiving speed and control.
- Retail price mark verification.
- Data discrepancy detection and reduction.
- Elimination of turn-around documents.
- Key entry savings.
- Automated discrepancy analysis.
- Elimination of statement processing.

The UCC has also developed NEX/UCS (Network Exchange/ Uniform Communication Standard). NEX/UCS is a natural extension to the work of the UCC, linking office computers by telephone lines to facilitate transfer of delivery authorization and other vendor information. Benefits to be gained from implementing NEX/UCS include:

- Efficient and timely file maintenance.
- More effective use of promotions.
- Reductions in file and costing discrepancies.
- Automated payables and receivables accounting.

Software and Hardware

Exhibit 10.8 represents the use of EDI and DSD in the total retail environment. RF-based, hand-held terminals are indispensable in this application. When an order is delivered, the receiver enters the required purchase order information by key or bar code scan. Now each

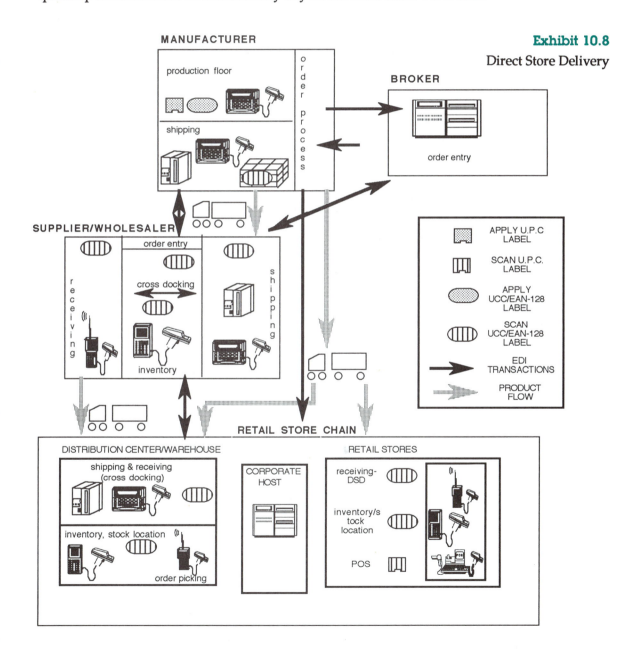

Exhibit 10.8

Direct Store Delivery

container label is scanned against the order, with an item count manually entered if the container label does not contain this information. If the delivered goods do not match the purchase order, a message is displayed to the receiving clerk through the hand-held terminal display.

Most systems available today are driven by software residing on store-level PCs or minicomputers. The DSD controller must then be linked to the central computer for mainframe level data coordination.

Labels

In the past, the majority of DSD applications were installed in supermarkets and convenience chains. DSD applications have expanded rapidly in all retail fields as a result of emerging standards for case labels. Both VICS and FACT (Federation of Automatic Coding Technologies) have been developing standards which can facilitate DSD. Exhibit 2.8 in Chapter 2 (p. 35) represents the case label currently recommended by VICS. Exhibit 10.9 is just one example of a case label which facilitates DSD and EDI.

Exhibit 10.9

UCC/EAN-128
Case Label for Shipping

(Courtesy of Standard Register)

OTHER RETAIL APPLICATIONS ■

Shelf Price Auditing

A shelf price audit (SPA) system assures pricing integrity among the prices marked on the shelves, on the products, and in the store's POS system file. Using RF-based, hand-held bar code scanning devices for manual audit and correction can yield a significant reduction in time spent performing this necessary routine.

To perform this bar code driven SPA, a clerk scans the bar code label on each stock item with a hand-held RFDC (radio frequency data collection) terminal, and then either keys or scans the unit price information. This record is transmitted to the host computer at that store. The unit price entered for that item is checked against the POS price database. If the prices do not match, a decision must be made regarding the current price. Then, either the database on the central computer is updated or the clerk takes the necessary steps to reprice the items on the shelves or racks.

As an alternative and less costly SPA application, you could utilize portable, hand-held terminals without the RF transmitting function. The clerk first scans the item identification and enters the price marked on the shelf and unit label for a batch of items; then the clerk uploads the collected information. The store's host computer creates an exception report, listing any discrepancies. An audit trail of file maintenance and various performance reports can be generated through this procedure.

Having a password-driven security system in this application is desirable. A second-level password may also be desirable before someone can install a new item price in the POS database. SPA complements your POS system, and increasingly it is viewed as a vital step for bar code based retail system refinement. Exhibit 10.10 illustrates an employee carrying out a shelf price audit.

Inventory

Bar code driven POS and DSD systems, when used correctly, give the retailer the controls to maintain perfect inventory at the store level. The retailer can know exactly what was received, sold, and returned. In practice there are always some transactions that are performed incorrectly or incompletely. These mistakes can produce, over time, an

Exhibit 10.10

Shelf Price Audit
System

(Courtesy of Monarch Marketing Systems)

increasingly inaccurate store inventory file if adjustments and corrections are not made. Using portable bar code terminals can make inventory taking fast and accurate.

The inventory procedure will vary somewhat, depending on certain system features such as the following:

- Shelf labels with bar-coded item information.
- Case labels with product identity and quantity in bar code.
- Item labels which can be descriptive, or cross-referenced by serial number.

If item labels are product descriptive, the operator scans the bar code on the shelf or item and keys in the quantity after a manual count. If the items are uniquely serialized, every label must be scanned. To reduce the risk of losing data, you should upload portable scanners frequently, according to a defined schedule.

In addition to finding discrepancies in stock quantities, SPA can also perform a complete item cost audit. In this function, you must manage inventory files and perform POS transactions in multitasking mode. When each item from inventory is sold, the inventory file can reference the original cost of that item for inventory valuation adjustment. This step can be done simultaneously, or an inventory transaction file can be recorded for adjustment later. When new inventory is received, that item's data and its cost at receipt are added to the inventory file for later matching to a POS transaction. This application is most valuable for high-cost items where the cost basis varies. Of course, each item label must be serialized in bar code. Other applications which can be built into your inventory software include:

- Automatic replenishment or repurchase of items which fall below a reorder threshold.
- Detailed analysis of inventory turnover.
- Store transfers and returns.

The value and success of inventory management depends on the software in your mainframe computer. It is essential that the retailer carefully design the entire bar code control system before purchasing hardware or supporting application programs. You may decide to phase in various degrees of inventory control over several years, beginning with the most basic steps first. Even so, to avoid difficulties in future control refinement, you should have a master plan designed from the beginning.

You can review Chapter 9 for other inventory control features and design considerations. Compared with a bar code driven POS system, stock inventory control applications are less costly to install and usually provide more immediate cost recovery.

Time and Attendance

A large employee pool, working brief, irregular schedules, can create a timekeeping challenge. Bar code suppliers have responded by offering a number of time and attendance (T&A) packages. Some of these are intended to stand alone, while other packages can be integrated with related retail applications. Exhibit 10.11 presents a fully integrated system design that incorporates all principal functions of retailing. The most popular T&A features are:

- Manpower availability reports, on demand.
- Report of employee absences, highlighting employees with a poor "track record."
- Employee tardiness reporting.
- Overtime hours, per employee, by reporting period.
- Wages reporting, including overtime, vacation, holiday, and sick pay.

Not only can a record be kept of the number of hours the employee has worked, but this information can also be sorted by department, giving insight into employee and departmental efficiency. Such information, combined with sales data, can lead to refined staffing schedules, balancing the delicate profit-versus-service considerations for normal retail periods, as well as holidays.

Bar-coded ID badges are the key to T&A applications. Every badge is scanned at the start and end of each work shift, at the beginning and end of breaks, and when the employee begins a new department or work assignment. Badge scanning in place of punching a time clock provides more detail, security, and data timeliness.

Purchased T&A packages are frequently menu driven. Flexibility should be provided through user-defined reports, with manual overrides (if, for example, employees forget their badges). Your store manager or system administrator should also be able to authorize overtime pay, create temporary badges, and customize new payroll categories.

A modern T&A system should be expandable and permit an interface with the company's security access systems. Only certain employees, for example, would be allowed entry to certain stock areas or other restricted zones.

Exhibit 10.11
Integrated Retail System

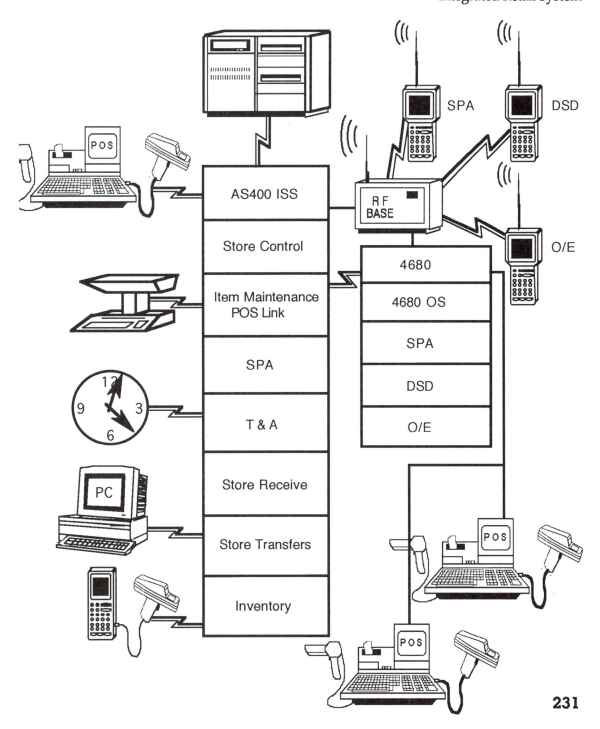

Distribution Centers

Distribution centers (DCs) provide the retail outlet with a continuous supply of items for store shelf stock display and sale to customers. Here, bar code systems play a vital role in coordination and increased productivity, reducing the time to replenish retail outlet stock and lowering overall inventory. Other benefits are a decrease in damaged goods and loss due to spoilage or obsolescence, and the ability to better accommodate highly fluctuating manufacturing schedules. As we have seen earlier, bar code control systems frequently depend on corporate mainframe support for their ultimate utility. In addition, bar code interface with EDI can further tighten DC support to retail outlets.

Distribution centers have been fertile sites for bar code applications, with significant gains in productivity continually claimed by users. Exhibit 10.12 presents a typical DC system. In this design, all purchase orders are entered into a mainframe computer at the distribution center. When each related shipment arrives, the items are scanned and verified against the purchase order. These same labels can be scanned for put away verification, location tracking, cycle counting and stock level tracking. Next, a program in the mainframe computer creates files which print bar code price tickets and assign goods for store distribution.

Unit and carton labels are printed at the DC. As cartons are picked and packed, bar code labels are applied to each item and finally to the carton itself. The cartons are placed on a conveyor, where they are scanned, recorded for manifest creation, and sorted to their shipment destination. Detailed shipping documents are automatically created and printed at the loading dock. The design and composition of carton labels require considerable reflection. You may wish to use a bar code label, which efficiently and economically integrates your DC with your retail stores. On the other hand, you may decide to follow the UCC/EAN-128 Standard with Application Identifiers. This labeling standard is designed to link to EDI and let trading partners control the management material in a coordinated effort. Chapter 14 covers Application Identifiers in detail. DCs can also benefit by installing extensive bar code driven inventory controls as described in Chapter 9.

Exhibit 10.12

Distribution Center System

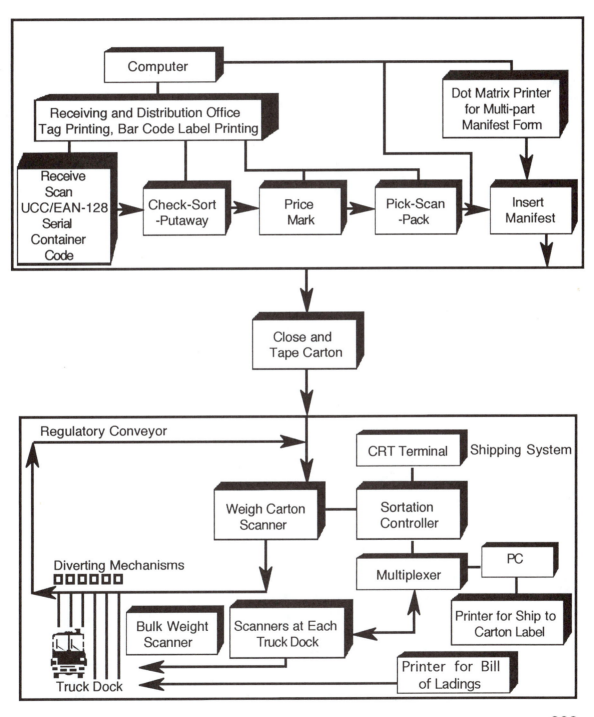

NOTE:

Several industry associations have become active in developing bar code related standards. The retailer should review these before making final label design and system decisions. The following associations should be contacted for their latest recommendations and standards affecting the retail industry:

- FASLINC (Fabrics and Suppliers Linkage Council)
  (202) 862-0500
- ICRDA (Independent Cash Register Dealers Association)
  (704) 376-8516
- AAMA (American Apparel Manufacturers Association)
  (703) 524-1864
- National Retail Federation
  (212) 244-8780

Refer to Chapter 13 for additional information on sources for standards and resources available to the bar code systems implementor.

■ SUMMARY

The "quick response" concept has been heartily adopted throughout the retail industry. In broad terms, it is a method by which retailers can gain a competitive advantage through improved customer service. In more specific terms, it is the ability of the retailer to have items on hand when they are needed — not before, resulting in excess inventory, and not later, when the demand has passed. VICS has guided business to take full advantage of the increased information flow available through data integration, use of bar code, and EDI. A continuous connection between the supplier and the retailer is now possible. POS, DSD, DEX/UCS, and NEX/UCS are all key components of quick response.

Whether you adopt bar code retail control for a small shop with a limited item selection, or for a giant retail chain with all the integration of the quick-response movement, bar code can streamline operations to a degree not possible in a previous era of data and material control.

Chapter 11

Tracking

Chapters 9 and 10 presented suggested system designs for two bar code applications — inventory control and retail operations. This chapter introduces tracking, a third application for bar code. As a category, tracking covers a broad variety of commercial functions, including the following:

- personnel time and attendance
- library circulation control
- tool crib management
- work in process management
- product warranty and repair services
- hospital x-ray, patient record, and specimen tracking

Many beginning users of bar code decide to implement this type of application first, because tracking systems require minor integration with other operations, simplifying connecting software. This feature keeps system costs low, and quick payback becomes the rule.

DESIGN CONSIDERATIONS

To list every combination of label and scanner useful in each tracking category is beyond the scope of this book. However, guidelines for practical software features, desirable hardware capabilities, and general label requirements are presented here.

Software and Processor

Many fine software packages have been developed and packaged commercially to handle common tracking applications. As in the case of inventory control software (covered in Chapter 9), some software packages utilize a commercially "popular" database, adding their own communications software to transfer data in batch mode.   Other software packages have been created to fit a specific tracking problem exactly and are offered as a complete and efficient canned package.

Regardless of how the software has been designed, it is important that collected data be shared with a host or mainframe computer. Data collected at the scanner-based tracking locations can be merged into accounting software for more accurate asset depreciation schedules, project accounting detail, or customer billing. Tracking data, once collected, is often converted into ASCII file format and uploaded in batch mode to a host or mainframe computer for accounting or control software to operate on. In a more sophisticated system, scanners would be on-line to a PC or host where software would link each item scanned to related data through shared files.

Other software features that have proved useful in bar code tracking systems are able to perform the following tasks:

- Customize data collection and reporting routines.
- Provide data verification and validation criteria, such as message length and format.
- Generate files of overdue items by a responsible individual or department. Some systems take this feature one step further and routinely generate reminder memos on overdue items.
- Produce an audit trail of all entries to the database.
- Include a security system to limit access to certain files or items. Database inquiry access is often controlled as well. Personnel screening for limited use of report generator or database editing may also be desirable.
- Allow all entries to be entered manually or scan entered. Here, bar code menus can improve data entry when routine information is added to item identity.
- Provide for the import or export of ASCII data files to other computers and applications.

tracking systems. Transaction volumes are generally moderate, so an 80386-based PC running under MS-DOS or Windows provides sufficient host capability. A multitasking operating system may be more costly than necessary, since queries into the database and report runs can be scheduled at times when item scanning is not required. A parallel port on the PC is required for report generation. At least one serial communications port should be available to accept data from a portable data collection device, as well as to provide batch transfer of data to a mainframe. A second serial port is required if a multiplexor is used to network scanners. As with all bar code data collection systems, you should provide a floppy disk drive or CD ROM to back up collected data.

If you are going to query your database from only one location, then a single PC is sufficient. Data entry tracking terminals with bar code scanners can be distributed to other locations as required. If several departments in different locations need access to the database, a PC network will have to be created, with scanners wedged to each PC, or networked as described earlier. Exhibits 11.1 and 11.2 present these two architectures.

Exhibit 11.1

PC Network-Based File Tracking System

PC NETWORK-SHARED DATABASE

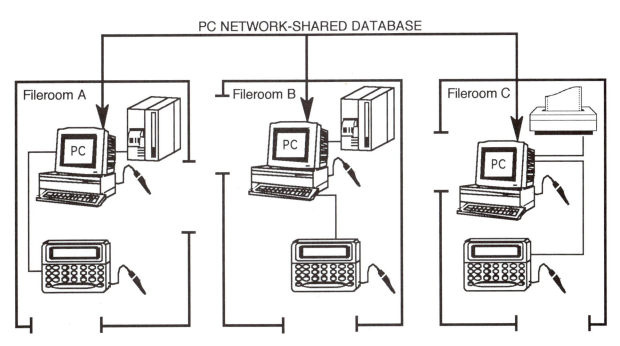

Exhibit 11.2

Networked Tracking of Laboratory Samples

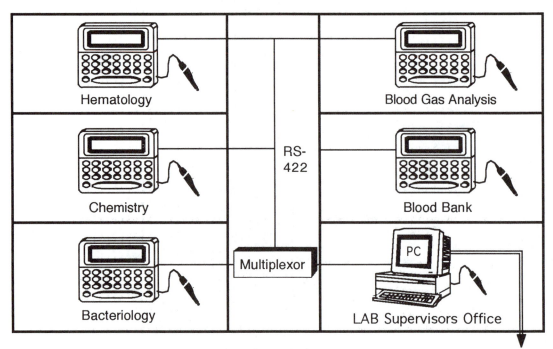

Your system design, including software, hardware, and database characteristics, should be based on the number of tracking transactions, the volume of collected data, the number of scanning locations, and any communication requirements with other processors. Fortunately, the popularity of bar code tracking applications provides users with a number of supplier choices.

Scanners

The bar code scanning needs of most tracking applications can be met using low-cost wand scanners. These are often connected directly to the PC through a keyboard wedge device or through a decoder box interfaced via an RS-232C serial communications port. For remote scanning sites, a bar code terminal with a two-line display can increase data collection accuracy, with the PC providing prompt instructions for the user. If many item tags are missing or unreadable, alphanumeric keyboard decoders can be considered. You should choose a wedge or decoder device that can also support a hand-held laser scanner for those special locations where the added cost is justified.

Some tracking applications may require that items be scanned away from fixed scanning stations. An example would be having to perform a physical inventory covering fixed assets. Here, a portable bar code data entry terminal can be used, as we saw in the general inventory system described in Chapter 9. Programming your portable tracking device to prompt the user through data entry, with verification as data is entered, will provide a higher level of tracking reliability. When data collection is complete, the information is batch loaded to the PC. As noted earlier, a software routine must be available to accept data from a portable terminal into the PC's application database.

Printers and Labels

Tracking files, books, x-rays, patient records, tools, and assets requires that labels be scanned many times over an extended period of time. Durability and service life are important qualities for labels, in addition to a high first-read rate. Consider using off-site photocomposed labels, which may be printed on laminated paper, vinyl, plastic, or metal. These labels will hold up to repeated contact scans without deterioration. Additional qualities to seek are resistance to dirt, UV (ultraviolet) resistance, and a compact bar code using an "X" dimension of the order of 10 mils. If the labels have a security component, you should also use a material that will self-destruct if someone attempts to remove the label.

Labels used for laboratory specimens, warranty repair, and work in process do not require the high resistance to abrasion just discussed; nor are they required to last for several years. These labels can be printed on demand at a work or inspection station and be applied when the item is created. Consider a laser printer or thermal printer because of its excellent image quality and quiet operation. An inexpensive dot matrix printer may seem appealing, but the dot row tolerance may be uneven and present a low first-read rate, leading to scanning abrasion and a shortened label life.

Some applications, such as printed circuit boards tracking, require very small labels that are resistant to high temperature and caustic chemicals. Many commercial label suppliers have developed special materials which can easily survive in this environment.

Keep in mind that for bar code tracking, as in other bar code applications, it is necessary to scan enter the operator identity when records are collected or the database is reviewed. The simplest way is to supply every employee with his or her own identity number bar coded inside a laminated ID badge. Exhibit 11.3 illustrates an asset tracking application.

Exhibit 11.3

Asset Tracking Application

(Courtesy of Hewlett-Packard Company)

TRACKING APPLICATIONS ■

The following sections give insight into some typical features of popular tracking systems and offer guidelines on printers, scanners, software, and host selection. Each bar code tracking solution described here can be adapted to several other related tracking applications.

File Tracking

Under the general heading of file tracking, we can itemize some specific applications such as the following:

- office file tracking
- library circulation control
- x-ray and patient record tracking
- tool crib management
- videotape circulation control

The first feature of all these systems is the ability to record what was borrowed, by whom, and when. Important information needed to complete a record can include the date the item will be returned, the location (file cabinet or shelf) to which the item will be returned, where the item is going, and who is next in line to receive the item. If the item, for example, an office file, goes to a new borrower while it is in circulation, there must be some way to update the database with this new information. For a tracking system to be effective, users must log all item transfers through a scanning station so that the database continually reflects exact status information.

Depending on the composition and capacity of the database, additional information about each tracked item can be made available for reference. In a library application, for example, the date of purchase, price, and publisher of each book may be provided, as well as cross-references for ISBN number and Library of Congress Cataloging Number (LCCN). For x-ray tracking, the date and the type of x-ray are important. As was stated earlier, the advantage to using a "popular" database within a bar code data collection application is the extended ability to enhance user information. With on-line access to a continually current database, many reports and control checks are now available to the system user.

> **NOTE:**
> When installing a bar code tracking system that contains a large inventory of files, x-rays, or books, apply labels to existing items the first time each item is checked out under the new system. When new items enter your system, apply a label immediately.

Exhibits 11.4, 11.5 and 11.6 illustrate reports that have been generated by a bar code tracking system. To find an example of a bar code tracking system in your local area, check your neighborhood video rental store. Many of these merchants have eagerly adopted bar code tracking and have reaped many benefits, including improved customer service and satisfaction. Exhibit 11.7 is an example of tracking library books.

Exhibit 11.4

Database Audit Trail

General Hospital - Patient Records Departments
Database Audit

current date: 07/10/90

DATE	CREATED	CHECKED OUT	CHECKED IN	RESERVED	ARCHIVED	DELETED
06/01/90	7	5	0	1	0	0
06/04/90	3	4	6	0	0	0
06/05/90	3	7	2	1	0	0
06/06/90	3	7	5	0	3	1
06/07/90	1	12	14	0	0	0
06/08/90	3	8	5	1	0	0
06/12/90	2	7	7	0	0	0
06/13/90	1	7	14	0	0	0
06/14/90	0	6	0	0	0	0
06/15/90	1	4	10	0	0	0
06/18/90	2	16	9	0	0	0
06/19/90	1	6	1	0	0	0
06/20/90	1	11	18	1	0	0
06/21/90	0	1	0	1	0	0
06/22/90	0	2	2	0	3	0
07/10/90	0	0	0	0	0	0
TOTAL	28	103	93	5	6	1

Exhibit 11.5

File
Status Report

```
                              FILE REPORT
06/10/90

File Title: SMITH, WILLIAM AND ALICE  1-8-1976
Description: SMITH et al vs. ABC Widget Co.


        Status:  Out
     Folder ID:  123-456-789              Bar Code ID:  123456
    Originator:  Test User               Creation Date:  05/01/90
    Department:  Cival                    Waiting List Flag:  Set
      Location:  CF                       Reserved Flag:  clear
  Signed Out to:                          Last Activity:  05/22/90
         ID #:
         Dept.:


                      FILE HISTORY (last 10 transactions)


Users                      Check-out Dates          Check-in Dates

  BROWN,  THOMAS A.            05/22/90                  /  /
  STEELE,  RICHARD J.          05/12/90                05/13/90
  BROWN,  THOMAS A.            05/07/90                05/08/90
  WARREN,  SALLY               05/06/90                05/07/90
```

Exhibit 11.6

Past Due List for Library Tracking System

```
                              Public Library
                            - Past Due List -
current date: 9\27\90
```

name/ library card #	tel #/ address	book title/ bood ID	date-out	date-due	previously notified
John Smith 0144736	555-1153 21 Main St. Duxbury	How to Build a Porch 562513	9-07-90	9-21-90	
Jane Dunn 0344162	555-0142 4 Elm St. Duxbury	Microwave Cooking 143442	8-24-90	9-17-90	9-24-90
Sue Jones 0413628	555-7914 367 Oak St. Duxbury	Art in the 19th Century* 446537	9-14-90	9-26-90	

* reserve request pending

Exhibit 11.7
Library Book Tracking

(Courtesy of Symbol Technologies, Inc.)

Laboratory Specimen Tracking

The hospital or clinic setting is a good place to begin when discussing laboratory specimen tracking. Progressive health institutions have benefited greatly from using bar code tracking. Processing of lab samples is more efficient, and concerns about sample mix-up have virtually disappeared. An added bonus is the lab's ability to provide patient billing information to the accounting department immediately following each test .

The bar code driven tracking techniques that work efficiently in a health care setting can be transferred to other laboratory situations. For example, consider an environmental lab that performs biological and chemical tests on hundreds of soil and water samples. When technicians are sent to the field, they can take with them bar code printed forms and labels for each sample they collect. After taking a sample, the technician applies a bar code label to the sample's container. The technician then completes a corresponding form, printed with an identical bar code number, specifying the tests to be performed and pertinent field details. When the samples and documents arrive for processing at the lab, the bar codes link information concerning the sample with the sample itself. Here the host computer plays the vital role of coordinator, linking items and information which may have been physically separated for some time.

All forms and labels can be generated by a laser printer or impact matrix printer. If the sample is to be subdivided after it enters the laboratory, a technician with a bar code driven label printer can generate multiple labels when and where needed. By scanning the label on the primary sample, the technician can create a new coordinated label for the subdivided sample. This label can be identical to the original, or appended with a special code designating the item as a subsample.

The adhesive quality of the label must be examined if the samples are to be applied in extreme temperature conditions or in a dirty or oily environment. Do test label material for worst-case conditions before you approve your final tracking system design. The general approach of this tracking problem can be adapted to related applications, such as patient record tracking through many hospital departments.

Asset Tracking

The ability to track assets from the time of acquisition until retirement is crucial for high productivity and accurate financial reporting in business. In the past, asset tracking has been inaccurately performed while consuming expensive personnel resources over an extended period of time. Companies that have replaced traditional asset tags with bar code labels report reductions in inventory expense of as much as 75 percent, with far greater record accuracy.

While asset tracking using bar code has many features in common with those listed for other tracking designs in this chapter, consider the following advantages as well:

- Transportable assets can be checked and assigned easily.
- All fixed and transportable assets are under continuous management.

- Asset reassignment by location or department is simplified.
- On-site asset verification by building, office, or individual can be performed quickly on an annual or cyclical basis.
- Standard reports covering valuation, aging, depreciation, location, contract assignment, discrepancies, and detailed inventory of all items in the system can be generated by continuous inquiry.

Physical assets that can be tracked include furniture, data processing equipment (terminals, PCs, typewriters, calculators), telephones, art work, and even modular offices. A PC or minicomputer host located in the controller's department can easily manage the processing involved. Assets are scanned and recorded in batches using a portable bar code terminal equipped with either a wand scanner or a hand-held laser gun. Assignable assets issued and returned through a central storeroom can be recorded with each change of assignment by a scanner and terminal that are networked to the host computer. In this design all assets are continually reported through a single database.

Some operations require tracking components within an asset. For example, a personal computer may have certain options, like extended memory or installed software, that are used for a time in one department but then reassigned to another. The labeling methods, software, and database selected for this application must be chosen with additional care to assure label visibility to a scanner and file structure capable of detailed subdivision.

As with other bar code based control systems, any tracking feature or configuration is possible. For your application, you must decide which features can be justified against the added costs or complexity of operating the system. Frequently, creating and operating several simple bar code systems, with data from each entered to a master database, is more practical than designing and operating a master system that does many tasks. For example, developing a master tracking system to manage an active tool crib and also maintain extensive corporate fixed assets in a shared network and database is impractical. Two separate bar code based systems will be much easier to design, implement, operate, and adapt to future functional changes.

Time and Attendance Tracking

Keeping track of personnel is usually a costly and inexact organizational challenge. Bar code based time and attendance (T&A) systems improve data accuracy, add improved levels of security and accountability, and usually integrate more easily with normal work procedures. In addition to recording your employees' presence, a typical T&A system can also record where your employees are working and what they are working on. A modern T&A system can report through a PC host, or directly to a mini- or mainframe computer. T&A information, or extracts of this data, must ultimately combine with mainframe files for payroll and cost accounting calculations. Due to the increased detail and reliability of bar code driven T&A records, sophisticated software can now handle more accurate staff planning by detailed employee profile, as well as identify employees needing more intensive training.

In a T&A bar code application, employees scan their bar-coded badges with a badge reader on arrival at work. Supplementary information about each job is then entered by wand scanner and menu card at every workstation, department, or point-of-sale device. Exhibit 11.8 illustrates a bar code menu for a T&A application. When an employee starts a shift or job number, the appropriate bar codes are scanned. The bar-coded numeric keypad permits entry of variable data, thus avoiding the expense of a more elaborate and costly keyboard. Scanner hardware remains simple and inexpensive.

Several levels of security can be built into a T&A system using passwords, special access codes, and, if necessary, special bar code badges. Frequently, T&A badges have a red filter over the bar code identity label to prevent the symbol from being reproduced on an office copy machine. This reduces unauthorized use of another's badge number. If a badge is lost or an employee leaves without returning a badge, the verification database must be adjusted immediately. A supervisor must be able to override the normal operation and link the employee to a temporary badge. Date and time information is, of course, automatically appended to all data entries.

Work in Process Tracking

A bar code based work in process (WIP) system provides the manufacturing manager with the ability to track all job locations and job progress accurately, with minimal impact on productivity. In contrast to other tracking systems, WIP system software usually resides on a mini- or mainframe computer. Some commercial packages have been developed to run on a PC-DOS-compatible host, with scanner terminals reporting through their own local area network.

Exhibit 11.8
Time and Attendance Bar Code Menu

The Mac-Barcode Company

TIME AND ATTENDANCE MENU

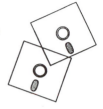

- **SCAN BADGE**

CLOCK IN   CLOCK OUT

- **SCAN JOB NUMBER**

- **SCAN JOB STATUS**

STOP- JOB COMPLETE   STOP- JOB INCOMPLETE

START JOB   RESET

1   2   3   4   5

6   7   8   9   0

YES   NO

A WIP system should have bar code scanner terminals at each job center. The type of terminal needed, from a simple read-and-beep decoder to an 80-column-by-20-line CRT with full alphanumeric keyboard, will depend on a variety of system factors incorporated in your manufacturing operations and tracking software. Design emphasis should be on simplicity, using serial labels and menu cards for information entry, and display decoders for prompting and verification. In most manufacturing and assembly operations, personnel are least productive when typing on keyboards or scrolling through lengthy, computer-driven screens.

A bar code serial number or identity label can be applied to the item being processed, to the carrier or kit which is transporting the item, or to the work order or ticket that describes the processes and paths the item must follow. Exhibit 11.9 shows a carrier containing a bar-coded label for WIP tracking. In any case, the label must be readable through all stages of processing, so care in choosing label media and print technology is important. In some WIP systems, the item label can, when

Exhibit 11.9
WIP Tracking

(Courtesy of Computer Identics)

scanned, trigger operator prompts through a terminal display for detailed work instructions on that piece. This item-and-process-driven software is elegant and permits close manufacturing tracking and control. However, expensive fault-tolerant processors are required for the host computer, since any host downtime would otherwise bring all work to a halt. A more forgiving system design would have a single host and use a work order with item identification and process steps in bar code. Now, scanner display terminals with sufficient RAM to continue to prompt, local edit, and store data for several hours will permit manufacturing to proceed and WIP information to be collected, even if host connectivity is lost.

NOTE:

Before installing a WIP system on your existing computer, you should carefully evaluate the impact of this new data flow on your CPU. It would not be surprising to find that WIP tracking will require more processing cycles and disk accesses than all of your other computer applications. Many existing systems are not able to handle the heavy interactive data and message traffic without experiencing severe performance degradation. For this reason, many companies have chosen to install a mini- or PC host dedicated to their WIP application, communicating with the corporate mainframe through batch file transfers.

A bar code based WIP system not only eliminates errors and delays in manual work tracking; it can also reverse the tendency to require skilled machinists and assemblers to spend unproductive time learning and operating arcane computer terminals.

Warranty Repair Tracking

The final tracking application to be considered is warranty repair, either by the original manufacturer or through a repair center. In a sense, this system is a hybrid of the other tracking applications we have considered. Features of importance here include the following:

- A file reference, by item, of warranty duration can be maintained, including the date of purchase or beginning of warranty, warranty term, and end date of warranty. In many situations, warranty duration may depend on the source or terms of purchase. In the absence of a timely warranty card return from the customer, a warranty cut-off date may be inserted through a file cross-reference, using an item serial number table.

- The item can be tracked as it progresses through the repair facility — for example, repair authorization number, evaluation, parts collection, repair in progress, final test, and shipment. Other related information that can be retained includes the date and time of receipt, correspondence with the owner, and the identity of the supervisor authorizing the repair.

- A database of warranties performed and ECO modifications, including a range of warranty periods for all categories of repaired products, can be maintained.

- A customer database, including the customer name, address, product application, and repair history, can be maintained — a particularly useful feature for guiding future product design.

Warranty repair tracking has a great deal of similarity to tracking laboratory samples. Although a few warranty repair tracking software packages are available, you can also consider customizing a more generic tracking program or create a highly tailored system around a commercially available database.

SUMMARY ■

The applications discussed in this chapter represent several of the most popular and successful examples of commercial bar code use today. Most tracking systems can be easily implemented if the design is kept

Exhibit 11.10   Cost Schedule for a File Tracking System

COMPONENT	PURPOSE	UNIT COST	QTY	OPERATING COSTS	TOTAL TO INSTALL
PC (or PC compatible) 80486 processor 4 MB RAM VGA monitor 1 Serial Port 120 MB Hard Disk 1.2 MB Diskette DOS or Windows OS Multiplexor	Host computer receieves scanned data	$1,500.00 [a] $1,000.00	1 1	maintenance agreement diskettes	$1,500.00 $1,000.00
PC (or PC compatible) 80486 processor 4 MB RAM VGA monitor 1 Serial Port 1 Parallel Port 120 MB Hard Disk 1.2 MB Diskette DOS or Windows OS	Host computer receieves scanned data	$1,500.00 [a]	1	maintenance agreement diskettes	$1,500.00
Software PC-based (network compatible)	receives scanned data maintains database generates reports	$7,000.00	1		$7,000.00
Keyboard Wedges	decodes input to PC transmits data to PC	$400.00	2		$800.00
Fixed Data Entry Terminals	prompts user allows manual input	$1,200.00	3		$3,600.00
Light Pens	performs scanning	$150.00	5		$750.00
Printer Laser	prints labels generates reports	$1,000.00	1		$1,000.00
					$17,150.00

a Network cabling required.

simple.   Attention to the item label and bar code menu of possible appended messages should be your primary focus. Exhibit 11.10 presents a typical cost schedule for the file tracking system displayed in Exhibit 11.1. Costs for any individual system can vary, of course, due to local complexities. However, the greatest payback frequently comes from applying bar code to tracking along the simplest and most straightforward design path.

PUTTING IT ALL TOGETHER

The previous sections of this book presented material covering bar code labels and scanning technology, systems software and related components that connect scan terminals to a host, and a design approach for each of three bar code applications. Part Four will guide you through the steps you should take to develop and install your bar code system. It will also provide you with a directory of resources you can consult when putting together a bar code system.

Two recent developments related to bar code use are presented in the final chapter. Application Identifiers (AI) and data identifiers (DI) are rapidly emerging as bar code preambles to permit the system designer to express bar code information with less chance for misinterpretation. Electronic data interchange (EDI) permits extended users of common documents and material to process items and information more rapidly, using bar code as the linking mechanism. A thorough data collection system designer should examine Chapter 14 to see if the use of AIs and EDI should play a part in future bar code connections with trading partners.

Chapter 12

Planning and Implementing Your Design

A successful bar code program requires not only making the right hardware and software choices, but also careful involvement and integration with the people in the organization. This chapter outlines five stages of a bar code program. A key group, or bar code committee, should be chosen and involved throughout all stages of implementation to assure the best fitting and most smoothly integrated system. Many bar code systems have failed to live up to their potential because some of the stages of program development were missing or poorly performed.

ESTABLISHING A BAR CODE PROGRAM ■

Companies that incorporate bar code scanning in their operation frequently make one or both of two fundamental mistakes at the beginning of their program. The first common and avoidable error occurs when management sets unrealistic schedules for completion of the new system. In this case the designer does not have enough time to plan, design, and install the system, including vital user training. The second error occurs when the system designer fails to adequately explain to all organizational levels what the bar code system is expected to accomplish. What may follow as a result of these oversights is a lack of confidence in the new technology, in the management who have elected to install it, and often in the suppliers who provide the chosen components.

257

A bar code plan should encompass the development of a number of bar code projects. A project can be either interdepartmental, such as a warehouse inventory control system, or intradepartmental, such as a production tool tracking system.   Exhibit 12.1 is a diagram of a complete bar code planning effort.

Bar code systems usually can be rapidly cost-justified, even in the most efficient operating environments. The bar code advocate can set the stage for management acceptance by presenting case studies of similar organizations that have installed bar code control in related applications. Such success stories appear frequently in data collection magazines or vertical industry technical journals. General justification arguments include:

- Instant and continuous availability of operating data, with maximum value for management guidance.

- Significant reduction in paperwork quantity and time to prepare, producing large cost savings and increased efficiencies.

- Elimination of data entry errors and the multiple costs associated with operating on, and eventually correcting, misinformation.

- Reduction of tedious and costly data entry positions.

- Elimination of data verification delay and expense.

- Improved organizational image, in that bar code users are seen by their peers as progressive and efficient to deal with. Increasingly, suppliers that fail to bar code in their operations are eliminated from bidders' approval lists.

FIVE STAGES OF A SUCCESSFUL BAR CODE PROGRAM

The five distinct stages of bar code program development are planning, design, implementation, training, and upkeep (Exhibit 12.2).   Each stage should be thoroughly executed to assure complete bar code program success.

Exhibit 12.1

Bar Code Development Program

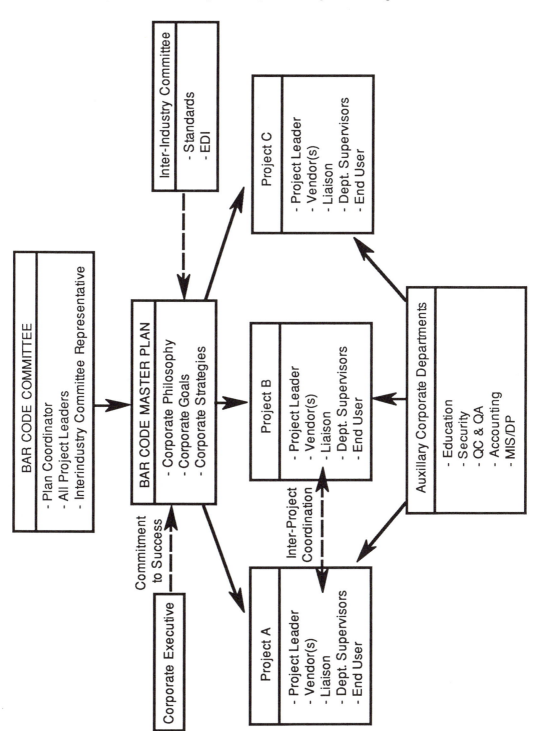

Exhibit 12.2

Five Stages of a
Bar Code Master Plan

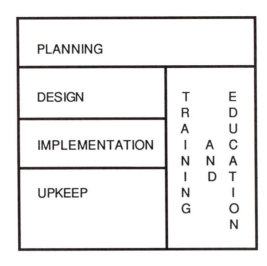

Stage 1: Planning

Once a decision has been made to incorporate bar code scanning into your operation, the planning process begins. The first step in this process is to appoint a bar code team. The team should represent all departments and every employee level that will have any contact with the program. While a system designer will play the lead role, department managers, supervisors, and other key user personnel will also have input. It may not be necessary to have a top executive as a regular member of this team, but it is important to communicate progress or obstacles regularly to this level. A comprehensive bar code program often requires examination of outdated or unworkable policies and procedures that stand in the way of system simplicity. Continuous executive involvement will go a long way toward solving these problems quickly if they arise.

The next step in the planning process is to agree, in writing, to an overall, long-range objective at the start of the bar code program. For example, "to apply bar code identity to each item manufactured" is not a proper program objective. An appropriate objective would be "to install a system that enables the corporation to keep timely and accurate records of all items manufactured, inventoried, and shipped." Here, continuous tracking of bar code labeled items is just one step in achieving the broad objective. When choosing your long-range objective, make sure it is farsighted and clearly consistent with essential good management practice for your industry. The least successful bar code projects are those that were chosen hurriedly in response to a temporary problem.

After a long-range objective has been agreed to, it is time to create a master plan for departmental bar code use. Each department of your operation that creates or uses repetitive data should be considered for a bar code project application. After a list of potential departmental projects has been assembled, prepare an estimate, including time, cost, and payback of each eligible project. Then prioritize the individual bar code projects according to the role each project plays in reaching the long-range objective. Only now can you prepare the schedules illustrated in Exhibit 12.3 and Exhibit 12.4.

Exhibit 12.3

Master Plan Cost Schedule

PROJECT	START DATE	TIME TO COMPLETE
Automatic Production Scan	July	4 Months
Pallet Bar Coding	September	4 Months
Distribution Shipping System	October	6 Months
Distribution Tracking	November	4 Months
Retail Tracking	Future	Unknown

Exhibit 12.4

Master Plan Time Schedule

PROJECT	COST	PAYBACK TIME
Automatic Production Scan	40000	12 Months
Pallet Bar Coding	36000	18 Months
Distribution Shipping System	68000	3 Months
Distribution Tracking	56000	36 Months
Retail Tracking	High $	Unknown

Note that although a distribution shipping system has the most attractive payback period, it would not be practical to implement that system first. Labels needed to verify shipping should be applied at the time the items are manufactured and packaged. Labels applied at this stage are then available for continuous tracking through manufacturing, finished goods inventory, and shipping. Also note from Exhibits 12.3 and 12.4 that not all projects need to be firmly scheduled at the beginning of your long-range bar code master plan. There are, sometimes, valid reasons for not specifying all project dates. However, it is usually possible to at least anticipate that a project will eventually be scheduled. If so, it deserves inclusion in your master plan.

Stage 2: Design

The design phase of a bar code program is the important second stage in making your system a reality. Before design can begin on each approved departmental bar code project, the existing data collection procedures must be critically reviewed and evaluated. This exercise will often tell you how much of the data presently collected in this project is useful, and what is not. It will also give your bar code team a chance to look for gaps in the data content which a bar code label could now fill. For example, a new bar code driven, open-stock hospital supplies system may now require that all items used and the related patient identification label be scanned and correlated for closer control. Previously, this combination of information was not practical to collect. In practice you cannot bring the patient out to the supplies cabinet each time an aspirin is removed, but you can have a continuously updated bar code list of patients from that floor on a menu and use a wand scanner to collect the combined data.

A valuable exercise in bar code project design is to create data flow diagrams. These diagrams should represent item movement with related data as well as forms and ticket flow. Current transaction volumes and cost of transactions should be calculated at this time. Exhibits 12.5 and 12.6 show simple examples of product flow and paper flow for an authorized material returns activity.

After the manual data collection system has been examined, you can write your project's functional specifications. Before you meet with potential vendors, you should have a first draft of this document; the draft should reflect the project coordinator's summary of the team's input and opinion on how to apply bar code to this application.

Exhibit 12.5

Product Flow Diagram

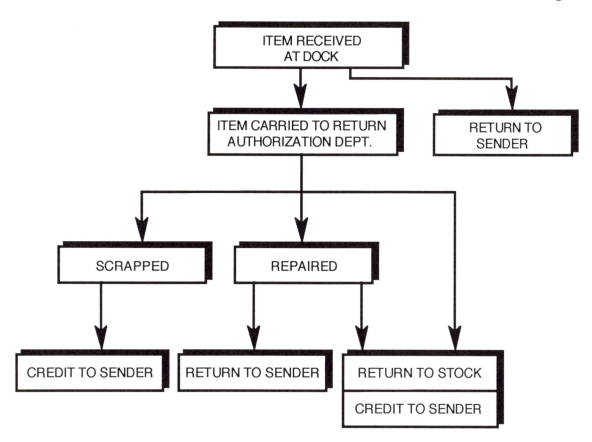

The next step is to invite two or three vendors to quote on each contract you intend to place. If you will be performing the systems integration in-house, then you will want to invite several companies that offer each of the major hardware and software components of the project to review the functional specifications and submit their quotation. If you intend to award an overall project contract to a systems integrator, you can deal directly with this vendor group and let it, in turn, deal with the component suppliers.

A period of two weeks is about appropriate for the vendor group to review the specification and submit quotes with alternative designs if it chooses. Make it clear that you respect the vendor's experience and solicit any suggestions for alternative approaches. Vendors have

Exhibit 12.6

Paper Flow Diagram

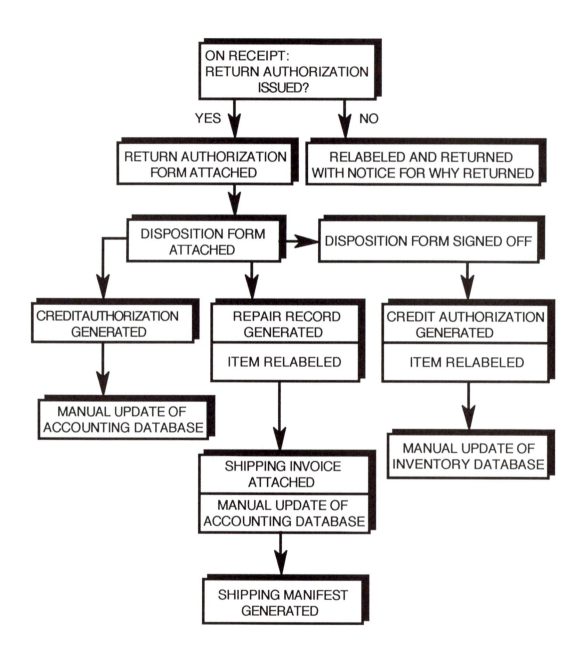

biases toward their corporate strengths and higher-profit components, but their advice can often be beneficial and lead to lower costs and smoother integration.

At this point it would be unusual for a clear picture of the best system and best supplier to emerge. More likely, your project team will see in the vendor responses a new and interesting solution path unfold which was not previously explored or perhaps not fully developed in earlier in-house discussions. Take your time and request a requote against newly modified specifications. It may even be desirable to repeat this cycle a third time. Remember, do not rush the project design stage of bar code data collection. Time spent here will be offset by the benefits of a superior system that will have a longer service life and be more easily integrated into existing operations.

NOTE:

If you have made a decision to purchase an "off the shelf" software package, now is the time to review each available package against your requirements. Remember, if you choose to use canned software, you must expect to make some modifications to your system design. However, you should not have to make major concessions to project functionality. If that seems to be the case, perhaps you should choose to investigate "customized" software.

If you have decided to develop your system in-house, all managers or supervisors who will be affected by the new system should participate in all cycles of the vendor review process.

After the functional specifications have been modified and matched to a selected vendor or vendors, the system design and equipment (SD&E) specification can be generated. If you have elected to use an outside systems integrator for your project, this vendor group will generate the SD&E document. Otherwise, it should be produced by your project team. The SD&E document should include the following information:

- Choice of symbology.
- Label design, including data message, human readable information, graphic enhancement, and label placement on item or form.

- Choice of printer, printer location, and special enclosure required, if any.
- Choice of scanning devices, including decoder and any terminal level prompt or validating programming required.
- Software design, including documentation standards.
- Report formats.
- Host computer hardware requirements, including multiplex or network controller.
- Cabling requirements.
- Test plan, at vendor's location (if appropriate)/ and on site.

The system or components delivery dates, acceptance criteria, warranty period, and postacceptance support policy should also be included in this document. Once the SD&E is completed and signed off with the vendor, a realistic schedule can be established, including a final bar code system startup date. This schedule should include a time allotment for installation, testing, and operator training.

Stage 3: Implementation

The implementation phase of a bar code project covers the time between approval of the design specification and the acceptance of the system from the vendor or the project team. If an "off the shelf" selection of equipment and software has been made for this project, you should complete the following steps:

1. Acquire labels ready to print on site or select an approved off-site vendor and product.
2. Wire, power, and test hardware installation.
3. Integrate and test computer hardware and software.
4. Simulate data collection and reports.

If you are implementing a "customized" system, the period following design approval becomes critical, whether you have chosen a systems integrator from outside, or your project team has played this role. Schedules must be reviewed and adjusted at regular weekly meetings, with all bar code team members participating. Progress reports and problem identification and resolution should be the focus of these sessions.

Periodic off-site testing of components and software at a vendor location may take place during this phase. The project team will have an opportunity to correct any misunderstanding regarding components and their interaction before the system is installed. The project team should select one of its members who has a knack for detail to conduct all tests following a plan prepared in advance and shared with the vendor.

Other constructive steps that can be taken during the software coding period to prepare for installation include the following:

1. Finalize all label and forms issues.

2. Be sure any PC or mainframe software development which may be needed to control item label serialization and data formatting has been assigned and accomplished.

3. Find out if special scanner mounting brackets have to be fabricated.

4. Examine the need for protective enclosures for printers and the host computer if they are going to be located outside the office environment.

5. Check data line capacity and quality, and upgrade to a higher standard if necessary.

Once your system has been delivered, assembled, and installed, final acceptance testing can begin. The system should be tested under the worst case data rates, although you may have to use some ingenuity to simulate this scenario. Many bar code data collection systems appear to work well under a light load but fail to perform adequately during normal or peak loads. System testers should try to make the system fail, and push transaction combinations through in unexpected and invalid ways to see the consequences. The purpose is not just to discover system shortcomings, but to prepare for the important on-line cut-over and to eliminate any unexpected problems at that time.

Testing should be done off-line, and then, for a short time, in parallel with the existing manual data system. If bugs are found, the testing procedure may have to be restarted from the beginning. After the bugs have been worked out and the system has passed final acceptance, all operations are switched over to the new system.

> **NOTE:**
> In the experience of the authors, some resistance to switchover is common among operating personnel. It may be that all bugs, or "unexpected results under certain conditions," may take a long time or cost a great deal to eliminate. A decision to use a bar code driven data collection system with some bugs remaining may make sense if the new system works better, even with the bugs, than the manual system it is replacing. If that time comes, go ahead and put your new system on-line.

Stage 4: Training

Of all the stages in a bar code program, training is the one most frequently neglected. Unfortunately, that neglect can burden your system with a significant loss of performance. Training should start before the system is installed. Department personnel in the bar code project and all others who may be affected by the new system should receive background information covering the bar code technology in general, why the system has been developed, and what the system will accomplish. After that, you should encourage the personnel involved to get acquainted with the bar code scanner hardware. There is no substitute for direct education here. You will gain immediate enthusiasm for the project and user support in the vital switchover process.

The training program should cover managers, supervisors, and operators, with written procedures identifying initial training responsibility and training of new employees in the future. Although the bar code vendor or systems integrator will provide some documentation, the project team should create a project-specific training document to guide users through their operating steps.

At intervals during the system test period, job training must be scheduled. This training might be combined with volume load simulations necessary for the thorough testing of system performance. At first, supervisors would work with each operating employee on a one-to-one basis. Later, an evaluation of procedures and retraining can take place if necessary. Trainers must be cautious not to make assumptions about the operator's prior knowledge and adaptability. Remember, except for bar code grocery applications, scanning is a new technology for almost everyone. Proper initial system training, with a continuing program of maintenance of operator skills, will result in the rapid integration of this technology throughout your operation. Everyone wants to work in a well-managed business, and bar code data collection is strong, visible evidence of good management.

Stage 5: Upkeep

As with any new system or procedure developed to satisfy a current requirement, your bar code data collection project will require periodic review and occasional upgrade. For some time after complex bar code systems have been accepted and put in use, certain combinations of activity may still produce a surprising result or even a system lockup. When this happens, it is critical for users to record clearly all activities and conditions just prior to the error incidence. If a log is maintained in this manner, an analyst will be better able to identify the problem and develop a quick cure.

When users are comfortable with their system, a follow-up meeting should be scheduled. Managers, supervisors, and operators can now critique the application and explore possibilities for even greater efficiency in modified use, or even system expansion. The best time to do this is about three months after start-up. Enthusiasm is usually quite high, application details are fresh in the minds of the project team, and software documentation is current.

NOTE:

If you've decided to go to an outside systems integrator as your vendor source, be sure to negotiate a software modification fee (per hour) at the time of the initial contract award. This should be a "not to exceed" figure that would prevail for 24 months after system acceptance.

The following are some other steps which you should take to assure consistent system operation:

- Establish a spares depot in-house. Unless you have a maintenance agreement which provides for substitute equipment while a defective component is out for vendor repair, it is necessary to have at least one back-up unit for each type of hardware component in your system. If your bar code system has a number of separate projects, you may be able to minimize back-up devices by sharing between departments. To estimate the need for spares, ask your vendors for their failure experience with equipment in an application like the one you are implementing. If they say their equipment never fails, get a new vendor.

- For some reason software documentation is particularly difficult to store and keep current, so it is important to maintain original and back-up copies of software and software updates in media form and hard copy. Keep other documentation, including hardware manuals, maintenance contracts, operator procedure manuals, and service call logs in a library established for this purpose. Only copies of this material should ever leave the library.

- Quality assurance testing of a bar code system includes periodic evaluation of the accuracy and completeness of collected data. Evaluate operators of scanning devices for proper procedures and techniques. Also, periodically review new employee training procedures. Finally, routinely test labels for readability, and check and verify label data. Whenever a bar code system exhibits unusual behavior, examine the label quality and content first!

■ SUMMARY

If you follow the five stages of bar code system development covered in this chapter, you will implement a successful and professionally satisfying program. If possible, start with a small and simple system. That experience will give your project team valuable insight into the process of bar code project management and help them to plan future projects with balanced emphasis and more realistic scheduling. Exhibit 12.7 is a time schedule for one project within the bar code plan. You can see from this schedule how a project which only takes four months to execute can span a year from initiation to wrap-up.

Exhibit 12.7 Project Time Schedule

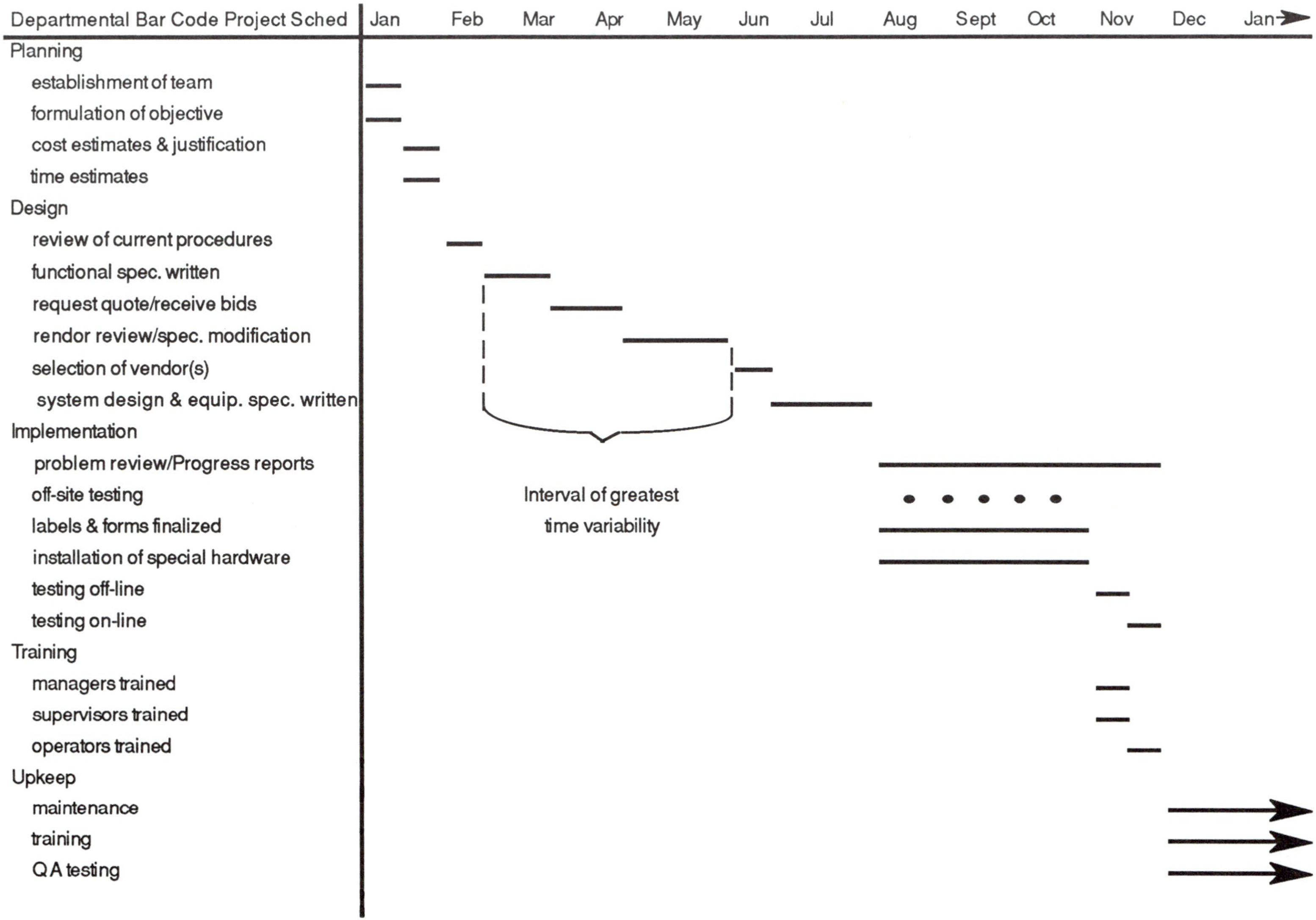

Chapter 13

Sources and Resources

The bar code industry has exploded in the past few years, and this trend shows no signs of slowing. The continual expansion of applications is healthy and brings benefits to businesses and organizations that can now move forward with new or expanded bar code data collection systems. The bar code supplier market has many players, and in a climate of predictable business expansion these suppliers are investing heavily in improved products and services. At the scanning terminal and printer level, equipment has become more powerful and "user friendly." Flexible software tailored to adapt to many applications is available from a number of experienced companies.

However, with rapid growth comes continual change, and this may create some confusion or apprehension among new or traditional users of bar code. Our intent in this book is to present this technology and its application in a clear and systematic manner for instruction and for reference. What we cannot do for you is give a single system design and component configuration to apply to all problems you will have to solve. Bar code technology is a flexible and adaptable science. While there is no wrong way to apply it, some design approaches will be more productive than others.

As you have seen in earlier chapters, bar code symbologies have to be chosen, and then labels and forms designed. After that, decisions must be reached concerning scanners and printers, host computers and communications networks, and software and reports. Finally, integration of departmental bar code applications has to take place with corporate mainframe computers. Expanded database contents must be woven into existing structures.

The purpose of Chapter 13 is to describe the sources of additional information that will allow a more detailed investigation into bar code technology. These sources are particularly important to explore if you are considering an interindustry application or bar code use between trading partners.

■ VENDOR CLASSIFICATIONS

In this section we provide descriptions of the different vendor classifications you will choose from, and their basic characteristics. Guidelines are offered which will help you choose one class of vendor instead of another for your component or system purchases. While there are exceptions to some of the points made below, the information will assist in helping you set realistic expectations.

Manufacturers

Manufacturers are the companies that actually design and produce scanner and printer components. For the most part, manufacturers concentrate on offering the marketplace increasingly modern and cost-effective hardware. Although the bar code supply community has no dominant manufacturer, several of the larger vendors are now beginning to capitalize on their emerging market strength by adding to their newer products added software value. User demand certainly exists for more equipment integration from manufacturers, and by maintaining a staff of application programmers some manufacturers provide this service, which profits both seller and buyer. For instance, while in this book we advise the development of portable bar code terminal prompt software by users in-house, many customers are reluctant to acquire that skill. Consequently, several fast-growing manufacturers have developed application programming teams located regionally for responsive customer application programming.

Other manufacturers that are faced with the need to develop software to tailor their products to customer requirements rely on regional value-added resellers (VARs) or local consulting software engineers. It is not easy to predict which arrangement will be most satisfying for you. Too much depends on the workload and skill of the individual who actually performs the program coding. The best approach to this issue of vendor selection is to examine vendor references.

When components are purchased directly from the manufacturer, you are assured that the seller has a complete knowledge of the product's capability. In addition, you'll find that most manufacturers offer comprehensive service agreements, provide expert warranty and repair service, and have the ability to deliver spares overnight in an emergency. If you will be purchasing large quantities of devices, you may be able to negotiate a better price when dealing with the manufacturer directly, and also influence design features of the product you've selected.

Dealing directly with the manufacturer is not always practical. Since more bar code component suppliers sell through distributors than directly to the customer, you may have to buy through this type of intermediary. Or, perhaps you're located in a section of the country not covered by a direct sales staff and the manufacturer cannot afford direct coverage for you. Such a situation should not really pose an impediment for your bar code project. In fact, working through a distributor of several product lines has its advantages.

Distributors

Distributors are sales organizations that purchase and stock equipment from manufacturers for local promotion and resale to the end users in their territory. In some rare cases they may represent a single bar code supplier. More frequently, they handle several compatible, or somewhat overlapping, product lines. The distributor, who may also perform installation and offer extended warranty agreements, usually performs some repair service. For serious repair or equipment upgrade support, the distributor usually returns your item to the factory.

The product knowledge that distributors have is not as comprehensive as the manufacturer's direct sales team due to the fact that distributors usually represent from five to fifteen manufacturers. This stretches their product knowhow beyond the breaking point at times. To work around this distributor shortcoming, you can call the factory and ask the technical support department any question you like. A smart distributor will stock a line of excellent products from a broad range of manufacturers and assemble working combinations of components that already have all the interface problems solved. If your bar code project is in the mainstream of applications for a user in your geographic area, it is likely that a local distributor has the various components and can at least offer you integrated hardware. Few distributors at this stage of the technology's development can offer much in the way of a sophisticated application software department that would be willing to take on complex software customizing. To add this skill you will have to seek a software consulting house, or perhaps explore the choice of a VAR who has seen your project at other companies and specializes in providing a packaged solution.

Value-Added Resellers (VARs)

VARS are vendors that have chosen to service a particular "niche" in business. They align themselves with one or several manufacturers of bar code equipment and develop the market for one or several focused applications, providing a turnkey solution for the customer. In some ways they are specialized systems integrators. VARs may offer canned or customized software packages, depending on the application and depth of their technical staff.

By concentrating on one application, sometimes within one geographic region, VARs can efficiently focus marketing and technical resources to quickly become a dominant and preferred supplier, providing at least one of your application solutions. The major drawback for you to consider is the possibility that the one "best fit" solution to your generic application, purchased from the VAR supplier you chose, may lead you down an architectural path not suited for integration with other bar code projects. Nonetheless, VAR suppliers are expanding rapidly in the bar code marketplace, and their efforts have frequently provided a vital link between component manufacturers and successful users.

Systems Integrators (SIs)

Systems integrators are broad-based application problem solvers. They should have the skill to take each of your bar code project plans and generate a system design and equipment (SD&E) specification, and then deliver a complete, documented, functioning solution at a fixed price. They must possess hardware, software, communications, and project management skills, and be able to translate those skills across a broad variety of available components and sources. Their profit derives from favorable purchasing terms with the supply community, and a fee from their customers for their expertise and integration services. A number of SIs, although not all, will write the vital software linking tailored applications with components, operating systems, and databases. Some SIs will contract the software to outside suppliers. A skilled systems integrator can be a valuable resource to you by accelerating your bar code implementation with minimum impact on your scarce in-house resources. Since some distributors, manufacturers, and VARs represent themselves as systems integrators, the Automatic Identification Manufacturers (AIM) have attempted to clear up any possible confusion by classifying SIs by three categories: applications served, services provided, and project size/capability.

Since there is a chronic shortage of systems integrators with broad skills, most companies serving as systems integrators specialize in one or two applications. They can serve as a valuable source of information when you are putting together the functional specification for a project. Their background should guide you in adding useful features that may have been overlooked by the project team, and prevent the specification from having serious design errors.

As bar code data collection systems grow in complexity and degree of integration with other business applications, they may become quite complex. It is our opinion that a qualified systems integrator is well worth any apparent premium charged above the cost of software and components alone. Avoiding missteps and saving time in bringing a project to prompt and successful completion are benefits that more than offset the fee. If there is any risk to using an SI on your projects, it is in gaining the necessary assurance that your choice is truly qualified.

There is no easy way to evaluate the qualifications of an SI. The customer must take some pains to distinguish between component integrators, software integrators, and true systems integrators. Companies that manufacture or distribute equipment have an understandable bias toward their own components. The true systems integrator should be willing to view your project objectively and choose broadly from available industry components to assemble the most responsive and effective system for you. We recommend that you thoroughly research qualifications before selecting a systems integrator. Local customer references may provide the single best source for referrals.

Summary of Vendor Classifications

Before making a final decision on project implementation and supplier choices, reflect on the following questions:

- What is your overall experience with bar code technology? Do you have the available skills on your staff to perform the systems integrator role?
- Will you need to modify your operating environment project objectives to use a vendor's proposed system?
- What is the proposed SI's or VAR's experience with similar applications? Contacting three previous customers will go a long way toward removing any doubts you may have about qualifications.

If your application is simple and straightforward, using an SI may complicate the program and raise costs unnecessarily. If your SI is not local, the interval between meetings will become awkward, and the cost to conduct meetings may become a burden over a lengthy contract.

■ TRADE ORGANIZATIONS

In the United States today hundreds of trade organizations offer assistance to retailers, manufacturers, hospitals, and many other identifiable affinity groups. These organizations sponsor trade shows and seminars, publish guidelines and specifications, and address the concerns and problems shared by members of a particular industry. The growth of bar code has caught the attention of many such associations. Within these associations, bar code committees or working groups have been created to smooth the path for their members to make productive use of this technology. We have grouped here a brief list of associations for your guidance, explaining their target audience and major application interest.

Automatic Identification Manufacturers (AIM)

AIM USA
634 Alpha Drive
Pittsburgh, Pennsylvania 15238
(412) 963-8588

AIM was founded in 1972 and is supported by manufacturers and suppliers of automatic identification products and services. Members include the principal vendors of bar code devices, but the association also includes strong representation from suppliers of voice recognition, RF data capture, optical character recognition, and magnetic stripe technology as well. AIM was first established as an American organization, AIM USA, but has since spread around the world; AIM International affiliates are in every major industrial trade zone.

AIM's mission is to increase awareness of the benefits of automatic identification technologies and provide reliable information on these data collection techniques. While the original focus of AIM education was the industrial manufacturing and distribution communities, AIM has lately provided valuable support to the growth of bar code within the retail environment. Together with VICS (Voluntary Interindustry Communications Standards), AIM sponsors a seminar called Quick Response for integrating bar code with EDI (electronic data interchange) to simplify and accelerate products flowing to retail markets. Another AIM activity is the sponsorship of the Teacher's Institute, which is designed to aid college instructors who are incorporating automatic identification technologies into their engineering curriculum. AIM also sponsors the Technical Symbology Committee, which addresses symbol quality and tolerances and is the source of symbology standards documents.

Uniform Code Council (UCC)

UCC
8163 Old Yankee Road, Suite J
Dayton, Ohio 45458
(513) 435-3870

The UCC is a nonprofit trade association formed from within the grocery industry to support the voluntary standard bar code we now know as UPC. While this symbol was first created to facilitate the use of automated checkstands in retail grocery stores in the United States, the popularity of retail bar code use has greatly expanded the scope of this organization. The UCC now administers the (VICS), Uniform Communications Standards (UCS), and VICS EDI.

The UCC is responsible for assigning UPC supplier or vendor numbers. The association also publishes numerous manuals for symbol specifications and their preferred location, and application guidelines. The UCC conducts other educational services as well. Exhibit 13.1 is the commonly recognized UCC logo.

Exhibit 13.1
Uniform Code Council Logo

UNIFORM CODE COUNCIL, INC.

8163 Old Yankee Road, Suite J
Dayton, Ohio 45458

(Courtesy of the Uniform Code Council, Inc.)

■ TRADE JOURNALS

In addition to services sponsored by trade organizations, information concerning automatic data collection can be obtained from a number of professional trade journals. Some of these address the general bar code and automatic identification industry, while others are published for vertical groups representing a particular trade or industry. These latter publications present bar code in the context of their readership's most important applications and principal benefits. Trade journals frequently list upcoming bar code seminars and trade shows for further guidance. They also announce new products and offer reader response cards which quickly provide you with direct supplier follow-up. Editorials offer insight and interpretation concerning future bar code technology trends. Overall, trade journals are the best continuing link to new developments in this field. There is, frequently, no subscription charge to qualified professionals.

Listed below are the better-known publications covering bar code components and applications, with an identification of the focus of each journal:

Automatic ID News
1 East 1st Street
Duluth, MN 55802
1-800-346-0085
(general)

ID Systems
174 Concord Street
PO Box 874
Peterborough, NH 03458
(603) 924-9631
(general)

Adams Chronicle
2101 Crystal Plaza, #203
Arlington, VA 22202
(703) 548-8261
(general)

Retail Information Systems
(RIS News)
One West Hanover Ave., #108
Randolph, NJ 07926
(201) 895-3300
(retail)

Managing Automation
5 Penn Plaza
New York, NY 10001
(212) 629-1511
(industrial)

Manufacturing Systems
191 S. Gary Avenue
Carol Stream, IL 60188
(708) 665-1000
(industrial)

Stores Automatic Identification
100 West 31st St.
New York, NY 10007
(212) 244-8780
(retail)

Scan Newsletter
11 Middle Neck Road
Great Neck, NY 11021
(516) 487-6370
(general)

Material Handling Engineering
1100 Superior Avenue
Cleveland, Ohio 44114
(216) 696-7000
(industrial)

Industrial Engineering
25 Technology Park / Atlanta
Norcross, GA 30092
(404) 449-0460
(industrial)

APICS Magazine
Lionheart Publishing
2555 Cumberland Parkway
#299
Atlanta, Georgia 30339
(404) 435-2849
(industrial)

Modern Materials Handling
Cahners Publishing
275 Washington Street
Newton, MA 02158
(303) 388-4511
(industrial)

■ TRADE SHOWS

Trade shows, or expositions, provide an excellent window into bar code technology for the newcomer to this field. For users who want to expand their knowledge, trade shows — and the seminars usually held in connection with them — provide a forum for discussion about bar code driven applications of interest described by experts or user peers who have been through the experience of implementing a bar code system.

Trade shows with significant bar code content are sponsored by a number of associations or agencies and are held throughout the year. There is a concerted attempt to move these shows around the country and involve the broadest cross section of potential new users. Some shows focus on automatic identification technology, in which bar code is predominant, while other shows focus on vertical user subjects of interest, such as health care. In these shows bar code represents a fraction of the seminar program and exhibit space.

If you have decided to implement bar code driven data collection in your operations, attending a trade show is another efficient way to get familiar with key issues and new developments. You can easily establish contact with component manufacturers, VARs, or systems integrators and at the same time collect initial vendor impressions and data sheets. For first-time users of bar code, trade shows offer a practical, inexpensive, and broad educational experience.

The following trade shows are those we consider the most important. Since each is held in a different city at a different time each year, it's not possible to list their schedules. However, that information, as well as the seminar program for the current year, can be obtained from the sponsor or from listings in the trade journals referenced in this chapter.

SCAN-TECH

SCAN-TECH is the earliest and one of the two largest automatic identification shows in the country. Sponsored by Reed Exhibitions, SCAN-TECH is traditionally held in the fall. Hundreds of manufacturers, VARs, distributors, and SIs exhibit their latest product offerings. Bar code scanners, printers, software packages, technical publications, media, and supporting services are on display. Alternative automatic identification technologies to bar code are well represented also, and overall exhibit area growth has averaged 20 percent from year to year.

In addition to the SCAN-TECH exhibits, seminars are presented over a three-day period. These seminars are divided into four learning tracks: case studies, specific applications, new technology, and an introductory course on bar code basics.

ID EXPO

ID EXPO is held in the spring, traditionally in Chicago, and is sponsored by Advanstar Expositions. Advanstar Communications publishes Automatic ID News magazine.

ID EXPO also runs seminars which feature lectures by acknowledged industry pioneers and leaders covering all fundamental subjects such as scanning, printing, or processing. In addition, about forty case studies or application surveys are presented over a three-day period. Seminars are scheduled to permit all attendees to spend adequate time on the exhibit floor.

AUTOFACT

AUTOFACT, sponsored by the Society of Manufacturing Engineers (SME), is a yearly conference promoting automated, integrated factories incorporating the use of bar code data entry devices as well as other automatic identification technologies. First held in 1977, AUTOFACT has grown to include over three hundred exhibitors and four days of useful seminars and conferences. The number of bar code suppliers exhibiting in this show, however, will be fewer than the number that exhibit in the SCAN-TECH and ID EXPO shows. A new addition to the show is the "Partnership for Integration" exhibit — a large-scale, working computer integrated manufacturing (CIM) demonstration which addresses topics of concern for both small and large manufacturers.

The stated mission of the Society of Manufacturing Engineers is to assist in developing the skills needed to meet the combined challenges of manufacturing engineering, design engineering, production control, assembly, network communications, and business finance. SME can be contacted for more information at: One SME Drive, PO Box 930,

Exhibit 13.2
AUTOFACT Logo

(AUTOFACT is a registered trademark of the Society of Manufacturing Engineers.)

Dearborn, MI 48121-0930 at (313) 271-1500. Exhibit 13.2 represents the AUTOFACT logo. The exact date and location changes each year.

Quick Response (QR)

Quick Response is co-sponsored by AIM USA and VICS. Initiated in 1988, this show presents in its seminar sessions case studies that show the multiple benefits for suppliers to retailing and retailers alike of using bar code and EDI together. The show started modestly and was staged in Dallas for its first three years. Plans for 1991 and future years call for varying its location. More than the other shows mentioned, QR has heavy user involvement and influence.

The quick response philosophy — that when linked, bar code and EDI are the technologies that provide access to QR — is preached and illustrated during this show. Better and faster collection and communication of business information produces more timely and accurate ordering. Retail sales are greater, inventories are smaller, and customer satisfaction is improved using the quick response strategy. The QR seminars cover the basic tools and implementation techniques, as well as successful applications. Although relatively new, this show has quickly gained prestige and is particularly useful for retail merchants and their suppliers.

TRADING PARTNER STANDARDS ■

Throughout this book frequent reference has been made to the growing need to be aware of industry bar code labeling standards. This section contains a partial list of significant trade groups or associations that are exerting a major influence on future voluntary or mandatory label standards.

Automotive Industry Action Group (AIAG)

AIAG
26200 Lasher Road, Suite 200
Southfield, Michigan 48034
(313) 358-3570

The AIAG is a not-for-profit trade association of the major North American vehicle manufacturers and their suppliers. They are organized to provide members with information and research updates and to coordinate standards and guidelines for improving manufacturing methods and practices.

The AIAG was one of the first organizations to realize the benefits of providing standardized bar-coded container labels among traditional trading partners. Due to its early advocacy of a standard vendor-to-manufacturer label, the AIAG has had a significant influence on other industry associations in this regard. The AIAG has also been an early champion of data identifiers.

Suppliers to the automotive industry are certainly aware of the bar code label standards they must meet on order shipment to this customer group. Exhibit 13.3 is an example of the AIAG standard case label. Newcomers to the automotive vendor ranks would be wise to obtain specifications for bar code use from AIAG, as well as EDI message standards.

Exhibit 13.3

AIAG Case Label

PART NO. (P)

2468097531

QUANTITY (Q)

168923

PURCHASE ORDER NO. (K)

PESP22058

SUPPLIER (V)

F1505C0

ENGINEERING CHANGE

002

DELIVERY LOCATION

T.L. ASHFORD & ASSOCIATES

525 W.5TH STREET

COVINGTON, KENTUCKY 41011

SERIAL (S)

00000030

DESIGNED & PRINTED USING T.L. ASHFORD SOFTWARE 1-800-541-4893

(Courtesy of T.L. Ashford & Associates)

American National Standards Institute (ANSI)

ANSI
11 West 42nd Street
New York, NY 10036
(212) 642-4900

ANSI is a not-for-profit organization charged with developing national standards covering a wide variety of technical disciplines. These standards are usually the result of a voluntary committee report. ANSI is a member of the International Organization for Standardization (ISO) and the International Electrotechnical Commission (IEC). Through these affiliations, ANSI has had a major influence on technical standards worldwide.

In 1980 the Material Handling Institute formed a committee to develop an ANSI standard for bar code symbols on unit loads and transport packages. Members of the committee were drawn from a wide field of representation, including users of bar code technology, carton manufacturers, printers, consultants, and bar code equipment manufacturers. The resulting document specified Code 39, I 2of5, and Codabar symbologies, as well as application standards. ANSI has continued to keep current on significant bar code innovations since that time. ANSI has also published documents specifying standard transaction sets for purchase orders, invoices, receiving, shipping, and a number of common business exchanges.

Health Industry Business Communications Council (HIBCC)

HIBCC
5110 N. 40th Street, Suite 250
Phoenix, Arizona 85018
(602) 381-1091

HIBCC was created in 1984 to develop bar code standards for use throughout the health care field. Later, the HIBCC charter was enlarged to include all practical automated business communications systems for health care. HIBCC bar code label recommendations influence hospitals and other health care facilities, as well as manufacturers and distributors of health care products and pharmaceuticals.

HIBCC provides a forum for education and discussion of bar code and other automation technologies that might prove useful in providing accuracy and efficiency within the health care delivery system. HIBCC has standards which support codes 128 and 39, as well as UPC in certain applications. Currently, HIBCC is studying codes 16K and 49 for possible use on unit dose labels.

Uniform Code Council (UCC)

UCC
8163 Old Yankee Road, Suite J
Dayton, Ohio 45458
(513) 435-3870

The UCC was established as the central management and information center for producers and retailers that are influenced by point-of-sale bar code labels using UPC symbology. As stated earlier in this book, the Uniform Code Council has set up strict label standards for the retail and grocery industries. The UPC symbology has been chosen for unit labels and coupons. Code I 2of5 and Code 128 play a role in identifying containers of retail-directed products. UCC also publishes guidelines on bar code and EDI applications and on label location.

Recently, UCC has led the way in promoting standards for EDI and DSD. UCS (Uniform Communication Standard) is the EDI standard used within the grocery industry and other general merchandise sectors. While UCS was initiated by the grocery industry, it has now been adopted by hundreds of companies, including manufacturers, retailers, wholesalers, and brokers. It is spreading to the food service, mass merchandising, wholesale drug, and service merchandising industries. Other UCC influences extend to UCS/DSD-developed message standards to exchange delivery information between the DSD supplier and the retailer, and the UCS/WINS (Warehouse Information Network Standard) message format and the communications standards to be used when communicating directly to a warehouse.

U.S. Government

LOGMARS COORDINATING GROUP (DOD)
Director AMCPSCC
Attn: SDSTO-TA
Tobyhanna, Pennsylvania 18466-5097
(717) 894-7146

The LOGMARS Program (Logistics Applications of Automated Marking & Reading Symbols), established in 1976, is charged with coordinating the use of bar code over all Department of Defense (DOD) applications. These include shipping, receiving, inventory, quality assurance, self-service retail, and asset management.

The DOD specified Code 39 as the principal bar code symbology to be used in all military data transactions. LOGMARS has developed military standards for bar code labels used with items such as ammunition, shipping containers, packing lists, and property tags. All labels must be generated within the exact tolerances specified by LOGMARS. Standards have also been set concerning the adhesive used on pressure-sensitive labels.

SUMMARY ■

Chapter 13 has provided a description of four vendor classifications, as well as a partial explanation and list of resources that are available as you go forward with bar code in your workplace. Perhaps with this book for reference and a subscription to a trade journal, you will have the confidence and perspective needed to implement a long-term bar code driven program. On the other hand, you may want to attend a trade show or two to keep your product familiarity up to date without depending on a single vendor to educate you.

If your business falls under the influence of one of the many trade associations that are encouraging the placement of a bar code label on shipping containers, you can turn to the organizations listed above for more specific details. Of course, the list of organizations developing trading partner standards is constantly growing and currently numbers nearly thirty. We have highlighted only five.

As your bar code program progresses, keep looking outside your organization to your trading partners to see how their requirements will influence your bar code activity. Then cooperate willingly. Remember, bar code data exchange is just as valuable between your business and the outside world as it is between the departments in your company.

Chapter 14

Electronic Data Interchange, Data Identifiers, and Radio Frequency Identification

Electronic data interchange (EDI) is the practice of providing routine business transactions over standard communication lines between computers within a company, or from your computer to a trading partner's computer. To make this practical, EDI messages must adhere to strict structure and content format rules. For maximum industry usefulness of EDI, companies should share the same format rules for similar transactions.

EDI has rapidly become a companion technology to bar code in the interindustry use of automatic data collection. EDI accelerates routine message exchanges between companies where it has been installed. More important, it eliminates keystroke errors and expense, since EDI messages flow from one computer to another over standard communication lines under error detection and correction control.

Although you can implement a bar code system without using EDI, many companies that have already put bar code systems in place are now looking at the combination of bar code and EDI to gain new advantages in efficiency. The Automatic Identification Manufacturers (AIM) has stated that "the full benefits of EDI cannot be realized without bar coding." This chapter explores the benefits of these two technologies when used in partnership.

Application Identifiers (AIs) and data identifiers (DIs) are message prefixes incorporated in bar code that assist in data verification and permit a certain degree of local data editing, usually without reference to a database. DIs have been used in bar code labels for a number of years without consideration of outside, or trading partner, applications. Now, standards committees are beginning to encourage trade association membership to use DIs and AIs in interindustry labels. The UCC has published the UCC/EAN Code-128 Application Identifier Standard, which has applicability to intra- and interindustry transfers of goods and information on a global scale. This chapter presents the benefits of the proper use of data identifiers.

Radio Frequency Identification (RF/ID) is also discussed in this chapter. A proven, reliable technology, RF/ID is preferred for applications where the use of bar code, magnetic stripe, optical character recognition, or traditional identification has limitations. The key to a successful RF/ID application is designing a solution that meets data collection requirements at minimum cost and within the tolerances of the product chosen. Although sophisticated RF/ID tools are already available, refinements in the existing technology and expansion of appropriate applications will continue.

■ ELECTRONIC DATA INTERCHANGE

Although using EDI in conjunction with bar code systems is a fairly recent development, the practice of EDI began almost twenty years ago. Initially, EDI was utilized inside a company. For example, data that was key entered in the order entry department was electronically transferred to the shipping and accounting departments. When bar code applications started to become widespread, it made sense to link these two technologies.

EDI takes data automation a step further. Bar code based systems capture a large number of short data messages and build accurate databases quickly, while EDI eliminates time, costs, and inaccuracies in transferring documents between users. Combining EDI and bar code based applications often enables a company to process its business continuously, based on current and accurate data. Among the first industries to adopt EDI were the automotive, textile, and general merchandise industries. Faced with pressing foreign competition, they turned to EDI to reduce the normal order fulfillment cycle and lower inventory expense. A big boost to the general acceptance of EDI is the recent government initiative into EDI. The General Services Administration, the Department of Defense, and major retail chains have developed several milestone EDI projects.

Since EDI is the exchange of formatted business data, it is influenced by software at several levels. EDI software can be viewed as having three principal components:

- Application link software performs a translation of an existing application data file into a predefined, fixed-length, formatted data file.

- Translation software takes these formatted files and converts the information in them to a standard format. Headers and trailers for control and data identification are appended. The applicable standard specifies several transaction types, each with its own unique identifier. Each standard also has its own data element dictionary, which defines the type of data element and the minimum and maximum length of the element. Data elements must appear in segments in a particular order. ANSI X.12 is an example of an EDI standard.

- Communication software establishes the link between the computers and detects transmission success or failure. IBM's *3780 Bisynchronous Protocol* is an example of this type of component.

Of course, both partners to an EDI transaction must have a shared communication carrier between them. Public networks frequently provide this capability. Popular services include McDonnell Douglas's *EDI*NET*, Sterling Software's *ORDERNET*, Control Data Corporation's *REDINET*, and IBM's *Information Network*.

Electronic data interchange practices are still evolving, and the benefit to each party in an EDI transaction set will vary with the degree of user experience and supporting data automation on each side. Overall, though, the benefits of EDI fall into the following categories:

- Improved order-entry procedures through elimination of key entry and related data errors. The actual data transfer is fast, accurate, and predictable.

- Reduced personnel role in routine document processing. The steps of forms generation and handling, copying, filing, and mailing are reduced or eliminated.

- Process cycle periods are shortened. Purchase orders can be placed weekly rather than monthly, as an example.

- Closer relationships are established with critical partners using EDI. If new sources or destinations for material or end products are required on either side of a partnership, EDI can easily adapt. You are not dependent on new personnel hiring and training as business relationships expand.

- Audit trails and activity reports are readily available with EDI software. Details can be stripped from your standard transaction files for summary reporting, or for reanalyzing material usage or cash flow.

Companies that wish to use EDI should start off gradually, and in conformity with a standard transaction set promoted by the industry or trade association, if possible. The selection sequence for initiating EDI may be chosen from within the operation as a result of a carefully thought-out cost-benefit analysis. Or, a company may find itself scrambling to install EDI to retain a major customer. Either way, the following guidelines are important if you are considering EDI:

- Automate your material or product handling and tracking using bar code.

- Use EDI to control transactions involving high-volume items first.

- Establish EDI links between suppliers and customers with whom your company has had a stable relationship.

- Limit early EDI transactions to straightforward buyer/seller, and material management stages of supply.

- Do not link your EDI transactions automatically to your company's internal data processing system. Data should be passed to and from EDI software and communications network via independent files.

Intracompany EDI can be implemented more easily than intercompany transactions. Once the format of the transaction files has been agreed to and controlling software obtained, you only need a data to begin. Looking at EDI applications within your company, the following examples let you pass along valuable files internally without a highly structured information architecture:

- Purchase order details can be shared through EDI with order entry and order processing departments, the accounting department, and sales management, to update sales reporting and trend analysis.

- Customer information and product requests can be forwarded to your distribution warehouse.
- Stock reorder information can be sent to the purchasing department for generation of replenishment orders.

Exhibit 14.1 presents an example of EDI within a large intracompany organization.

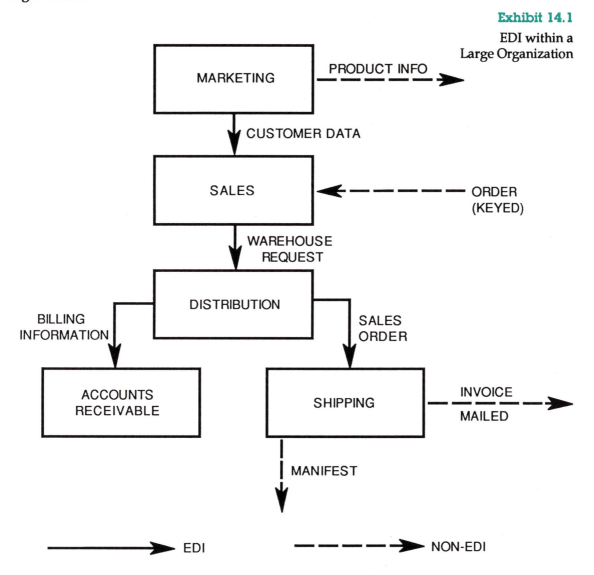

Exhibit 14.1

EDI within a
Large Organization

Exhibit 14.2
EDI with Trading Partners

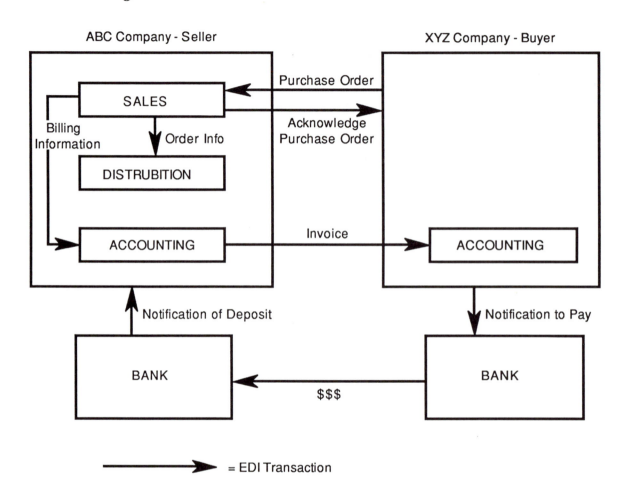

Intercompany EDI is far more complex, and its success depends on adherence to strict format and procedures. Exhibit 14.2 illustrates such an application. Since the more interesting and rewarding bar code related EDI applications are between trading partners, or interindustry in nature, this chapter will devote more attention to this emerging use.

EDI Standards

Most interindustry EDI development in the United States today is evolving around the standard known as ANSI X.12. While there are

EDI applications outside this specification, the list of X.12 advocates is impressive and includes these industries:

- Automobile industry via AIAG
- Retail industry via VICS
- Electrical industry via EDX
- Chemical industry via CIDX
- Electronics industry via EIDX
- Office products industry via ICOPS

In addition to the X.12 standard and its subsets, some EDI standards have been developed to support specific transaction types, regardless of the industry affiliation. UCS/WINS (Uniform Communication Standard/Warehouse Information Network Standard) is a standard developed to coordinate the grocery merchant and supporting distribution center. WINS is gradually merging its standards with the ANSI standards, defining a subset of transactions for use by warehouses nationwide, regardless of the industry. TDCC (Transportation Data Coordinating Committee) is the predominant EDI standard which supports transportation functions between shippers and their motor, rail, ocean, and air transportation carriers. ANSI X.9 is the standard which defines many transactions for banking and similar financial institutions.

NOTE:

The ANSI X.12 dictionary and other materials are available from the following sources:

Data Interchange Standards Association
1800 Diagonal Road, #355
Alexandria, VA 22314

(703) 548-7005

Transportation Data Coordinating Committee
TDCC
1800 Diagonal Road
Suite 280
Alexandria, VA 22314

(703) 838-8042

Exhibit 14.3

ANSI X.12 EDI
Transactions

812	Credit/Debit Adjustment
820	Remittance Advice
846	Inventory/Inquiry Advice
852	Product Activity Data
855	Purchase Order Acknowledgement
856	Ship Notice/Manifest
875	Purchase Order
876	Purchase Order Change
880	Invoice
882	Statement
885	Receiving Advice
893	Item Information Request
896	Product Dimension Change
994	Administrative Message

EDIFACT is an international standard that supports electronic trade transactions across national boundaries. Transaction sets are defined for administration, commerce, and trade. Exhibit 14.3 represents a partial list of EDI transactions common to many industry groups.

Although EDI transaction standards have been developed for many industries, a number of companies have developed proprietary transaction standards and are reluctant to move from them. To continue to trade with such a partner, you may have to conform to their transactions. Sometimes you may find yourself in an awkward and costly administrative crossfire of incompatible electronic data interchange standards. Since widespread adoption of EDI across many transactions is still some time off, it might not be too late to convene a group of organizations in a similar bind and establish a consensus to avoid duplication.

Many companies are supplying customers or purchasing from sources across several industry boundaries. The time may come when a substantial level of preprocessing will be needed to tailor and prepare for EDI document exchange, due to varying standards which are in conflict. This situation would be unfortunate, in that it would add new cost and delay to a process that has a simple foundation. Even so, EDI is here to stay and represents a progressive step in data automation.

> **NOTE:**
> EDI is still in the early stages of application. Currently, most EDI transactions are one-way transmissions which simply replace paper forms. In the future, sharing of all trading partner information must be conducted in both directions. This would require a realtime connection between the application programs running on each of the partner company's computers.

EDI Systems

Companies that choose to implement EDI have three possible paths to follow. They can develop EDI translation software in-house, purchase a complete EDI system from an outside vendor, or subscribe to a third-party service. The direction a company opts for should be based on the company's level of expertise with its computer systems, the availability of human resources, and the time and budget allotted for the implementation of EDI. The most efficient EDI implementation usually contains the fewest components, with the translation and communications software installed on the same computer as the application program.

In-House EDI Software Development

If you decide to write EDI software with your own programming staff, take care to follow the industry standard explicitly. Monitor new developments and changes in the standard closely and integrate these changes into the software as they evolve. You must plan on making a long-term commitment to provide resources for planning, implementation, and administering the EDI system. Corporations that are planning to write their own EDI soft-ware would also profit from joining the EDI standards committee representing their industry. FACT will assist any industry in establishing an appropriate EDI standard.

EDI Software Suppliers

Most companies do not have the technical expertise or the resources to implement an EDI system independently. Several software vendors have developed comprehensive EDI software packages to fill this void. These systems are designed to run on PCs as well as on IBM and DEC mini- and mainframe computers. The software is frequently menu driven and should provide translation to and from all the current standards. Other features that are sometimes provided in these programs include the following:

- Support of bisynchronous and asynchronous communications.
- Back-up and recovery of transmitted data.
- Various levels of security, including password control access and data encryption.
- Flat file interface for integration with other application software.
- Automatic, unattended data transmission.
- Standard and custom report generation. These reports can be set to run automatically or on demand.
- Audit trail of all incoming and outgoing transactions, with time and date stamps.
- Realtime and batch (mailbox) data transmission.
- Application link utility providing a code generator that will allow EDI data to be inserted into user application software.

When choosing a software vendor, it is important to examine the vendor's ability to support new EDI standards, should you ever be required to adopt one. Since EDI is a relatively young practice for many industries, there is almost certain to be a period of evolution and modification ahead. Your vendor of choice should have the software engineering staff to track developments in this field and continually provide contemporary products. Then, too, you may have a need to call on your vendor for some custom-tailored feature beyond the scope of the standard product. Finally, make sure the vendor will be available to advise and support installation and help you troubleshoot any initial transaction difficulties.

Third-Party EDI Service Providers

As the benefits of EDI use become better known and as industry standards develop or change more gradually, some vendors are beginning to offer turnkey EDI services. These suppliers provide their customers with communications connectivity, application translation for popular EDI standards, and even attractive service features such as toll-free 800 access and the efficiency of a packet switch network. These suppliers also assume the following responsibilities:

- Provide all communications refinements such as line speed matching and conversion protocol matching (asynchronous, bisynchronous). They will even connect you with destination companies that are not among their customers.

- Maintain security and verification of data transmissions, including reports that cover all activity, with time and date detail provided.

- Assure full data back-up and recovery during EDI transactions.

- Supply all hardware and software needed to complete your EDI transactions with your third-party provider.

Optional features that third-party service providers sometimes offer include the following:

- *Media conversion.* Here your supplier provides a back-up document from your electronic data files. This service is particularly useful to companies that are required to support both EDI- and non-EDI-based trading partners.

- *Standards translation.* This feature refers to the translation of data received under one EDI standards format into another EDI format.

- *Database services.* Transferred EDI data will be stored and made available to you in your provider's database for secondary applications such as market research information or sales management detail.

- *Consulting services.* Your provider should help you evaluate the benefits and costs of implementing EDI. This feature would require developing an implementation plan specifying hardware and software required to complete your EDI links. You may even choose to have this vendor play the intermediary role with the EDI experts at your trading partners' headquarters.

Before making your final decision regarding EDI implementation, you should consider that with a third-party service provider you can avoid the transaction processing and communications overhead that may overload your current computer system or limit its responsiveness during peak transaction periods. This path also represents a lower investment initiation into EDI than does a full in-house effort. Also, you will have gone down a reversible path. A self-developed system in the future, when detailed cost-benefits are known, is still possible. While it is true that a third-party provider profits from your transaction business, that does not mean that your costs are higher than if you did this task yourself. Bundled communications providers sometimes bring such economies of scale into communications services that the casual user may face significantly higher costs when buying unbundled pieces of data transmission capacity.

The Future of EDI

As corporations become more familiar with EDI and are more comfortable with its capabilities, they are beginning to look for more sophisticated and powerful EDI software. One new feature which is gaining popularity is data mapping. Inbound and outbound data is "mapped" from the applications database to the EDI standard without extensive manual intervention. Some software programs have the ability to map a single user file to several different transaction sets. Through data mapping you can eliminate the application link portion of EDI software.

Another modern service that is gaining popularity is the conversion of EDI data transmissions into several media, including E-mail, fax, and document form. This option is appealing when your trading partners are divided between EDI and non-EDI procedures.

Certain legal and auditing issues are still not fully resolved. A number of standards committees are focusing on these, including TDCC-EDIA and ANSI X.12. EDI software vendors are sensitive to certain risks and are providing extensive multilevel security, detailed audit trails, data back-up and recovery, transmission verification using error-detecting protocols, and data validation. Some vendors even offer data encryption. The specter of filling a large order received via EDI from a nonexistent customer is no greater than if the order had arrived in the mail, misaddressed to you. Moreover, once data security has been put in place within EDI software, that software will function exactly the same way for years or decades, examining each transaction in detail. The same cannot always be said about human clerks assigned a similar function within a paper-based system.

EDI has proved to be a durable and effective means of automating the exchange of structured messages among trading partners. Increasingly, these same trading groups are using bar code to identify their material shipments with container labels using formatted information, often including an EDI message serial number. A receiving clerk can thus scan an arriving shipment label and call up the shipment detail from a supporting computer where the EDI shipment detail has been waiting. This combination of EDI and bar code is certainly where the future lies for a large segment of the business and commercial community. You should be cautious and methodical in your implementation plans for programs incorporating these technologies, however. First establish a bar code program master plan and successfully implement one or two basic projects such as inventory control or POS scanning. Then bring EDI on-line with a basic transaction, such as purchase orders, first. Now you should be ready to correlate bar code and EDI through a project such as advanced shipment notification, where an EDI message is sent to each major customer as a by-product of a bar code driven shipping verification project. Regardless of how your company chooses to implement EDI, success will be dependent on the level of commitment to this project, and the ability of your company to accept technological change.

DATA IDENTIFIERS ■

A data identifier (DI) is one or several characters connected to a bar code message intended to classify the bar code message by category or use. In other words, DIs identify the "type" of data you are scanning. Examples of data types include measurements, quantities, transport carriers, container types, dates, locations, and personnel identification. DIs can, in principle, be used with all bar code symbologies as well as other forms of automatic identification technology, such as radio frequency identification (RF/ID). DIs may prove to be particularly useful in the new stacked symbologies such as Code 16K and Code 49, which permit rather generous message capacity.

If you are designing a bar code program for use solely inside your organization, you may decide that a data identifier character would strengthen the ability to perform terminal-based message editing. In this case no reference to outside standards is necessary. Label design is entirely an internal organizational decision, and data identifiers should be as simple and straightforward as possible.

UCC Application Identifiers

If you are considering using bar code in interindustry material or forms exchange, you will probably adopt some type of standard label. In that case, you should explore the use of Application Identifiers. Step one should be to contact the UCC. The new UCC/EAN-128 symbology with AIs was introduced in Chapter 2. This symbology has been adopted because manufacturers, suppliers, and distributors from a wide range of industries were expressing frustration with existing standards for shipping container labeling. Industry leaders were interested in coding additional information such as ship-to location, sell-by date, production date, and lot number, to name a few. They felt the addition of these fields would greatly enhance the value of the label — a label which would serve many purposes while further enhancing the value of EDI. Information required for a particular operation would be extracted during scanning at various points.

In response to this input, the UCC performed an extensive survey of companies and trade associations to determine their data requirements. The result is 46 Application Identifiers which have been defined and approved by the UCC/EAN. Exhibit 14.4 is the current list of Application Identifiers and their formats as defined by the UCC/EAN. Each prefix precisely defines the data. Note the existence of identifiers to be used for internal applications as well as AI 99, which can be used for any data types not included in the list. The most commonly used AIs are two digits, whereas less widely used AIs are four digits. AIs are numeric, which enables maximum use of the double dense version of Code 128.

When trading partners adopt the UCC/EAN-128 AI data formats, all parties have a common understanding of the data content, field length, and numeric or alpha-numeric makeup of the codes in the bar code string. Trading groups have chosen subsets of the total list of AIs as standards for their industry. For example, the meat, poultry, and turkey industries have selected manufacturer and product identifiers as follows: weight, production, sell-by or expiration date, and serial number. All this information is concatenated into a single bar code. The UCC/EAN-128 format is predicted to be the dominant shipping container labeling standard for the next ten years.

UCC/EAN Application Identifiers

00	Serial Shipping Container Code...	n2+n1?
01	Shipping Container Code...	n2+n14
10	Batch or Lot Number..	n2+an..20
11(*)	Production Date (YYMMDD)...	n2+n6
13(*)	Packaging Date (YYMMDD)...	n2+n6
15(*)	Sell BY Date (Quality) (YYMMDD)..	n2+n6
17(*)	Expiration Date (Safety) (YYMMDD)...	n2+n6
20	Product Variant..	n2+n2
21	Serial Number..	n2+an..20
22	HIBCC - Quality, Date, Batch and Link......................................	2n+an..29
23(**)	Lot Number (Transitional Use)..	n3+n..19
30	Quantity...	n2+n..8
310(***)	Net Weight, Kilograms..	n4+n6
311(***)	Length or 1st Dimension, Meters..	n4+n6
312(***)	Width, Diameter or 2nd Dimension, Meters................................	n4+n6
313(***)	Depth, Thickness, Height or 3rd Dimension, Meters...................	n4+n6
314(***)	Area, Square Meters..	n4+n6
315(***)	Volume, Liters..	n4+n6
316(***)	Volume, Cubic Meters..	n4+n6
320(***)	Net Weight, Pounds...	n4+n6
330(***)	Gross Weight-Kilograms..	n4+n6
331(**)	Lengh or 1st Dimension, Logistics...	n4+n6
332(***)	Width, Diameter or 2nd Dimension, Logistics.............................	n4+n6
333(***)	Depth, Thickness, Height or 3rd Dimension, Meters, Logistics......	n4+n6
334(***)	Area, Square Meters, Logistics..	n4+n6
335(***)	Gross Volume, Liters, Logistics...	n4+n6
336(***)	Gross Volume, Cubic Meters, Logistics.....................................	n4+n6
340(***)	Gross Weight, Pounds...	n4+n6
400	Customer's Purchase Order Number..	n3+an..30
410	Ship To (Deliver To) Location Code Using EAN-13......................	n3+n13
	or DUNS (Dun & Bradstreet) Number using Leading Zeros	
411	Bill to (Invoice To) Location Code Using EAN-13.......................	n3+n13
	or DUNS (Dun & Bradstreet) Number using Leading Zeros	
412	Purchase From (Location Code of Party from Whom Good are Purchased........	n3+13
420	Ship To (Deliver To) Postal Code Within a Single Postal Authority.....................	n3+an..9
421	Ship To (Deliver To) Postal Code With 3-Digit ISO Country Code Prefix.............	n3+n3+an..9
8001	Roll Products - Width, Length, Core Diameter, Direction and Splices.................	n4+n14
8002	Electronic Serial Nubmer for Cellular Mobile Telephones.................................	n4+an..20
90	Mutually Agreed, Between Trading Partners...............................	n2+an..30
91	Internal - Raw Material, Packaging, Components........................	n2+an..30
92	Internal - Raw Material, Packaging, Components........................	n2+an..30
93	Internal - Manufacturers..	n2+an..30
94	Internal - Manufacturers..	n2+an..30
95	Internal - Carriers..	n2+an..30
96	Internal - Carriers..	n2+an..30
97	Internal - Wholesalers..	n2+an..30
98	Internal - Retailers...	n2+an..30
99	Mutually Defined Text...	n2+an..30

(*)   : To indicate only year and month, DD must be filled with "00"
(**)   : Plus one digit for length indication
(***) : Plus one digit for decimal point indication

Data Value Representation:

a	alphabetic characters	n	numeric characters
an	alpha-numeric characters	a3	3 alphabetic characters, fixed length
n3	3 numeric characters, fixed length	an3	3 alpha-numeric characters, fixed lenght
a..3	up to 3 alphabetic characters	n..3	up to 3 numeric characters
		an..3	up to 3 alpha-numeric characters

FACT and DI

FACT (Federation of Automated Coding Technologies) has also defined an extensive list of data identifiers. This bureau has provided much guidance in defining data categories and in assisting industry groups to establish standards. FACT also has a working group responsible for creating new categories and assigning the actual data identifier.

Why Use Data Identifiers?

The obvious use of data identifiers is to avoid the possibility of message confusion which could result when a bar code is scanned out of sequence in data collection. DIs give the host processor in a bar code system the ability to recognize each data field individually. This feature is especially useful when several bar codes within a label have the same length and format. Even when there is human readable information repeated with each bar code, there is a risk that an operator may scan the wrong bar code or scan a sequence of bar codes in the wrong order. Since this type of data entry error must be avoided, data identifiers have proved useful for message validation in connection with host computer processing.

Implementing DIs does have some drawbacks, however. The length of the bar code label, for example, must be increased to accommodate the identifier. If the data collected at the scan terminal is not validated until it reaches a host computer, then the data network is further burdened with overhead traffic. At this point the message can have the DIs stripped for efficiency, but the system designer must be consistent in this practice.

At present the use of DIs is minor in relationship to existing bar code applications. There are, however, influential bar code users who would like to broaden the base of this practice quickly. The following alternative approaches to using data identifiers are available to add dependability to data collection using bar code:

- Standardize your label formats and use a different message length or format for each bar-coded line of data. Validation tests will screen for message integrity.
- If message length or format cannot be varied, apply tests to the record collected to screen out illogical data, such as "quantity that makes no sense" or "invalid destination code."

- Use standardized label formats such as the AIAG case label. Each field is specifically defined as to location and content.
- Use well-designed labels and software. Labels can be designed using graphics and human readable text, which will eliminate all confusion.

As the use of UCC/EAN-128 Application Identifiers becomes more widespread, you may soon be required to incorporate these labeling standards within your business to satisfy customers. As a supplier, you will reap benefits from your bar code labels, also, through the product detail provided by AIs.

Radio Frequency Identification (RF/ID)

Radio Frequency Identification can be used in place of bar codes when a data collection application has no predictable line-of-sight between the scanner and the data label, or tag, or if the object lacks a surface suitable for traditional bar code labels. Possible situations might include the following:

- The environment is dirty, which would cause a bar code label to become unreadable.
- The environment is too hot for bar code labels. RF tags can be exposed to temperatures up to 200 degrees C (392 degrees F).
- Items that cannot be practically labeled — livestock, trees, and recycled pallets, for example.
- Items which cannot be placed in a scanner's "line-of-sight" or at a predictable depth of field.
- When security is a concern. Unlike bar code, RF tags are very difficult to counterfeit, and because of the proprietary nature of RF/ID systems, tags cannot be read by any transponder other than the original manufacturer's.

Applications ideally suited for the RF/ID include:
- Traffic management
- Production control
- Automatic vehicle tracking and anti-theft devices
- Copyright protection of videotapes, and software
- Laboratory tracking of samples and research animals
- Wildlife tracking of zoo animals, migration, and breeding

Exhibit 14.5

Auto Security System
Using RF/ID

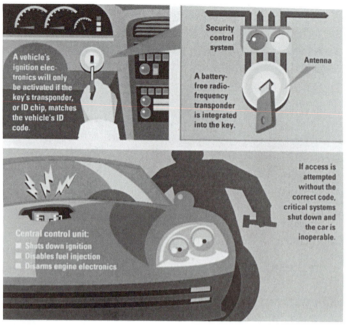

(Courtesy of Texas Instruments)

- Livestock control
- Shipping container tracking of pallets, totes, baggage, etc.
- Physical asset management

All RF/ID systems have essential hardware components: a transponder or tag with an RF receiver; an antenna or coil, with or without a decoder; and a transceiver or sender-receiver. Exhibit 14.5 illustrates an RF/ID application.

■ SUMMARY

EDI and DI are automatic data collection refinements that support bar code data collection and can carry bar code applications to a higher level of efficiency. There is continuing activity within industry standards committees on the status of EDI and DIs. A good system design will always accommodate future additions and modifications. RF/ID should be considered as a viable alternative when bar coded labels or tags would be impractical.

List of Acronyms

ACK/NAK	acknowledge, negative acknowledge
AI	Application Identifier
AIAG	Automobile Industry Action Group
AIM	Automatic Identification Manufacturers
ANSI	The American National Standards Institute
ASCII	American Standard Code for Information Interchange
BISYNC	Binary Synchronous Communication
CCD	charge coupled device
CIM	computer integrated manufacturing
CPI	characters per inch
CPU	central processing unit
CRT	cathode ray tube
CSMA/CD	Carrier Sense Multiple Access/Collision Detect
DBMS	database management system
DC	distribution center
DCE	data communications equipment
DDCMP	Digital Data Communication Message Protocol
DEX/UCS	Direct Exchange/Uniform Communication Standard
DI	data identifier
DOD	Department of Defense
DOS	disk operating system
DPI	dots per inch
DSD	direct store delivery
DTE	data terminal equipment
EAN	European Article Numbering System
EBCDIC	Extended Binary Coded Decimal Interchange Code
ECO	engineering change order
EDI	electronic data interchange
EDIFACT	International EDI Standard

EIA	Electronics Industry Association
ETB	end text block
FASLINC	Fabrics and Suppliers Linkage Council
FACT	Federation of Automated Coding Technology
HDLC	High-Level Data Link Control
HeNe	helium neon
HIBC	Health Industry Business Communications Council
ICRDA	Independent Cash Register Dealers Association
IEC	International Electrotechnical Commission
IGP	intelligent graphics processor
I/O	input/output
ILD	infrared laser diode
ISBN	International Standard Book Number Code
ISO	International Standards Organization
LAN	local area network
LCCN	Library of Congress Cataloging Number
LCD	liquid crystal display
LED	light-emitting diode
LOGMARS	Logistics of Marking and Reading Symbols
MAP	Manufacturing Automation Protocol
MICR	magnetic ink character recognition
MIS	management information system
MS-DOS	Microsoft's Disk Operating System
MSR	magnetic stripe reader
NEX/UCS	Network Exchange/Uniform Communication Standard
NiCad	nickel cadmium
NRMA	National Retail Merchants Association
OCR	optical character recognition
OEM	original equipment manufacturer
OSI	Open Systems Interconnection
PC	personal computer
PLU	price look-up
POS	point of sale
PROM	programmable read-only memory

QR	Quick Response
RAM	random access memory
RF	radio frequency
RFDC	radio frequency data collection
RFID	radio frequency identification
RTS/CTS	ready-to-send/clear-to-send
SAFLINC	Sundries and Apparel Linkage Council
SD&E	system design and equipment
SDLC	synchronous data link control
SI	systems integrator
SKU	stock-keeping units
SME	Society of Manufacturing Engineers
SNA-SDLC	System Network Architecture/Synchronous Data Link Control
SPA	shelf price audit
SQL	Structured Query Language
STX	start of text
T & A	time and attendance
TALC	Textile Apparel and Linkage Council
TDCC	Transportation Data Coordinating Committee
UCC	Uniform Code Council
UCS	Uniform Container Symbol
UPC	Universal Product Code
UPCC	Uniform Product Carton Code
USS	Uniform Symbol Specification
VAR	value-added reseller
VICS	Voluntary Inter-Industry Communication Standards
VFD	Vacuum Flourescent Display
WINS	Warehouse Information Network Standard
WIP	Work-in-progress/process
WYSIWYG	"what you see is what you get"

Glossary

AIAG Automobile Industry Action Group. An organization formed to coordinate automatic identification activities for the automobile industry.

AIM* Automatic Identification Manufacturers Incorporated. Organization supported by manufacturers and suppliers of automatic identification products and services.

Algorithm A finite number of steps, following a set of defined rules, for the solution to a problem or the completion of a task.

Alphanumeric* The character set which contains letters, numbers, and maybe other characters such as punctuation marks or control characters.

ANSI* The American National Standards Institute. A nongovernmental organization responsible for the development of voluntary industry standards.

ASCII* The character set and code described in the American National Standard Code for Information Interchange, ANSI X3.4-1977. Each ASCII character is encoded with 7 bits (8 bits including parity check). The ASCII character set is used for information interchange between data processing systems, communications systems, and associated equipment. The ASCII set consists of both control and printing characters.

Aspect ratio*   In a bar code symbol, the ratio of bar height to symbol length.

Asynchronous communication Also referred to as "start/stop" transmission. Every character transmitted has special bits attached, telling the receiving device when the data begins and ends.

Autodiscrimination*   The ability of bar code reading equipment to recognize and correctly decode more than one symbology.

---

*Copyright © Automatic Identification Manufacturers, Inc. 1990.

Bar* The darker element of a printed bar code symbol.

Bar code* An automatic identification technology which encodes information into an array of varying width parallel rectangle bars and spaces.

Bar code character* A single group of bars and spaces which represent an individual number, letter, punctuation mark, or other symbol.

Bar code density* The number of data characters which can be represented in a linear unit of measure. Bar code density is often expressed in characters per inch.

Bar code label* A label which carries a bar code symbol and is suitable to be affixed to an article.

Bar code message overhead The bars and spaces representing the start, stop, and check characters required by some symbologies, increasing the length of the bar code but not affecting the message content.

Bar height* *See* Bar length.

Bar length* The bar dimension perpendicular to the bar width. Also called bar height.

Bar width* The thickness of a bar measured from the edge closest to the symbol start character to the trailing edge of the same bar.

Baud rate Communication speed measured in the number of bits per second.

Bidirectional* A bar code symbol capable of being read successfully, independent of scanning direction.

Binary* The number system that uses only 1's and 0's.

Bit* An abbreviation for binary digit. A single element (0 or 1) in a binary number.

CCD Charge coupled device. Scanning is accomplished with an array of LEDs flooding the bar code with light.

Character* 1. A single group of bars and spaces which represent an individual number, letter, punctuation mark or other symbol. 2. A graphic shape representing a letter, numeral or other symbol. 3. A letter, digit, or other symbol that is used as part of the organization, control, or representation of data.

Character set* Those characters available for encodation in a particular automatic identification technology or symbology.

Check character* A character included within a message whose value is used for the purpose of performing a mathematical check to ensure the accuracy of that message.

Check digit* *See* Check character.

Codabar* A numeric-only bar code, in which each number is represented by seven black and white bars.

Code 128* A full alphanumeric bar code capable of encoding all 128 ASCII characters.

Code 16K* An extremely compact code where a long message is broken into sections and "stacked" one upon another similiar to sentences in a paragraph.

Code 39* A full alphanumeric bar code consisting of nine black and white bars for each character symbol.

Code 49* An extremely compact code where a long message is broken into sections and "stacked" one upon another similiar to sentences in a paragraph.

Continuous code* A bar code symbology where all spaces within the symbol are parts of characters. There is no intercharacter gap in a continuous code. Code I 2of5 is an example of a continuous code.

CPI Characters per inch. A common measurement for bar code density.

Data identifier Message prefixes, conforming to standards that are incorporated in a bar code that define the general category or intended use of the data that follows.

DBMS Database management system. A place for stored data to be integrated and shared.

Decoder* As part of a bar code system, the electronic package which receives the signals from the scanner, performs the algorithm to interpret the signals into meaningful data, and provides the interface to other devices.

Depth of field* The distance between the maximum and minimum plane in which a bar code reader is capable of reading symbols.

DEX/UCS Direct Exchange/Uniform Communication Standard for linking the computers of supplier and retailer at the receiving dock.

Discrete code* A bar code symbology where the spaces between the characters (intercharacter gap) are not part of the code.

DOS Disk operating system. PC-DOS and MS-DOS are the two most common operating systems found on IBM PCs and PC look-alikes.

Dot matrix* A system of printing where individual dots are printed in matrix-forming bars, alphanumeric characters, and simple graphics.

EAN* European Article Numbering System. The international standard bar code for retail food packages.

EBCDIC Extended Binary Coded Decimal Interchange Code. Developed by IBM, it is used primarily for communication with byte-oriented computers.

EDI Electronic data interchange. Intercompany, computer-to-computer communication of data in a standard format, performing a standard business transaction.

EDIFACT The international standard that supports electronic trade transactions across national boundaries.

Electrostatic* A method of printing utilizing a special electrostatic paper or a charged drum, both of which attract toner to the charged area.

FACT* Federation of Automated Coding Technology. An inter-industry organization responsible for overseeing the assignment of data identifiers.

Film master* A photographic film representation of a specific bar code or OCR symbol from which a printing plate is produced.

Fixed beam scanner* Either a visible light or laser scanner reading in a fixed plane. Requires a more exact positioning of a bar code than a moving beam scanner.

Font* A specific size and style of printer's type.

Formed font impact* A printing method for labels consisting of a rotating drum etched with raised bars and characters. A one-time ribbon and the label move between the drum and a micro-controlled hammer.

Infrared laser diode Used in some hand laser scanners to project a light beam invisible to the human eye.

Helium neon laser* A type of laser commonly used in bar code scanners. It emits coherent red light at a wavelength of 633 nm. Commonly referred to as He-Ne.

HIBC Health Industry Bar Code. The format and symbology for automated data collection within the health industry.

Horizontal bar code* A bar code or symbol presented in such a manner that its overall length dimension is parallel to the horizon. The bars are presented in an array which looks like a picket fence.

Impact printing* Any printing system where a microprocessor-controlled hammer impacts against a ribbon and a substrate.

Infrared The band of light wavelengths too long to be seen by the human eye. Represented by waves that are between 750 and 4 million nanometers.

Ink jet* A method of printing using liquid ink projected a drop at a time against a substrate.

Intercharacter gap* The space between two adjacent bar code characters in a discrete code.

Interleaved bar code* A bar code in which characters are paired together using bars to represent the first character and spaces to represent the second. An example of an interleaved bar code is I 2of5.

Ion deposition* *See* Electrostatic.

Kilobyte KB. 1024 bytes.

LAN Local area network. A high-speed data communications architecture facilitating the sharing of resources (files, databases) and devices (printers, hard disks, PCs).

Laser An acronym for Light Amplification by the Stimulated Emission of Radiation. Components include an energy source, the material to convert the energy to light, and the optics to direct the beam of light into a narrow cone.

Laser diode A laser made from a semi-conductor material and powered by applying electrical power to the material.

Laser scanner* An optical bar code reading device using a low-energy laser light beam as its source of illumination.

LED* Light-emitting diode. A semiconductor that produces light at a wavelength determined by its chemical composition. The light source often used in bar code scanners.

Light pen*   In a bar code sytem, a hand-held scanning wand which is used as a contact bar code reader held in the hand.

LOGMARS*   Logistics of marking and reading symbols. A Department of Defense program to place a Code 39 symbol on all federal items.

Megabyte   MB. 1024 kilobytes.

MICR*   Magnetic ink character recognition. An example of magnetic ink characters can be found on the lower left of bank and personal checks.

MIS   Management information system. The MIS group within a corporation is responsible for operating and maintaining all the computer-related devices, software, and databases.

Misread*   A condition which occurs when the data output of a reader does not agree with the data encoded in the bar code symbol.

Modem   An acronym for modulator/demodulator. Device used to convert binary digital data to audio tones suitable for transmission over phone lines and vice versa.

Moving beam scanner*   A scanning device where scanning motion is achieved by mechanically moving the light beam through the bars.

NEX/UCS   Network Exchange/Uniform Communication Standard for linking office computers by telephone lines to facilitate transfer of delivery and other vendor information.

Non-read*   In a bar code system, the absence of data at the scanner output after an attempted scan due to no code, defective code, scanner failure, or operator error.

Numeric*   A character set that includes only numbers.

OCR-A*   Character set used in optical character recognition and automatic identification. Described in ANSI Standard X3.17-1981. It is both human and machine readable.

OCR-B*   Character set used in optical character recognition and automatic identification. Described in ANSI Standard X3.49-1975.

Operating system   Software that controls the execution of programs and provides services such as resource allocation, CPU scheduling, input/output control, and data management.

Optical throw The horizontal distance from the aperture of the bar code reader to the leading vertical plane of the depth of field. It is the minimum distance a bar code can be away from a scanner and still be read.

Orientation The alignment of a bar code symbol with respect to the horizontal. Two possible orientations are horizontal with vertical bars and spaces (picket fence) and vertical with horizontal bars and spaces (ladder).

Overhead* In a bar code, the fixed number of characters required to start, stop, and check. For example, a symbol requiring a start/stop and two check characters contains four characters of overhead. Thus, to encode three characters, seven characters are required to be printed.

Parallel communication Data communicated one character at a time, over eight wires.

Pen scanner* A penlike device, either connected by wire to a device or self-contained, used to read bar codes. Requires direct contact with the symbol.

Photo composition* A system to produce very high quality labels by computer/photography.

Picket fence code* *See* Horizontal bar code.

Pitch* Rotation of a bar code symbol about an axis parallel to the direction of the bars.

PROM Programmable read only memory chip, whose contents cannot be changed by the user and remain in place when the computer is turned off. In some systems the PROM contains the program or utilities for instant access.

Quiet zone* A clear space, containing no machine readable marks, which precedes the start character of a bar code symbol and follows the stop chararcters.

QWERTY The standard keyboard configuration as seen on typewriters and computer terminals.

Radio frequency* An electromagnetic wave.

RAM Random access memory. Serves as the computer's work area, whose contents are changed by programs and user commands; when the computer is turned off, the contents are cleared.

Read rate* The ratio of the number of successful reads on the first attempt to scan to the total number of attempts.

Reflectance The light which is reflected back from the white spaces of a bar code during scanning. This light is converted to an electrical signal, amplified, and transmitted to a data entry terminal.

Resolution* In a bar code system, the narrowest element dimension which can be distinguished by a particular reading device or printed with a particular device or method.

Ribbon* A cloth or plastic tape with several layers of material, one of which is inklike, that produces the visible marks on a substrate. Used on formed font impact, dot matrix, thermal transfer, and hot stamp printers.

RS-232 A common interface standard that permits DTEs and DCEs to connect successfully.

Scanner* An electronic device to read bar codes that electro-optically converts bars and spaces into electrical signals.

Self-checking* A bar code or symbol using a checking algorithm which can be independently applied to each character to guard against undetected errors.

Serial communication Data transmitted one bit at a time, sequentially, over a single wire. The most common serial interface is RS-232C.

Skew* Rotation of a bar code symbol about an axis parallel to the symbol's length.

Space* The lighter element of a bar code, usually formed by the background between bars.

Space width* The thickness of a space measured from the edge closest to the symbol start character to the trailing edge of the same space.

SQL Structured Query Language. A common language used to acces data in a database management system.

Stacked code* 16K and Code 49 are examples where a long symbol is broken into sections and "stacked" one upon another, similar to sentences in a paragraph. These codes are extremely compact.

Standard* A set of rules, specifications, instructions, and directions to use a bar code or other automatic identification system to your profit. Usually issued by an organization, e.g. LOGMARS, HIBCC, UPC, etc.

Start-stop character*   A special bar code character that provides the scanner with start and stop reading instructions as well as scanning direction indicator. The start character is normally at the left-hand end of a horizontally oriented symbol. The stop character is normally at the right-hand end of a horizontally oriented symbol.

Substrate*   The surface on which a bar code symbol is printed.

Symbol*   A combination of bar code characters, including start/stop characters, quiet zones, data characters, and check characters required by a particular symbology, which form a complete, scannable entity.

Symbol density*   The number of data characters per unit length.

Symbol length*   The distance between the outside edges of the quiet zone.

Synchronous communication   Transmission of data which does not use special control bits, but requires a clock lead for coordination between the devices.

Thermal*   A printing system where dots are selectively heated and cooled and dragged upon heat-sensitive paper. The paper turns dark in the heated areas.

Thermal transfer*   A printing system like thermal except a one-time ribbon is used and common paper is used as a substrate; eliminates the problems of fading or changing color inherent in thermal.

TDCC   Transportation Data Coordinating Committee. The group responsible for setting the EDI standards for shippers and carriers.

Tilt*   Rotation of a bar code symbol about an axis perpendicular to the substrate.

UCC*   Uniform Code Council. The organization which administers the UPC and other retail standards.

UPC*   Universal Product Code. The standard bar code symbol for retail food packages in the United States.

UPCC*   Universal Product Carton Code. A standard administered by the UCC.

U.S. Bureau of Radiological Health (BRH)   The government agency which is responsible for setting the standards and classification for laser scanners.

USS Uniform Symbol Specification. The current series of symbology specifications published by AIM.

Verifier* A device that makes measurements of the bars, spaces and quiet zones and optical characteristics of a symbol to determine if the symbol meets the requirements of a specification or standard.

Vertical bar code* A code pattern presented in such orientation that the axis of the symbol from start to stop is perpendicular to the horizon. The individual bars are in an array appearing as rungs on a ladder.

VICS Voluntary Inter-Industry Communication Standards. Industry group formed in 1986 to initiate actions to improve mechanisms for automatic identification in the retail industry.

Visible laser diode Used in some hand laser scanners to project a beam of light visible to the human eye, simplifying the scanning process.

Void* An undesirable absence of ink in a bar.

Wand scanner* A hand-held scanning device used as a contact bar code or OCR reader.

Wedge* A device that plugs in between a keyboard and a PC. Includes a scanner allowing data to be entered either by a keyboard or scanner.

WINS Warehouse Information Network Standard. Defines the specific EDI transaction types for the warehouse industries.

WYSIWYG "What you see, is what you get" method for designing and printing graphics.

"X" dimension* The nominal dimension of the narrow bars and spaces in a bar code symbol.

XON/XOFF A communications protocol using two control characters (XON, XOFF) to start and stop data transmission.

Index